Instructor's Manual

for

Educational Research
An Introduction

Eighth Edition

prepared by

Meredith D. Gall
University of Oregon

Joyce P. Gall
University of Oregon

PEARSON

Boston New York San Francisco
Mexico City Montreal Toronto London Madrid Munich Paris
Hong Kong Singapore Tokyo Cape Town Sydney

ISBN 0-205-51363-8

Printed in the United States of America

10 9 8 7 6 5 4 3 2 1 10 09 08 07 06

CONTENTS

I. COURSE DESIGN

II. TEST ITEM FILE: CLOSED-FORM and OPEN-FORM TEST ITEMS, APPLICATION PROBLEMS, AND TEACHING ACTIVITIES SPECIFIC TO EACH CHAPTER

I. COURSE DESIGN

Organization of the Instructor's Manual

The purpose of this manual is to provide ideas and resources for teaching a course on educational research using the textbook *Educational Research: An Introduction,* 8th edition.

In this first section of the manual, we present ideas and to consider in course design. In addition to a sample syllabus and a form for outlining a research proposal, a new feature in this eighth edition of the Instructor's Manual are a set of teaching activities geared to the course as a whole. The second section of the manual is a test item file containing closed-form and open-form test items, application problems , and specific teaching activities for each of the 18 chapters of the textbook.

Factors to Consider in Designing a Course on Educational Research

Syllabus

Exhibit A, which appears near the end of this section of the manual, presents a syllabus that one of the authors (M. Gall) used in teaching a graduate course (a doctoral-level course that also included a few master's level students) using *Educational Research: An Introduction* as the course text. It is provided as a possible starting point to help you design your course on educational research and the syllabus for that course.

Content Coverage

Educational Research: An Introduction, 8th edition, contains 18 chapters and approximately 650 pages of text. This may well be too much content for students to master in a quarter-system course or even a semester-long course. If so, you can select some of the chapters to cover during the course and suggest to students that they read the other chapters after the course as the information becomes relevant to their research endeavors. In fact, instructors tell us that many students hold on to the textbook after they take the course and use it as a reference work. The glossary and the expanded coverage of research topics in the eighth edition (especially in the areas of proposal writing, literature review, and qualitative research) should make the book even more useful for this purpose.

Another approach to content coverage is to provide instruction on all or most of the chapters of the textbook but to assign only certain sections of each chapter. For example, the chapter on correlational research presents basic correlational designs in the first part of the chapter and more sophisticated designs (e.g., path analysis and hierarchical linear modeling) and statistical issues later in the chapter. You might require students to read only the first part of the chapter and then provide an overview in class of the material covered in later parts of the chapter. If you decide on this approach to content coverage, you can refer to the detailed table of contents in the textbook to decide which topics in each chapter to cover.

In contrast, the top-down approach involves starting the course by helping students develop the "big picture" of educational research. Later in the course you can help them fill in the details. Following this approach, you might start off with Chapters 1 and 2, which together help students develop an understanding of how research differs from other forms of inquiry and what is involved in doing a research study. Next, you might assign students to read Chapter 4 (Reviewing the Literature) and have them conduct a small-scale literature review on a topic of your or their choice. This will give them a feeling for what completed research studies look like, even if they don't understand all the research terminology and procedures involved. Because this is an initial foray into the research literature, you might have them read only abstracts, such as those in the ERIC database, rather than complete journal articles. The next step would be to assign chapters that present complete research designs, for example, descriptive and causal-comparative designs (Chapter 10), experimental designs (Chapter 12), case study research (Chapter 14),and action research (Chapter 18). Then you could teach particular aspects of the research process, such as sampling (Chapter 6) and collecting data with questionnaires and interviews (Chapter 8).

We do not know whether the top-down or bottom-up approach is superior. However, we are fairly certain that you need to focus on both the "big picture" and specialized procedures in order for students to develop a strong initial understanding of educational research.

Homework

The closed-form items, open-form items, and application problems within the test item file in this manual can be given as homework assignments. The application problems are particularly appropriate for this purpose. Also, there are a number of closed-form and open-form items for most of the objectives in each textbook chapter. Therefore, you might consider assigning some of the items for particular objectives as homework and using the other items for the same objectives in tests that will be graded.

When assigning textbook chapters for students to read as homework, you might advise them to read the objectives at the start of each textbook chapter before studying the chapter. After reading the chapter, students can check their mastery of the chapter by returning to the objectives and checking whether they can remember the concepts, procedures, and ideas associated with each objective. Students also can check their mastery of the textbook content by completing the self-check test at the end of each chapter.

You might advise students to take special note of the terms that are bold-faced in each chapter. Many of these terms are the subject of the closed-form and open-form items in this manual. Each boldfaced term is defined in the text of the chapter and also in the glossary at the end of the textbook.
Some instructors aim to encourage students ' personal response to research methodology. If this is one of your goals, you may wish to give students an assignment involving their writing a personal journal of reflections on their textbook readings.

Instruction in Statistics

Statistical analysis is an integral part of quantitative research. Even in qualitative research, descriptive statistics sometimes play a role. Also, in designing a qualitative study, the researcher will need to conduct a review of the literature, which is likely to include some quantitative studies. Students need to understand statistics in order to integrate these studies into their literature review.

Some students might have taken a course on statistical analysis prior to a research methods course. This is a desirable background to have before taking a course on research methods, unless the instructor focused on teaching statistical computations rather than helping students understand the role of statistics in research design. You might recommend that the students review their statistics textbook and notes as they encounter previously learned statistical procedures in the chapter on statistical techniques in *Educational Research: An Introduction*, 8th edition.

Many students benefit by taking a statistics course and a research course concurrently. Because the content of these two types of course overlaps to some extent, the students thus have an opportunity to see both statistics and research methods from different perspectives. Also, exposure to statistics in two courses during the same quarter or semester might facilitate a deeper understanding of statistical thinking.

If some students in your course have no background in statistics, you might wish to consider alternative ways for them to catch up with your students in the course who have some background in statistics. Among the options to consider are peer tutoring and independent study of a statistics textbook. If none of the students have had prior training in statistics, you can move through certain chapters of *Educational Research: An Introduction* (especially, Chapters 10-13) more slowly. Also, you can place particular emphasis on Chapter 5, which provides an overview of statistical techniques.

Assessment of Student Learning

One method of testing that we have found works well with graduate students is to assign take-home tests consisting of application problems, such as those we include in the test item file. These problems are sufficiently complex and open-ended that various responses are possible. You can allow students to study the problems together but require them to write individual responses to each problem. This procedure encourages students to think about the textbook content in depth, without the possible anxiety generated by the prospect of taking a sit-down test. Also, this procedure gives students the opportunity to work both collaboratively (they can study the problems together) and independently (they must write their own responses to each problem on the test).

Note to the Instructor

We welcome feedback on any of the ideas presented in this manual or in the textbook *Educational Research: An Introduction,* 8th edition. You can write to Meredith (Mark) at: University of Oregon, College of Education, Eugene, OR 97403, or to either Mark or Joyce (Joy) Gall at 4810 Mahalo Drive, Eugene, OR 97405. Alternatively, you can write to us at our e-mail addresses: mgall@uoregon.edu; joygall@comcast.net

Teaching Activities That Involve Having Students Prepare a Research Proposal

A large part of constructing a building involves creating a blueprint. The blueprint is, in part, a visual representation of construction details, In addition, it represents many design elements, each of which was created in response to the occupants' intended uses of the building and constraints such as budget, building codes, and weight loads.

In a similar manner, a research proposal is a blueprint for the actual conduct of a study. If the proposal is flawed, so will be the process of data collection, data analysis, and conclusions that can be drawn from the results. If the proposal is conceptually sound and sufficiently detailed, it is likely that the study can be successfully executed and will make a contribution to research knowledge. The proposal might not anticipate every problem that will arise as it is executed, but it should be able to anticipate most of them and state appropriate precautions and checks to ensure conduct of rigorous and sound research.

If you are teaching a course on research methods using our book as a resource, you might consider having students develop a proposal on a research problem of their choice, using the form in Exhibit B as a guide. In our many years of teaching a research-methods course for students who will be expected to complete a master's thesis or doctoral dissertation, we have found that this approach is valuable. Students develop a strong understanding of educational research by creating a proposal concurrently with reading chapters in the book. They appreciate this proposal-writing activity, because they realize that they actually need to create a proposal as part of the thesis or dissertation process.
The form in Exhibit B is helpful because it points students to key elements that must be specified in the proposal. However, that purpose in creating the form was not to require student to create a full-blown proposal of 20 or more pages. Rather, its intent is to help students produce a "sketch" of a proposal. A sketch contains key elements of the

research proposal, but its advantage is that it can be revised quickly as students get new ideas or respond to feedback from others. Furthermore, because a sketch does not require substantial effort, students will find it easy to abandon if they develop a new research problem that they find more compelling and doable. A proposal sketch might be only three to five pages and can be written in outline form with brief statements describing each design element.

The following are suggestions about how to use the form in Exhibit B as you assign each chapter of the book. We recommend that you take a few minutes now to read these chapter-by-chapter suggestions in order to get a sense of our approach. As you read them you might find activities that you like, or you might find that they serve as springboards for generating other activities that better suit your students and instructional purposes.

A common feature of the following teaching activities is that they have two parts. One is an assignment that students complete, and the other is use of class time for students to present design ideas from their emerging proposal. As selected students present their ideas in class, you can provide feedback in the form of constructive criticism and recommendations for revising the proposal. Students in the class also can be invited to provide feedback. You can point out to students that this feedback process is not an artificial activity, but rather an integral part of actual research.

Chapter 1 The Nature of Educational Research

Have students generate an idea for a research study. Have them state its purpose in one sentence (point 1.A of Exhibit B), The sentence should indicate whether the purpose is to describe, predict, improve, or explain. For example, "The purpose of this study is to determine whether the number of hours that high school students are employed during the school year predicts their grade-point average."

We find that if students have a clear idea about a study they intend to do, or might do, they can state its purpose in one sentence. If they can't do this, it might mean that they are not yet clear in their mind about what the study will focus on.

The next step is to ask students to specify their variables by completing point 6.A of Exhibit B. If their study involves a qualitative approach, you can advise students to read sections of Chapter 14 that pertain to the nature of cases and case foci.

In class, call on selected students to present their purpose statements. Provide feedback, and invite the class to provide feedback.

You can expand the activity by asking selected students whether their purpose statement reflects a quantitative or qualitative orientation, and why.

Chapter 2 The Research Process: From Proposal to Final Report

Ask students to take their purpose statement (1.A in Exhibit B) and make it more specific by generating research questions, hypotheses, and/or objectives, as called for bypoints 2.A and 2.B of Exhibit B.

You can extend the activity by having students state whether their study will be guided by a theoretical framework, and if so, what that framework is. This is point 2.C of Exhibit B.
In class, call on selected students to present their prepared statements. Provide feedback, and invite the class to provide feedback.

Chapter 3 Ethics and Site Relations in Educational Research

Ask students to examine their idea for a research study (see teaching activity for Chapter 1) for possible ethical threats to the research participants. Also have them consider actions they might need to take to seek entry to the research site and gain the cooperation of those affected by the study. Have them prepare their statements by completing points 9.A, 9.B, and 9.C of Exhibit B.

In class, call on selected students to present their prepared statements. Provide feedback, and invite the class to provide feedback.

Chapter 4 Reviewing the Literature

Reviewing the literature on one's research problem is arguably the most important part of the research-proposal process. Therefore, consider giving special emphasis to the following teaching activity.

Ask students to analyze their purpose statement (1.A of Exhibit B) and have them conduct a literature review to determine what previous research has been done on it. You can have them start by identifying appropriate descriptors and preliminary and secondary sources (points 3.A and 3.B of Exhibit B). Next, ask them to identify relevant studies by searching their selected preliminary and secondary sources. You might ask them to print and turn in to you 10 to 20 of the most relevant citations (author, title, journal name, abstract, etc), perhaps with a brief statement appended to each citation that explains its relevance to the proposed study.

The final step in this process would be to have students complete points 1.B, 1.C, and 1.D of Exhibit C.

In class, call on students to describe their experiences in doing the literature review, including problems they encountered and how the process helped them think about their proposed study.

Chapter 5 Statistical Techniques

Students might experience difficulty in thinking about statistical techniques for their research study until they have learned methods and designs covered in other chapters. Nonetheless, it is still worthwhile for them to take an initial plunge into statistical techniques in order to develop an initial understanding of what is involved.

Start by having students examine their idea for a research study (see teaching activity for Chapter 1) and any other sections of Exhibit B that they have completed. If some students have formulated a study that involves a qualitative approach, have them reframe it as a quantitative study for purposes of this activity.

Ask students to generate a hypothetical data set that might result from their purpose statement and their hypotheses, questions, or objectives (2.A and 2.B in Exhibit B). For example, suppose a student's primary hypothesis is that assigning retired teachers to supervise student teachers will lead to greater student-teacher satisfaction and higher teaching-effectiveness ratings than assigning doctoral students to do the supervision. The student can be asked to generate a set of data (in our example, a set of satisfaction scores and teaching-effectiveness scores for each of the two experimental groups) that might result from a study designed to test this hypothesis.
Once students have generated their data set, you can ask them to complete point 8.A of Exhibit B (the part pertaining to statistics).
In class, call on students to present their data sets and statistical analysis procedure. Because data sets are better seen than described, you can review data sets that have been handed in as class assignment and then select several to copy in sufficient quantity for the entire class and use as the basis for class discussion.

Chapter 6 Selecting a Sample

Start by having students examine their idea for a research study (see teaching activity for Chapter 1) and any other sections of Exhibit B that they have completed. Then ask them to complete Part 5 (A, B, C, D, E) of Exhibit B.

In class, call on students to describe their experiences in formulating a sampling procedure, including problems they encountered and how the process helped them think about their proposed study. Provide appropriate feedback

Chapter 7 Collecting Research Data with Tests and Self-Report Measures

Start by having students examine their idea for a research study (see teaching activity for Chapter 1) and any other sections of Exhibit B that they have completed. If they have not completed point 6.A of Exhibit B, ask them to do so. This section requires students to think through the variables that they will examine in their research hypotheses, questions, and objectives. If a student's research problem involves a qualitative approach, ask the student to restate it from a quantitative approach for purposes of this activity.

Next, have the students complete points 7.A and 7.B of Exhibit B.

It might be that some students have identified variables that are not appropriately measured by tests and self-report measures of personal characteristics. For these students, consider giving them a research problem and variables that you have formulated, so that they can develop an understanding of the relationship between variables and their measurement by tests and self-report measures of personal characteristics.

In class, call on students to describe their variables and their intended measurement. Provide feedback, and invite the class to provide feedback.

Chapter 8 Collecting Research Data with Questionnaires and Interviews

Start by having students examine their idea for a research study (see teaching activity for Chapter 1) and any other sections of Exhibit B that they have completed. If they have not completed point 6.A of Exhibit B, ask them to do so. This section requires students to think through the variables or aspects of cases that they will examine in their research hypotheses, questions, and objectives.

Next, have the students specify appropriate questionnaire and interview items by completing points 7.A and 7.B of Exhibit B.

It is possible that some students will have identified variables or aspects of cases that are not appropriately measured by questionnaires and interviews. If so, you can ask these students to expand their research problem to include several variables or aspects of cases that can be measured by these techniques.

In class, call on students to describe their variables or case aspects and how they can be measured by questionnaires or interviews. Provide feedback, and invite the class to provide feedback.

Chapter 9 Collecting Research Data through Observation and Content Analysis

Start by having students examine their idea for a research study (see teaching activity for Chapter 1) and any other sections of Exhibit B that they have completed. If they have not completed points 6.A of Exhibit B, ask them to do so. This section requires students to think through the variables or aspects of cases that they will examine in their research hypotheses, questions, and objectives.

Next, have the students specify appropriate observational or content-analysis techniques by completing points 7.A and 7.B of Exhibit B.

It is possible that some students will have identified variables or aspects of cases that are not appropriately measured by observation or content analysis. If so, you can ask these students to expand their research problem to include several variables or aspects of cases that can be measured by these techniques.

In class, call on students to describe their variables or case aspects and how they can be measured by observation or content analysis. Provide feedback, and invite the class to provide feedback.

Chapters 10-18

A student's research problem, as specified in point 1.A of Exhibit B, will require, in all likelihood, one of the research designs covered in Chapters 10-18. Therefore, if you assign some or all of these chapters, only one will be pertinent to the research-design section (4A-D) of Exhibit D.

One approach would be for students to complete this section (4A-D) only for the chapter that is pertinent to their research problem.

Another approach would be to ask students to reframe their research problem so that it is appropriately addressed by the research design covered in each assigned chapter in Parts IV-VI (Chapters 10-18) of the book.

Teaching Activities That Involve Having Students Apply the Findings of Research

For some education instructors, the major goal of their research methods course is to help students develop understanding of how research findings can inform and improve their professional practice. This is a worthwhile goal, but different from the goal of preparing students in the research skills required for a master's thesis or doctoral dissertation.

Focus on Problems of Practice

We believe that there are two major approaches to achieving this goal. One is to have students learn how to read published research studies and literature reviews and then explore how the reported findings can be translated into practice. The other approach is to start with problems that arise in professional practice and then teach students how these "problems of practice" can be solved, at least in part, by examining the research literature.

Both approaches have value, but focus on problems of practice is particularly appropriate if your students' goals include becoming better professional practitioners. In his classic book *The Reflective Practitioner*, Donald Schön observed that practitioners' work involves "complexity, uncertainty, instability, uniqueness, and value-conflict" (p. 39). However, researchers typically assume a stable reality about which generalizations can be made (most quantitative research), or they study a local situation whose applicability to other settingsis uncertain (most qualitative research).

Given the different realities in which researchers and practitioners reside, how do we motivate practitioner-students to see value in educational research? One answer to this question is to start with your students' actual problems of practice, and then show how research findings are relevant to them. This approach is supported by a large-scale review of the literature on how medical doctors and educators make use of research findings. One finding of this review, as summarized in an ASCD *Research Brief*(October 26, 2004, vol. 2, no. 2) is that, "Teachers reacted more favorably to research that matched their own personal experiences." (We have more to say about ASCD's *Research Briefs* below.)

Thus starting with their problems of practice can motivate practitioners to learn about, and then apply to their practice, relevant research findings. For example, in your course you can ask students to provide examples of their problems of practice at the start of the course. Then you can give them a major assignment, completed during the course, in which they are asked to search for research findings in primary and secondary sources that relate to a problem of practice that particularly concerns them, and write a paper that summarizes and critiques these findings and explores their implications for solving the problem.

You can stimulate students' thinking about problems of practice by giving them examples from current education publications, such as *Educational Leadership* or *Phi Delta Kappan*. The free online publication *ASCD SmartBriefs*, published daily, is a topical source of problems of practice. *ASCD Research Brief*, published monthly, another free online publication, focuses on problems of practice and research studies that are relevant to them. You can access both publications at <http://www.ascd.org>. Click on "Publications" in the top horizontal bar, and scroll down to "Free Newsletters" on the next screen.

The following are sample items from *ASCD Research Brief* that we came across recently. After each item, we summarize the problems of practice that it suggests.

> 5/15/06
> U.S. students continue to seek remote tutoring services from companies in India and other Asian countries, despite concern about some foreign coaches being unqualified. Burck Smith, CEO and co-founder of a Washington online tutoring company, believes American schools will eventually outsource office hours, review sessions and other functions to foreign teachers. (Problems of practice: Are tutoring services, including those that are outsourced, effective in improving student learning? How prevalent are tutoring services, and are they receiving a positive reception by educators, students, parents, and others? What qualifications should tutors have to help improve the achievement of U.S. students and thereby compete in the global marketplace?
>
> 5/12/06
> The California Senate endorsed a bill Thursday that would require social-science textbooks, beginning in 2012, to include the historical contributions of lesbian, gay, bisexual and transgendered individuals. Supporters say the measure would help create a more hospitable climate for gay and lesbian students, while opponents question the need to mention a historical figure's sexual orientation. (Problems of practice: How would the proposed textbook revisions create a more hospitable climate for gay and lesbian students? Would the revisions antagonize other groups? More generally, how much does the content of textbooks affect students' perceptions of school and of themselves?
>
> 5/4/06
> Voter support is waning for a June ballot initiative that proposes California fund a universal preschool program for 4-year-olds. Opponents point out research indicates universal preschool doesn't raise test scores and argue that the money involved would be better spent on K-12 schools. (Problem of practice: Should educators support the funding of preschool programs? If yes, how can they counter the claims of opponents of these programs?)
>
> 5/4/06
> Wake County, N.C., schools may change to a multitrack, year-round calendar to cope with surging student enrollment. A poll of teachers indicates 20% say they may leave if the district adopts the new schedule. (Problem of practice: Would the adoption of a multitrack, year-round calendar have positive or negative effects on students and their teachers?)

5/4/06
Hoover Institution analysts Brian Jacob and Lars Lefgren probe the issue of whether principals, if required to reward or sanction teachers under a merit-pay program, could accurately determine the effectiveness of those teachers. They conclude that elementary school leaders are quite adept in identifying teachers who will produce the most and least gains on standardized achievement tests, but less able to distinguish among those in the middle of the pack. (Problem of practice: Should principals be given primary responsibility for hiring and salary decisions involving the teaching staff?)

5/8/06
The Sims, one of the world's most popular video games, allows players to create and care for a virtual suburban family. Some psychologists look at the game as a great way for children, especially girls, to explore relationships and unleash their creativity. (Problem of practice: Should teachers include the use of video games as a standard element of their instruction? If so, what assistance might be needed for students who have not used such video games previously?)

4/19/06
A new Manhattan Institute for Policy Research study of the Class of 2003 breaks down high-school graduation rates in various ways, including by race and gender, by state and by the 100 largest school districts in the country. Among the nationwide findings: 72% of girls graduated that year, compared with 65% of boys, while black and Hispanic girls had graduation rates nine to ten percentage points higher than those of their male counterparts. (Problem of practice: What can be done to close the achievement gap between male and female students?)

4/17/06
Maryland's first official report on bullying in schools reveals most incidents of bullying and other forms of harassment involve middle-schoolers and consist of name-calling or threats. However, one state education official says the data may be skewed because districts vary in how aggressively they report such incidents. (Problem of practice: How can educators reduce the incidence of bullying in schools? Just how big is the incidence of bullying? Does failure to curb bullying put schools at risk for more severe incidents of violence?)

Each of these news items links to the newspaper or other source that reported the problem.

Focus on Reading Research Studies and Literature Reviews

As we explained above, another approach to helping students develop an understanding of how research findings can inform and improve their professional practice involves a focus on reading research studies and literature reviews. The emphasis is is on close analysis and critique of particular research studies and literature reviews, accompanied by an exploration of the implications of their findings for professional practice.

If you choose this approach for your course, you might select four to six recent publications that all students would read, for example, (1) a correlational prediction study, (2) an experimental study, (3) a case study, (4) a historical study, and (5) a literature review. The students would read these publications early in the course, so that you can refer to them as you assign and discuss in class particular chapters of *Educational Research: An Introduction.*

Many education journals are now available online and can be accessed without cost by anyone or without cost if your institution has an online subscription. A comprehensive list of these journals is available at a web site maintained by the American Educational Research Association (http://aera-cr.asu.edu/ejournals/).

The following are examples of journals that can be found at this web site:

Bilingual Research Journal
Computers and Composition: An International Journal for Teachers of Writing
Contemporary Issues in Technology and Teacher Education
Education Policy Analysis Archives
Electronic Journal of Science Education
Innovate: Journal of Online Education
International Journal for Education Policy and Leadership
International Journal for Mathematics Teaching and Learning
International Journal of Behavioral Consultation and Therapy
International Journal of Education & the Arts
International Journal of Special Education
International Review of Research in Open and Distance Learning
Journal for Critical Education Policy Studies
Journal of American Indian Education
Journal of Philosophy and History of Education
Journal of Research for Educational Leaders
Journal of Research in Rural Education
Journal of Vocational and Technical Education
Perspectives on Urban Education
Practical Assessment, Research and Evaluation
Reading Online: An Electronic Journal of the International Reading Association
Research in Middle Level Education Online
Teaching English as a Second Language

You can examine recent issues of these or other journals listed at the web site for research articles that are suitable for your purposes.

It is important to help students identify, read, and apply literature-review publications (secondary sources) in addition to research studies (primary sources). Table 4.2 on pages 108-109 in Chapter 4 of *Educational Research: An Introduction* contains a list of secondary sources that you can examine in order to find one or more literature reviews that you can ask students to read and discuss in class.

You might consider using two forms in *Educational Research: An Introduction* to help your students learn how to read research articles with a critical perspective. They are in Appendix A (Questions for Evaluating Quantitative Research Reports) and Appendix B (Questions for Evaluating Qualitative Research Reports).

In Part II, the Test Item file, we have retained the teaching activities specific to each chapter that appeared in the Instructor's Manual for *Educational Research: An Introduction*, 7th edition. You can decide whether you wish to use any of those activities to supplement the teaching activities described in this section of the Instructor's Manual that focus on the course as a whole.

Exhibit A: Example of a Syllabus for a Course on Educational Research

CI 612 INTRODUCTION TO RESEARCH DESIGN
CRN 7172 224 Education Hall
Tues and Thurs 3:30-4:50 PM

Fall 20--

Instructor: ____________
Office: ________ (phone: ________)
My office hours are ________.

Overview

This course has three goals: (1) to increase your understanding of research concepts and procedures, (2) to develop your appreciation of the importance of research in education, and (3) to develop your skill in preparing a research proposal for the doctoral dissertation. I will emphasize how research concepts and procedures apply to dissertation-level studies in education.

Research typically involves several stages: planning (e.g., the dissertation proposal), pilot study and development of measurement tools, data collection and analysis, and report-writing (i.e., writing the dissertation). This course cannot develop your skill in completing all these stages of a research study. These skills are best developed through actual practice in doing research, preferably guided by an experienced researcher. Therefore, the course will focus on the preparation of a dissertation proposal. This is one of the most critical phases of research, because it provides the *blueprint* for all the later stages of the study. The later stages will be covered in this course insofar as they relate to the research proposal.

Course Objectives

This course is intended to help you develop:

1. Understanding of the nature, purposes, and types of educational research.
2. Understanding of procedures for reviewing research literature.
3. Understanding of sampling procedures.
4. Understanding of procedures for selecting and administering tests and other measurement devices
5. Understanding of concepts and procedures relating to: descriptive research, causal-comparative research, correlational research, experimental research, case study research, and R & D studies.
6. Understanding of statistical techniques appropriate for analyzing data from different research designs
7. Skill in preparing the various parts of a dissertation proposal.

Course Assignments

The course text is: M. D. Gall, W. R. Borg, & J. P. Gall, *Educational Research: An Introduction*, 8th Edition (Boston: Allyn & Bacon, 2007). The following chapters are required reading: Chapters 1, 2, 3, 4, 6, 7, 8, 10, 11, 12, 14, and 15.

EDUCATIONAL RESEARCH: AN INTRODUCTION

Your mastery of these chapters will be tested by sets of take-home application problems. I recommend that you read the other chapters, too, to become familiar with their content for later reference. In addition, you are expected to read a set of 9 research reports that will provide the basis for class discussion. These reports can be purchased as a reading packet from _____ .

A set of take-home application problems will be given to you approximately every two weeks. You can discuss the problems in study groups if you wish, but you need to write your own responses. The application problems are directly related to the objectives at the beginning of each assigned chapter in the text. <u>Follow the word-processing rules at the end of the syllabus in writing your answers.</u>

Another course requirement is to prepare a research proposal. The proposal does not have to be your actual dissertation problem, although dissertation problems certainly are welcome. Your proposal can be the completion of the outline included in your reading packet or a regular narrative proposal covering the same points as in the reading packet outline. In either case, the assignment must be typed using the word-processin rules. (If you use the outline, include the headings of the outline in your proposal.) This assignment is due on the last scheduled meeting of the course (<u>date</u>). To help you complete the proposal, you will be asked to complete a set of brief exercises based directly on the proposal outline in the reading packet. Each exercise is due one class meeting after the topic to which it pertains has been covered in class.

Class time will be spent in lecture and discussion of actual research studies, dissertation proposal writing, and difficult concepts presented in the textbook.

<u>Grading</u>

Mastery-level performance on the application problems, and a satisfactory research proposal are required to receive an "A." If you do poorly on any assignment, you will be given the option of doing it again.

<u>Class Presentations</u>

The following is a list of topics that will be covered and the textbook chapters to which they are keyed. The dates on which the topics will be discussed are approximate.

	<u>Read beforehand</u>	
1. Sept. 24	Introduction to course	
2. Sept. 26	Nature and purpose of educational research	Chapter 1
3. Oct. 1	Comparison of quantitative and qualitative research	Studies 1 & 2
4. Oct. 3	Formulation of a research problem, variables, hypotheses, questions	Chapter 2
5. Oct. 8	Formulation of a research problem, variables, hypotheses, questions	

6. Oct. 10	Reviewing the research literature	Chapter 4 Study 3
7. Oct. 15	Measurement	Chapter 7 Study 1
8. Oct. 17	Measurement	Chapter 8 Study 2
9. Oct. 22	Sampling methods	Chapter 6 Studies 1 & 2
10. Oct. 24	Descriptive research	Chapter 10 Study 1
11. Oct. 29	Causal-comparative research	Chapter 10 Study 4
12. Oct. 31	Correlational research	Chapter 11 Study 5
13. Nov. 5	Correlational research	
14. Nov. 7	Experimentation	Chapter 12 Study 6
15. Nov. 12	Case study research	Chapter 14 Study 2
16. Nov. 14	Case study research	
17. Nov. 19	Qualitative research traditions	Chapter 15 Study 7
18. Nov. 21	Qualitative research traditions	Study 8
19. Nov. 26	Qualitative research traditions	Study 9
20. Dec. 3	Human subjects review procedures	Chapter 3
21. Dec. 5	Reflections on educational research	

WORD-PROCESSING RULES

1. Type all assignments.

2. Type double-space or space-and-a-half with at least an inch margin on the right or left side.

3. Type using a twelve-point font. To put it another way, please use a font big enough to read easily.

4. Type your name, date, and course title on a cover page or on the upper-right corner of the first page.

5. Paginate the paper. In other words, put a page number on each page of the paper.

6. Use a staple or clamp on the upper left corner to hold the paper together. Do not use clear plastic folders with plastic strip spines to hold your paper together.

7. If you want your paper returned in a confidential manner, submit it in an envelope.

8. If you want your paper mailed to you, submit it in a stamped, self- addressed envelope.

Exhibit B: Form for Outlining a Research Proposal

Note: You can give this form to students at the beginning of the course, and ask them to complete various parts of it as you cover concepts, procedures, and ideas that are relevant to those parts.

1. PURPOSE OF STUDY

   A. (One sentence only.) The purpose of this study is to ________ .

   B. What study or literature review is your study most directly based on? (Give citation.)

   C. How does your study build on previous research? (No more than 3 sentences.)

   D. How will your study contribute to knowledge about education? (No more than 3 sentences.)

2. RESEARCH QUESTIONS, HYPOTHESES, AND OBJECTIVES

   A. In what form are you stating your research purposes? (Check one or more.)
   ____ Questions ____ Hypotheses ____ Objectives

   B. List your research questions/hypotheses/objectives.

   C. Does your study relate to a particular theoretical framework? If it does, describe the framework, and indicate how your research questions, hypotheses, or objectives relate to it. If the study is qualitative in nature, indicate whether you plan to use a grounded theory approach.

3. LITERATURE SEARCH

   A. List the descriptors that you will use initially in your literature search.

   B. List the preliminary sources that you will use in your literature search.

4. RESEARCH DESIGN

   A. Describe the research design that you selected for your study: descriptive,causal-comparative, correlational, experimental, case study, historical, evaluation, or action research , a particular qualitative research tradition, or educational research and development.

   B. If the study is quantitative in nature, what are the threats to the internal validity of your research design? What will you do to minimize or avoid these threats?

   C. If your study is quantitative in nature, what are the limitations to the generalizability (i.e., external validity) of the findings that will result from your research design? What will you do to maximize the generalizability of your findings?

   D. If your study is qualitative in nature, what criteria for ensuring its soundness and rigor and what steps to ensure its applicability do you consider to be relevant to your research design?

5. SAMPLING

   A. If your study is quantitative in nature, describe the characteristics of the population that you will study. If your study is qualitative in nature, describe the phenomenon you wish to study and the cases that comprise instances of the phenomenon.

   B. Identify your sampling procedure (e.g., simple random sampling), and explain why you selected it.

   C. Indicate the sampling unit (e.g., individual students or a class of students).

   D. Indicate the size of your sample, and explain why that sample size is sufficient.

   E. Indicate whether the sample will be formed into subgroups, and if so, describe the characteristics of the subgroups.

6. VARIABLES

   A. If your study is quantitative in nature, list the variables that you will study. For each variable, indicate whether it is an independent variable, a dependent variable, or neither. If the study is qualitative in nature, describe the aspects of the cases on which data collection and analysis will focus.

7. METHODS OF DATA COLLECTION

   A. List the measures that you will select or develop for your study.

   B. If your study is quantitative in nature, indicate the variables that each measure will assess. For each measure, indicate which types of validity and reliability are relevant and how you will check them.

   C. If your study is qualitative in nature, indicate the themes and patterns that it possibly will explore. Also, indicate whether your data collection will focus on etic or emic perspectives, or both. Explain whether and how you will collect data on the context in which the research participants function. Explain, too, your role in the data collection process.

8. DATA ANALYSIS PROCEDURES

   A. What statistics, if any, will you use to analyze your data? If your study is qualitative, indicate whether you will use an interpretational, structural, or reflective method of analysis.

9. ETHICS AND HUMAN RELATIONS

   A. What threats, if any, does your study pose for your research participants? What steps will you take to minimize these threats?

   B. How will you gain entry into the setting in which you will collect data?
   C. How will you gain the cooperation of your research participants?

10. TIME LINE
   A. Create a time line listing in order all the major steps of your study. Also indicate the approximate amount of time that each step will take.

II TEST ITEM FILE AND TEACHING ACTIVITIES

Introduction

This section of the manual contains test items for each of the 18 chapters of *Educational Research: An Introduction*, 8th edition. The test item file for each chapter is organized as follows:

a. Closed-form Test Items. These items are multiple-choice and matching items that test students' knowledge of specific concepts, procedures, and ideas related to educational research. The items are keyed to the objectives listed at the start of each textbook chapter. For example, if an item begins 1. (obj. 1), that means it is the first item for the chapter and it covers information related to Objective No. 1 in the list of objectives at the beginning of the chapter. The answer is provided below each item.

b. Open-form Test Items. These are short-answer items that test students' knowledge of specific concepts, procedures, and ideas related to educational research. The items are similar to the question stems of the closed-form test items, but generally are more challenging because students must construct an answer. Also, each item generally covers more of the content presented in the textbook. Like the closed-form items, each open-form item is keyed to one or more of the objectives listed at the beginning of each textbook chapter. An answer is provided below each item; it often includes more points than the item requests, any of which are acceptable. If desired, you can also include a request for an example in students' answers to the open-form items. Some of the open-form items in the Manual already are written to require an example. For example, item 6 for chapter 3 states, "Explain desensitization, and give an example of a type of study in which it would be necessary." The answer to this item defines desensitization and also provides an example of a type of study that would require this procedure. If you modify items to request examples, it is up to you to judge the acceptability of examples that students give as part of their answers.

c. Application Problems. These are the most challenging test items, because students must draw on their knowledge of different parts of the chapter in order to answer them. They generally require more higher-cognitive thinking and judgment than the open-form test items. Because each application problem tests for students' mastery of several concepts, procedures and ideas covered in the chapter, they are not keyed to specific chapter objectives. Application problems can have a variety of acceptable answers, and we include a sample answer to each problem to illustrate an acceptable answer.

d. Teaching Activities. These teaching activities, retained from the Instructor's Manual for the seventh edition of *Educational Research: An Introduction*, for the most part are activities specific to each chapter. You can decide whether you wish to use any of these activities to supplement the teaching activities described in Part I of the Instructor's Manual that focus on the course as a whole.

In this edition the number of closed-form items represents a 22-percent increase, and the number of open-form items represents a 19-percent increase compared to the 7th edition. In creating test items, particularly the closed-form items, we have focused on the actual content of each textbook chapter. We encourage you to modify the test items as you wish or to generate additional items that relate to the course objectives as stated in each chapter. Also, to the extent that you present additional content in your course, you may wish to develop other test items to reflect that content.

If you or your students question our judgment as to the correct answers for specific closed-form items, or the suggested answers for specific open-form test items or application problems, we would appreciate receiving your feedback so that we can improve the Instructor's Manual.

EDUCATIONAL RESEARCH: AN INTRODUCTION

CHAPTER 1
THE NATURE OF EDUCATIONAL RESEARCH

Note: The phrase in parentheses following the item number for both closed-form and open-form items, for example, "(obj. 3)", refers to the textbook chapter objective to which the item is keyed.

CLOSED-FORM ITEMS

1. (obj. 1) Studies that seek to identify the students who will drop out of high school or the students who will do well in college are examples of
   a. descriptive research.
   b. intervention-oriented research.
   c. prediction research.
   d. theory-building research.

Answer: c

2. (ob. 1) Studies that seek to assess how well students are mastering different curriculum subjects are examples of
   a. descriptive research.
   b. intervention-oriented research.
   c. prediction research.
   d. theory-building research.

Answer: a

3. (obj. 1) Which of the following statements best reflects the current status of improvement-oriented research?
   a. Researchers have discovered only a few interventions that improve learning.
   b. Researchers have discovered many different types of interventions that improve learning.
   c. Researchers have conducted few improvement-oriented studies in education.
   d. Researchers have not yet conducted studies on forms of cultural oppression that affect student learning.

Answer: b

4. (obj. 2) "Intelligence is that which is measured by intelligence tests." This statement is an example of
   a. an operationally defined construct.
   b. a constitutively defined construct.
   c. a theoretical law.
   d. grounded theory.

Answer: a

5. (ob. 2) Theories are considered "small" or "large" depending on
   a. how much research evidence is available to support them.
   b. how many phenomena they can explain.
   c. the number of constructs they contain.
   d. the number of scientific laws they contain.

Answer: b

6. (obj. 2) Unlike the "grounded theory" approach, a research hypothesis in the conventional "scientific method"
   a. can be proved or disproved by a single study.
   b. only can be tested if the constructs have been constitutively defined.
   c. is formulated after the data have been collected.
   d. Is formulated before the data have been collected.

Answer: d

7. (obj. 3) To date, research has had the most impact on educational practices involving
   a. teacher decision-making.
   b. school organization.
   c. assessment of students' academic achievement.
   d. individualization of instruction.

Answer: c

8. (obj. 3) The findings of a well-done educational research study
   a. will be value-free.
   b. nonetheless will be value-laden.
   c. nonetheless will have no generalizability beyond the situation that was studied.
   d. will yield clear prescriptions about what ought to be done to improve educational practice.

Answer: b

9. (obj. 3) Richard Schön's model of reflection-in action as a guide to practice
   a. precludes the use of research knowledge as a basis for professional action.
   b. supports the assumed relationship between research and practice posed by the technical rationality model.
   c. assumes a stable, consistent reality about which generalizations can be made and applied.
   d. involves experimentation based on practitioners' analysis of each unique situation.

Answer: d

10. (obj. 4) Which of the following is *not* an example of basic research in education?
   a. Research to identify the parts of the brain that control memory
   b. Research on physiological changes in students during test-taking situations
   c. Research on the effects of a pharmaceutical drug on the classroom attention span of students diagnosed with attention-deficit disorder
   d. Research on factors that explain artistic aptitude

Answer: c

11. (obj. 4) In their study of research on the treatment of heart diseases, Julius Comroe and Robert Dripps found that
   a. medical doctors have more confidence in basic research than applied research.
   b. important advances in the treatment of heart diseases resulted from basic research.
   c. most advances in the treatment of heart diseases resulted from applied research.
   d. basic and applied research did not advance the treatment of heart diseases nearly as much as the informal research conducted by medical doctors in their daily practice.

Answer: b

12. (obj. 5) Karl Popper claimed that a theory
   a. is untestable through empirical research.
   b. can by proven correct or false if it survives replication tests conducted by researchers who are skeptical about the theory's validity.
   c. can be proven correct or false if research designed to test it has sufficient controls for researcher bias.
   d. can be proven to be false, but cannot be proven to be true.

Answer: d

13. (obj. 5) Postpositivists believe that
   a. physical and social research is independent of those who observe it.
   b. there is an objective reality, but it can only be known imperfectly.
   c. all epistemologies have equal value in the search for truth.
   d. generalizations from the research sample to other samples from the same population are impossible.

Answer: b

14. (obj. 5) Progressive discourse requires that researchers
    a. maintain a willingness to change their views in response to criticism and new research findings.
    b. conduct a replication study before reporting the findings of the original study.
    c. give equal weight to case studies and case research.
    d. all of the above.

Answer: a

15. (obj. 6) In writing a research report, the author includes her own reactions to the classrooms she has studied. This style of reporting typifies
    a. positivist research.
    b. scientific realism.
    c. reflexivity in research.
    d. postmodernism.

Answer: c

16. (obj. 6) Researchers who subscribe to constructivist epistemology believe that
    a. they might view social reality differently than the individuals whom they are studying.
    b. objectivity can be achieved if they take responsibility for collecting data, but leave the responsibility for data interpretation to the research participants.
    c. objectivity can be achieved through the use of a positivist reporting style.
    d. as individuals mature, they assimilate physical and social reality with more objectivity and less private interpretation.

Answer: a

17. (obj. 7) If a constructivist researcher was interested in the effects of cooperative learning, he most likely would select for study
    a. a large sample of teachers who were using this method.
    b. a few teachers who were using this method.
    c. every teacher in a school district who was using this method.
    d. a large sample of staff developers who were training teachers in this method.

Answer: b

18. (ob. 7) Positivist researchers believe that
    a. they should study cases in order to determine local interpretations of social reality.
    b. features of social reality retain a high degree of constancy across settings.
    c. if consistent findings are obtained from several case studies, these findings can be generalized to a population.
    d. an investigation starts with sample selection and ends with the determination of a population to which the findings apply.

Answer: b

19 . (obj. 8) Constructivist researchers typically deal with the shortcomings of numerical data by
    a. not subjecting such data to statistical analysis.
    b. collecting such data only on large samples.
    c. making pictorial representations of numerical data.
    d. relying instead on thorough verbal descriptions of phenomena.

Answer: d

20. (obj. 8) A constructivist educational researcher would most likely argue that
    a. features of the social environment retain a high degree of constancy across time and space.
    b. quantifiable features of the social environment do not reveal what is most important about teaching and learning.
    c. most of the significant advances in the physical and social sciences involve quantification.
    d. symbolism, mythology, and religion are the best guides to explain human events and physical phenomena.

Answer: b

21. (obj. 9) The view that the real world consists of layers of causal structures is a primary tenet of
    a. positivism.
    b. postpositivism.
    c. scientific realism.
    d. both postpositivism and scientific realism.

Answer: c

22. (obj. 9) The view that interpretations and intentions are causal agents in social reality characterizes
    a. constructivism.
    b. scientific realism.
    c. postpositivism.
    d. scientific realism and postpositivism.

Answer: a

23. (obj. 10) Postmodernists would argue that
    a. positivist research is not superior to literary studies.
    b. positivist research is superior to literary studies.
    c. literary studies has a privileged position in the search for truth.
    d. it is necessary to combine literary studies with positivist research in order to make scientific progress.

Answer: a

24 (obj. 10) Postmodernists believe that theories
    a. cannot be validated.
    b. can be validated.
    c. can only be validated by cross-cultural research.
    d. can only be validated through objective observation.

Answer: a

25. (obj. 11) *Qualitative research* is sometimes called
    a. interpretive research.
    b. case study research.
    c. constructivist research.
    d. all of the above.

Answer: d

26. (obj. 11) Quantitative and qualitative researchers
    a. differ in their reliance on variables and holistic observation.
    b. differ in their methods of data analysis, but agree on report-writing procedures.
    c. share the belief that social reality can be studied objectively.
    d. share the belief that they should become personally involved with their research participants.

Answer: a

27. (obj. 11) Advocates of mixed-methods research believe that
   a. studies should be designed using qualitative-research epistemology and quantitative-research statistics.
   b. quantitative and qualitative methods can be combined in a study, but only if the data are collected from an emic perspective.
   c. quantitative and qualitative research methods can be combined in a study to generate useful findings.
   d. different quantitative methods can be combined in a study, but these methods cannot be combined with any qualitative methods.

Answer: c

OPEN-FORM ITEMS

1. (obj. 1) Briefly describe four types of knowledge yielded by educational research.

Answer:
   1. *Description.* This is the initial step in new fields of investigation. It depends heavily on the state of measurement in the science.
   2. *Prediction.* Description often reveals relationships between variables. These observed relationships can be used to make predictions with varying degrees of accuracy.
   3. *Improvement or control.* Once predictions of events are possible, researchers can attempt to influence their occurrence by designing appropriate interventions. In education, interventions often have the goal of improving a learning outcome.
   4. *Explanation.* This the ultimate goal of research. The explanations often take the form of theories.

2. (obj. 2) State two reasons why theories are useful.

Answer (any 2 OK):
   1. They identify commonalities among phenomena that otherwise appear unrelated.
   2. They can be used to make accurate predictions of future events.
   3. They can be used to design or implement interventions that have known consequences.

3. (obj. 3) How is D. C. Phillips's distinction between *is* and *ought* relevant to the application of educational research to practice?

Answer:

Research tells practitioners what is but cannot tell them what they ought to do. Knowledge about what is helps practitioners by contributing to their dialogue about what ought to be.

4. (obj. 4) A common criticism of basic research in education is that it seldom leads directly to improvement in educational practice. What are two reasons that basic research nonetheless should be supported?

Answer (any 2 OK):
   1. Even though its immediate impact may be slight, its eventual impact may be great.
   2. Without basic research, we have little chance of gaining a better understanding of the underlying processes involved in education.
   3. Studies in other sciences such as medicine show that basic research contributes more to important advances in practice than all other kinds of investigation.

5. (obj. 5) Describe two distinctive beliefs of researchers who subscribe to postpositivist epistemology, and explain why
you think these beliefs have merit or are misguided.

Answer (any 2 OK):

1. Belief in the creation of concepts and procedures that are shared and publicly accessible.
2. Belief in the importance of replication research.
3. Belief in the refutability of knowledge claims.
4. Belief in the importance of controlling for errors and biases.
5. Belief in the boundedness of knowledge claims.
6. A moral commitment to progressive claims.

The instructor will need to judge the soundness of the student's argument in support of, or against, the beliefs listed in the answer.

6. (obj. 6) Why do constructivist researchers distinguish their perspective from the perspectives of the individuals whom they study and of the individuals who will read their research reports?

Answer:

Constructivist researchers believe that individuals construct their own interpretations of social reality. Therefore, researchers must bear in mind that (a) their interpretations of a social phenomenon may be different from those who participated in the phenomenon and that (b) the way they write their research reports will affect how readers interpret the findings.

7. (obj. 7) Give one reason why constructivist researchers study cases rather than samples or populations.

Answer (any 1 OK):

1. Constructivist researchers believe that social reality is constructed locally. Therefore, one must do in-depth study of local instances of a phenomenon. Each such instance is a case.
2. Constructivist researchers believe that social reality is highly variable and changeable, and therefore one must study particular instances of it. Each such instance is a case.

8. (obj. 8) State one criticism of relying on numerical data to measure variables in educational research.

Answer (any 1 OK):

1. Numerical data tend to involve variables that may be of trivial significance in education.
2. The assumption that a numerical value (e.g., the number of students in a classroom as a measure of class size) has the same meaning for all individuals may not be tenable.

9. (obj. 9) Explain one way in which constructivists and scientific realists differ in their explanation of the causes of social phenomena.

Answer (any 1 OK):

1. Constructivists believe that individuals' interpretations of the social environment are the causes of social phenomena, whereas scientific realists believe that layers of causal structures are the causes of social phenomena.
2. Constructivists believe that interpretations are constructed by individuals, whereas scientific realists believe that causal structures are real objects that exist independently of individuals.

10. (obj. 10) Explain why postmodernists would be critical of educational research as a basis for describing, predicting, improving, or understanding educational phenomena.

Answer: (any 1 OK):

1. Educational research claims to produce valid, replicable, and useful findings about educational phenomena, but postmodernists doubt that any method of investigation can lay claim to such an authoritative, privileged position in the search for truth.
2. Postmodernists suspect that any method of inquiry, including scientific inquiry, is not neutral, but instead serve particular political and societal interests.

11. (obj. 11) State two key differences between quantitative and qualitative research.

Answer (any 2 OK; other answers based on Table 1.2 in the textbook are also acceptable):

1. In quantitative research, the social environment is an independent reality; in qualitative research, the social environment is constructed by individuals.
2. In quantitative research, samples are studied; in qualitative research, cases are studied.
3. In quantitative research, numerical data are emphasized; in qualitative research, verbal data are emphasized.
4.. In quantitative research, instruments are used to measure variables; in qualitative research, the researcher is the "measuring instrument."

12. (obj. 11) State one assumption that must be satisfied in order to use quantitative research to verify the findings of a qualitative research study.

Answer (any 1 OK):

1. The social phenomena being studied must be stable across time and place.
2. It must be possible to represent the concepts discovered in the qualitative study by a measure that yields numerical scores.

APPLICATION PROBLEMS

Problem 1

Formulate a small theory about education, that is, an explanation of an observed set of phenomena in terms of a system of constructs and laws the relate these constructs to each other that you believe to be true. Generate a plan for a research study that would allow you test this theory that includes the following three steps:

1. Formulating a hypothesis based on your theory.
2. Deducing observable consequences of the hypothesis.
3. Testing the hypothesis by collecting research data.

Sample Answer:

The theory is that students learn better under conditions of positive reinforcement than under conditions of negative reinforcement.

1. Hypothesis: Students will learn more when they are rewarded for their positive efforts than when they are punished for their mistakes.
2. Observable consequences: When solving mathematical problems, students who receive praise and criticism or correction during each step of the process.
3. Data collection: Two groups of students will receive the same set of mathematical problems to solve individually. Observers in the first group will praise and encourage students at each step they take to solve the problems, while observers in the second group will criticize or correct students at each step. The average number of correct problem solutions will be calculated for each group and group means will be compared.

Problem 2

Suppose the federal government decides to fund a new program for training high school students in study skills. Some educators argue that all of the appropriated funds should be used to develop model programs and materials, to train teachers in summer institutes, and to hire additional school staff. Other educators argue that at least 15 percent of the appropriations should be allocated for research on study skills. What defense could you offer for the latter proposal?

Sample Answers:

a. The model programs and materials may be ineffective, in which case the appropriated funds would be wasted. Research is needed to sort out the effective programs from those that are ineffective.
b. Research may yield new insights about studying and study skills instruction that can be used to develop more effective programs and materials than any that are currently available. This increase in effectiveness is better in the long run than reaching more individuals with less effective programs and materials in the short run.

Problem 3
Suppose you are asked to design a study of teachers' attitudes toward recent school reforms. How would you select a sample and measure teacher attitudes if you were doing (a) a quantitative research study, or (b) a qualitative research study?
Sample Answer:

a. In the quantitative study, a large sample of teachers that is representative of a defined population would be selected, and their attitudes would be measured by a scale that yields numerical scores.
b. In the qualitative study, the researchers would select a small number of teachers (or perhaps just one teacher), each of whom would be a case, and their attitudes would be assessed by interviewing the teachers and recording their responses in detail.

TEACHING ACTIVITIES

Activity 1

Identify a report of a quantitative research study and a report of a qualitative research study that are fairly simple. Have students read each study as a homework assignment. In class, have students discuss how the design and the findings of the two studies differ. For purposes of this activity, it does not matter if students understand all the technical details of the study. This activity will help students to discover for themselves how quantitative and qualitative research differ, and to integrate these presented in chapter 1.

Activity 2

On page 10 of the textbook the authors state that, "putting a research finding into practice also means putting a particular set of values into practice." Assign a research article for all students to read as a homework assignment. In class, have students discuss how the authors' statement applies to this particular study. Having students read a report of an experimental study would be desirable for this particular activity.

Activity 3

On the first day of class, preferably before students have read Chapter 1, ask them (individually or in small groups) to write a definition of *research*. You can have them write their definitions on overhead transparencies, and them project each transparency so that the entire class can see all the definitions. You can ask students to look for commonalities and differences in the definitions. At various points in the term, you can ask students to revisit their definitions and decide whether they wish to revise the definitions in light of what they are learning about research in your course.

CHAPTER 2
THE RESEARCH PROCESS:
FROM PROPOSAL TO FINAL REPORT

Note: The phrase in parentheses following the item number for both closed-form and open-form items, for example, "(obj. 3)", refers to the textbook chapter objective to which the item is keyed.

CLOSED-FORM ITEMS

1. (obj. 1) Research knowledge and personal knowledge in that
   a. they serve different purposes.
   b. are judged against different standards.
   c. research knowledge is cumulative across studies.
   d. all of the above.

Answer: d

2. (obj. 2) An advantage of theory-based research is that it
   a. allows the researcher to examine any question of personal interest.
   b. provides a rational basis for explaining the research results.
   c. enables the researcher to prove a particular hypothesis.
   d. greatly reduces the possibility of conflicting interpretations of research findings.

Answer: b

3. (obj. 2) If a number of studies produce evidence in line with a theory and no disconfirming evidence is found, the most reasonable conclusion is that
   a. the theory has been proved.
   b. the theory has been supported.
   c. more evidence is needed to prove the theory.
   d. none of the above.

Answer: b

4. (obj. 2) Theory in qualitative research typically involves
   a. discovering a set of constructs, themes, or patterns in the data.
   b. formulating a research problem based on an earlier researcher's findings.
   c. testing hypotheses derived from an existing theory.
   d. attempts to disconfirm previously held beliefs about educational phenomena.

Answer: b

5. (obj. 3) Replication studies in education
   a. sometimes are done to test the generalizability of the original study's findings to new settings and populations.
   b. almost always find corroborative evidence for the findings of the study being replicated.
   c. are invalid unless they follow the same methodology as that used in the original study.
   d. can be used to search for more effective interventions than the one originally tested, but cannot be used to search for more efficient interventions.

Answer: a

6. (obj. 3) Replication studies in education
   a. have little value because they usually investigate problems of no interest to practitioners.
   b. have little value because the important studies generally are well-funded and produce trustworthy results.
   c. are of no value unless they literally reproduce the methodology of the original study.
   d. can be considered "original" if they check the findings of an important study using different methodology.

Answer: d

7. (obj. 4) One of the main advantages of working on a team project in learning to carry out educational research is that
   a. all team members are likely to have similar experience and research interests.
   b. the research problem is likely to be closely allied with the student's interests.
   c. a team project provides insight into how research teams operate.
   d. nearly all research in education involves a team of researchers.

Answer: c

8. (obj. 5) A research proposal for a dissertation study
   a. is similar in many respects to the organization of the final dissertation.
   b. is not necessary for a qualitative investigation because of the emergent nature of the research design.
   c. needs to include the research problem, hypotheses, and research design, but not a literature review.
   d. should focus primarily on the research design, data-collection instruments, and probable method of statistical analysis.

Answer: a

9. (obj. 5) Match each section of a research proposal with the appropriate example of the information that is presented in that section.
   __ 1. Introduction
   __ 2. Review of literature
   __ 3. Research design
   __ 4. Research method
   __ 5. Data analysis
   __ 6. Human subjects protection
   __ 7. Timeline
   a. Whether the study will attempt to describe, predict, explain, or control the phenomena being studied
   b. The methods of data collection to be used
   c. Statement of the research hypotheses
   d. When each step of the study will be completed
   e. Critique of the methods used in previous research on the problem
   f. The statistical tests that will be carried out
   g. Description of how risks to participants will be minimized

Answer: 1 = c 2 = e 3 = a 4 = b 5 = f 6 = g 7 = d

10. (obj. 6) "There is no relationship between parental use of corporal punishment and the level of school misbehavior of third grade students." This is an example of a
   a. null hypothesis.
   b. research objective.
   c. research question.
   d. directional hypothesis.

Answer: a

11. (obj. 6) A directional hypothesis about the relationship between the type of reading instruction and reading comprehension might be stated in terms of
    a. a question as to whether students receiving whole-language instruction or students receiving phonics instruction will score higher on a measure of reading comprehension.
    b. a prediction that there will be no difference in the reading comprehension of students taught by phonics instruction and those taught by whole-language instruction.
    c. a prediction that there will be a difference in the reading comprehension of students taught by phonics instruction and those taught by whole-language instruction, but without specifying which form of instruction will be superior.
    d. a prediction that students taught phonics will have higher reading comprehension scores than students taught by the whole-language method.

Answer: d

12. (obj. 7) A pilot study of a proposed research study is desirable because
    a. it permits a thorough check of the planned data collection and analysis procedures.
    b. in a pilot study the researcher typically has greater control over the research procedures than in the actual research project.
    c. it permits the researcher to collect sufficient for the researcher to predict the likely outcomes of the actual study.
    d. if the results are positive, further data collection in the research project will be unnecessary.

Answer: a

13. (obj. 8) A dissertation is organized similarly to a research proposal except for the
    a. problem statement.
    b. literature review.
    c. research method.
    d. research findings.

Answer: d

14. (obj. 8) In writing a dissertation, the student should put in appendixes material that
    a. is critical to the study but may not interest all readers.
    b. presents statistical results that are essential to understanding of the study.
    c. presents information about measures that the student developed.
    d. all of the above.

Answer: c

15. (obj. 9) The most important step a researcher should take to ensure that her research study is worth doing is to
    a. establish the validity and reliability of the measures to be used.
    b. demonstrate that the findings of previous research in this area are inconclusive.
    c. show how the study builds on and will add to the research literature.
    d. provide evidence that the research presents no possible risk to research participants.

Answer: c

16. (obj. 9) A researcher should base the selection of a journal to which to submit a report of one's research primarily on whether
    a. the journal is willing to publish the report in its original form.
    b. the journal has published other studies dealing with your research topic.
    c. the journal is published by a professional association.
    d. the report covers a topic not previously addressed by this journal.

Answer: b

17. (obj. 10) If your proposal is accepted for presentation at a professional meeting, you have an obligation to
   a. prepare a paper for submission to a journal published by the association that is sponsoring the meeting.
   b. attend the meeting and present a paper.
   c. submit the paper you present to the appropriate ERIC clearinghouse.
   d. prepare a chart essay summarizing your findings.

Answer: b

OPEN-FORM ITEMS

1. (obj. 1) List the five stages of a research study.

Answer:
   1. Identifying a significant research problem
   2. Writing a research proposal
   3. Conducting a pilot study
   4. Conducting the main study
   5. Preparing a report

2. (obj. 2) Explain two of the following terms: *theory*, *construct*, *operational definition*, and *variable.*

Answer (any 2 OK):
   1. A theory is an explanation of observed events in terms of the structures and processes that are presumed to underlie them.
   2. A construct is a type of concept used by theoreticians to describe a structure or process that is hypothesized to underlie particular observable phenomena.
   3. An operational definition is the definition of a construct in terms of the procedures or operations needed to measure it.
   4. A variable is a construct that can vary in quality or quantity.

3. (obj. 3) List three purposes for doing a replication and extension of a previous study as one's research project.

Answer (any 3 OK):
   1. To check the findings of a "breakthrough" study, i.e. one that challenges previous theory or research
   2. To check the validity of research findings for a different research population than the one previously studied
   3. To check trends or changes over time in research findings on a phenomenon
   4. To check important findings by changing the methods or correcting methodological flaws that were present in the previous study
   5. To develop and test instructional interventions to the point where they are effective or efficient for practical application

4. (obj. 4) Give two reasons why working on a team project can be beneficial.

Answer (any 2 OK):
   1. There may be financial support to cover some needed materials or activities.
   2. It may be possible to receive a scholarship or research assistantship that covers most of one's expenses while completing graduate study.
   3. It provides the opportunity to participate in a larger, more sophisticated study than one you could do alone.
   4. You have a chance to learn about the dynamics of team research.
   5. You can learn from a variety of other research team members, each of whom brings unique training and experience to the project.

5. (obj. 5) Give two reasons why it is important to write a complete research proposal before undertaking a study.
Answer (any 2 OK):
1. Composing a proposal compels you to think through and record your planned research design and procedures.
2. You can more easily find and correct flaws in a written proposal than you can after you have begun collecting data.
3. University and college faculty usually want to see a complete proposal before authorizing you to begin your study.

6. (obj. 5) List two topics that typically are covered in the introductory section of a research proposal.
Answer (any 2 OK):
1. A complete statement of the research problem to be addressed
2. A description of how the proposed study is grounded in the research literature
3. Speculation about how the proposed study will contribute to research knowledge and educational practice
4. A list of the research hypotheses, questions, or objectives that the study will address

7. (obj. 6) Why do researchers often state a hypothesis in null form, i.e., that no relationship or difference will be found, even when they expect the opposite?
Answer:
The null hypothesis is used in performing tests of statistical significance.

8. (obj. 7) Describe the nature and purpose of a pilot study in educational research.
Answer:
A pilot study involves small-scale testing of the procedures that you plan to use in the main study. The purpose of the pilot study is to identify weaknesses in the planned procedures so that the researcher can design better procedures for use in the main study.

9. (obj. 8) List two ways to check whether you are using the correct format and writing style in preparing your dissertation.
Answer (any 2 OK)
1. Obtain a copy of the style manual approved by your institution for preparing dissertations.
2. Ask your dissertation chairperson to identify several outstanding dissertations completed at your institution that you can examine.
3. If you hire someone to type your dissertation, check whether he is familiar with the format requirements of your institution.

10. (obj. 8) List two of the topics that the discussion chapter of a dissertation should cover.
Answer (any 2 OK):
1. A brief restatement of the research problem investigated and of the method used to study it
2. An interpretation of each major finding
3. A discussion of the methodological limitations of the study
4. A summary of the implications of the findings for practice
5. Possible questions that could be addressed in further research

11. (obj. 9) Name two factors to consider in deciding on a journal to which to submit a report of your research study.
Answer (any 2 OK):
1. Identification of a journal that is most likely to publish studies on the problem that you investigate
2. The journal's reputation, i.e., how widely read and influential it appears to be
3. Whether it is a refereed journal

12. (obj. 9) Name two factors to consider in deciding on a journal to which to submit a report of your research study.
Answer (any 2 OK):
1. Identification of a journal that is most likely to publish studies on the problem that you investigate
2. The journal's reputation, i.e., how widely read and influential it appears to be
3. Whether it is a refereed journal

13. (obj. 10) Give one reason why a chart essay is a desirable format for presenting a paper at a professional meeting.
Answer (any 1 OK):
1. The chart essay simplifies the elements of a research study by using charts to focus the audience's attention on aspects of the study that are most relevant to policy making.
2. The chart essay makes the study more understandable to policy makers or practitioners, who have less familiarity with research methodology than most researchers.

APPLICATION PROBLEMS

Problem 1
A graduate student claims that it is not necessary for her to do a pilot study prior to conducting an experiment for her doctoral dissertation. Her experiment is primarily a replication of a previously published study on the effectiveness of a teacher inservice on classroom management, with a few modifications. Give at least two arguments in favor of her doing a pilot study under these conditions.
Sample Answer (any 2 OK):
1. The pilot study may help her develop new hypotheses to be tested about the effects of the classroom management inservice.
2. It may help her discover problems with teachers' application of what they learned that were not mentioned in the report of the previous study.
3. It may help her discover new classroom management procedures that are more effective than those that were tested in the previous study.
4. It would provide an opportunity to test the modifications in the teacher inservice procedures that she made to those used in the previous study.

Problem 2
Rewrite the following dissertation titles so that they are brief yet informative.
a. "A Study Investigating the Relationship between Selected Personality Factors in First-, Second-, and Third Grade Children and their Attitudes toward School at Various Intervals in the School Year."
b. "A Preliminary Investigation into the Effects of Participation in a High School Counseling Program on Student Perceptions of Various Aspects of College."

Sample Answer:
a. "The Relationship between Personality and Attitudes Toward School in Primary-Grade Children."
b. "Effects of a High School Counseling Program on Student Perceptions of College."

Problem 3

a. State three of your areas of interest in education.
b. Mention two problems in each of these areas that you think are worthy of research investigation.
c. Write (1) a null hypothesis, (2) a directional hypothesis, and (3) a research objective for one of the problems you mentioned.

Sample Answer:

a. Three areas of interest
   1. Evaluation of teaching effectiveness.
   2. Teacher supervision.
   3. Creativity.
b. Two problems in each area
   1. Development of classroom observation systems; The relationship between particular teaching techniques and student outcomes.
   2. Characteristics of effective supervisors; Typical interaction patterns between supervisors and teachers.
   3. Development of techniques for increasing creativity; School achievement of creative children.
c. For the problem of the relationship between particular teaching techniques and student outcomes
   1. Sample null hypothesis: Mathematics teachers who use specific feedback during math lessons and comparable teachers who use general feedback do not obtain different levels of student gain in mathematics achievement.
   2. Sample directional hypothesis: Mathematics teachers who use specific feedback during math lessons obtain higher student achievement gains than comparable teachers who use general feedback.
   3. Sample objective: The objective of this study is to determine whether there is a difference in mathematics achievement for the students of mathematics teachers who use specific feedback compared with those who use general feedback.

TEACHING ACTIVITIES

Activity 1

Give students several statements of research problems (e.g., the effects of parental involvement on the homework completion of primary-grade students). Ask each student to write a hypothesis, a research question, and a research objective for a research study that could be generated from the problem statement. Discuss the students' work in class, noting strengths and weaknesses of selected hypotheses, questions, and objectives.

Activity 2

Identify a doctoral student whose dissertation proposal has recently reviewed by his or her dissertation committee. Give the class an opportunity to ask the student about his or her experiences in developing the proposal (e.g., how did the student select the research problem that will be studied?) and in having it reviewed by the dissertation committee (e.g., what revisions to the proposal, if any, did the committee request that the student make?)

Activity 3

Ask students to identify at least one research article on a topic of interest to them. Have each student circle statements in the article in which the authors call for further research relating to their study and its findings. Have some students present a summary of their selected study and the circled statements, followed by a class discussion of how replication-and-extension studies could be designed as a follow-up to the selected study.

Activity 4

Have students review a program listing the presentations at a meeting of the American Educational Research Association or another major association. Ask them to find several presentations that appear relevant to the research

CHAPTER 3
ETHICS AND SITE RELATIONS IN EDUCATIONAL RESEARCH

Note: The phrase in parentheses following the item number for both closed-form and open-form items, for example, "(obj. 3)", refers to the textbook chapter objective to which the item is keyed.

CLOSED-FORM ITEMS

1. (obj. 1) Ethical practice requires the research investigator to
   a. protect participants from physical and mental discomfort, harm, or danger.
   b. refrain from the use of deception in any research study.
   c. develop a written contract defining the participants' obligations concerning their involvement in the study.
   d. provide access to data on individuals to other qualified researchers.

Answer: a

2. (obj. 1) Currently prevailing legal constraints on educational research include the requirement that
   a. school records on individual students will not be released under any conditions without parental consent.
   b. no unauthorized person can have access to the names of the students who participated in the study.
   c. a national government review board must approve all research projects involving human subjects.
   d. deception may not be used in experiments with children.

Answer: b

3. (obj. 2) Professional associations such as the American Educational Research Association have developed written codes of ethics primarily because
   a. many researchers have violated ethical principles.
   b. institutional review boards are required to use such codes in evaluating research proposals.
   c. public and governmental concern about the effects of research on human subjects has increased.
   d. all of the above.

Answer: c

4. (obj. 2) Procedures used in educational research to address ethical, legal, and human relations issues are primarily designed to
   a. standardize the research methods used to study human beings.
   b. ensure that researchers avoid or minimize possible misuse of their power.
   c. increase the participation of research participants in the design of research studies.
   d. clarify the forms of oppression that need to be remedied in society.

Answer: b

5. (obj. 3) A valid reason for using deception in some behavioral science research is that
   a. if participants knew the purpose of the study, they might respond differently and thus invalidate the results.
   b. some studies involve aversive experiences, and participants might refuse to participate if they knew this fact.
   c. many researchers are interested in the study of how individuals respond to the fact that they have been deceived.
   d. it increases the likelihood of significant differences between the experimental and control group participants.

Answer: a

6. (obj. 3) It is important to dehoax research participants at the end of an experiment involving deception in order to
   a. discourage the participants from revealing the true purpose of the experiment to other potential participants.
   b. help ensure that the deception will do no future harm to the participants.
   c. solicit data about the participants' post-experiment perceptions of the deception.
   d. explain the expected findings of the experiment.

Answer: b

7. (obj. 3) Desensitizing research participants after an experiment typically involves
   a. telling them that they were in the control group rather than the experimental group.
   b. pointing out that their behavior was unpredictable.
   c. suggesting that their behavior was due to the circumstances present in the experiment.
   d. pointing out their responsibility for their own actions.

Answer: c

8. (obj. 4) The main function of an institutional review board is to
   a. determine procedures for allowing institutionalized individuals to participate in research studies.
   b. review research proposals to ensure that they provide satisfactory protection of human subjects.
   c. review research proposals to ensure that the research will yield useful results for the sponsoring institution.
   d. review completed research studies to ensure that human subjects were adequately protected.

Answer: b

9. (obj. 4) Proposals for research that are defined by federal regulations as eligible for expedited review are those that
   a. receive funds from a U.S. government agency.
   b. involve fewer than 10 research participants in each group.
   c. involve minimal risk to human subjects.
   d. will be conducted entirely within the institution that is reviewing the proposal.

Answer: c

10. (obj. 5) To reduce the potential vulnerability of the members of a research population of interest, a researcher should consider
   a. joint planning of the research with members of the population.
   b. intensive interviews with members of the research population to explore possible areas of vulnerability.
   c. doing qualitative research rather than quantitative research.
   d. all of the above.

Answer: a

11. (obj. 5) The best solution to avoid the ethical issue resulting from the control group being deprived of the perceived benefits of an experimental treatment is to
   a. not inform the control group of the expected benefits of the treatment.
   b. randomly assign individuals to the control and experimental groups.
   c. schedule the control group for the same treatment after data collection has been completed.
   d. provide monetary compensation only to control group members.

Answer: c

12. (obj. 5) Disseminating research results in the "least publishable unit" rather than as a coherent whole is unethical because
   a. it distorts the meaning of the research.
   b. it gives authors excessive credit for the extent of their publishable work.
   c. it makes scarce reporting space less available to other authors.
   d. all of the above.

Answer: d

13. (obj. 6) Match each of the following procedures that is used to protect research participants with the appropriate example of that procedure.
    __ 1. Describe the conditions of participants' participation in the study.
    __ 2. Ensure that participants can exercise their right to withdraw from the study at any time.
    __ 3. Protect participants' privacy and confidentiality.
    __ 4. Assess the risk-benefit ratio.
    __ 5. Apply safeguards when using deception.
    a. Asking, "Would you like to stop now?"
    b. Telling participants at the outset who will have access to the data.
    c. Explaining to participants that their behavior during the study was not unusual.
    d. Sending an informed-consent letter.
    e. Doing a literature review to determine whether the proposed treatment has unanticipated side effects.

Answers: 1 = d 2 = a 3 = b 4 = e 5 = c

14. (obj. 7) A major advantage of using a coding or linkage system to ensure the confidentiality of data on human research participants is that
    a. data protected by a coding or linkage system have privileged legal status in the courts.
    b. this system guarantees research participants that no one can determine how they responded to the research instruments.
    c. this approach is more ethical than a completely anonymous procedure.
    d. if necessary, the researcher can identify participants who failed to respond or misinterpreted the instructions.

Answer: d

15. (obj. 8) Which of the following is *not* a legitimate request for the researcher to agree to when seeking approval of a research project from school personnel?
    a. The results will be useful to the schools in their district.
    b. The study will contribute to the profession of education.
    c. Any aspects of the research design that interfere with other school activities will be modified.
    d. Minimal extra time and effort will be required from students who participate.

Answer: c

16. (obj. 8) A research project involved individual administration of a new measure of nonverbal intelligence to low achieving children. The test identified a number of children with previously undiagnosed learning deficits. This example illustrates
    a. the possible advantages to the school district of research that uses special measures.
    b. the potential dangers of not ensuring anonymity of research participants.
    c. the importance of modifying the research design to accommodate school requirements.
    d. the need for obtaining prior approval from school authorities for all measures to be used in the research.

Answer: a

17. (obj. 8) In research done in school settings, it generally is wise for the researcher to
    a. get approval from the teachers who will be involved before contacting the superintendent or principal.
    b. conceal the true purpose of the research from the teachers whose students may be involved in it.
    c. maintain distance from school personnel in order not to bias the results.
    d. think of ways to ensure that aspects of the study will provide direct benefits to the school.

Answer: d

EDUCATIONAL RESEARCH: AN INTRODUCTION

OPEN-FORM ITEMS

1. (obj. 1) An investigator conducts a study of the effects of large vitamin doses on college students' problem-solving ability. When he describes the study to his philosophy class, all the students agree to participate. A week later a student tells the professor she does not want to finish the project because she feels she is taking too many vitamins. The investigator points out that the doses are well within safe limits established by the medical profession. The student still wishes to drop out. Because the student was fully informed before the study and volunteered, would it be ethical for the professor to penalize the student by giving her a lower grade in the class? Explain your answer.

Answer:

No, doing so would violate professional ethics. The professor must allow the student to withdraw from the study without penalty.

2. (obj. 1) Describe three unethical practices involving the reporting of research that researchers should avoid.

Answer (any 3 OK):

1. Partial publication, i.e., disseminating research results in the "least publishable unit" in order to inflate the author's list of publications
2. Dual publication, i.e., publishing the same research results in more than one publication in order to inflate the author's list of publications
3. Plagiarism, i.e., directly lifting another's words for use in one's own publications
4. Paraphragiarism, i.e., closely copying another writer's words or ideas without giving credit to the original author
5. Not giving all persons closely involved in the research an opportunity to be listed as co-authors

3. (obj. 2) Describe one of the topics that are covered by the Ethical Standards of the American Educational Research Association.

Answer (any 1 OK):

1. Researchers' responsibilities to the field in their generation of conclusions
2. Respect for research populations, educational institutions, and the public
3. Recognition of creative contribution as the basis of intellectual ownership
4. Use of fair but rigorous standards in editing, reviewing, and appraising research
5. Joint preservation of research integrity by the sponsors, policy makers, and other users of research
6. Appropriate induction of student researchers into the field

4. (obj. 2) Explain how the risk-benefit ratio is used in the review of a research proposal.

Answer:

If the proposed study is likely to expose research participants to possible physical, psychological, or legal harm, the researcher must demonstrate that it provides sufficient benefits to the participants, or to research knowledge in general, to outweigh the risk of harm to which research participants will be exposed.

5. (obj. 3) The use of deception in a research study requires the researcher to ask herself several questions, such as whether the potential benefits of the study justify the use of deception. Briefly describe two other questions the researcher should consider before using deception.

Answer (any 2 OK):

1. Do the researcher's personal ethics permit deception for any purpose?
2. Are there alternate procedures that would not require deception?
3. Will the deception undercut the research participants' rights to be informed about the potential risk of participation in the research?
4. Will the use of deception cause negative effects on the research participants, such as cynicism, resentment, or loss of self-esteem?
5. Have safeguards such as debriefing been included in the research plan to minimize potential negative outcomes?

6. (obj. 3) Some research projects require desensitization of research participants. Explain desensitization, and give an example of a type of study in which it would be necessary.

Answer:

Desensitization is the process of helping research participants deal with new information about themselves as a consequence of the behavior they exhibited during the experiment. For example, if participants are induced to exhibit dishonest behavior or to behave cruelly toward others in a research study, desensitization would be necessary.

7. (obj. 4) Describe one of the tasks typically performed by an institutional review board.

Answer (any 1 OK):

1. Determine whether a proposed research study provides adequate protection for human subjects.
2. Review research in progress to determine if human subjects are being adequately protected from risk.
3. Oversee provisions for human subjects protection in data collection carried out in another country.
4. Oversee provisions for human subjects protection in the use of data that were collected in a previous research study.

8. (obj. 5) Give one example of a prospective research sample that would fit the definition of a vulnerable population.

Answer (any 1 OK):

1. Individuals living in poverty
2. People in a transitional living situation
3. Individuals in an institution or community who are singled out for study because of some unique characteristic
4. Single occupants of an institutional status (e.g., the school's principal, or the lone kindergarten teacher)

9. (obj. 5) Describe one ethical issue that researchers need to consider when administering tests or self-report measures to individuals.

Answer (any 1 OK):

1. How to elicit participants' best test performance while minimizing their anxiety
2. How to elicit valid self-report responses while minimizing threats caused by self disclosure
3. Perceived threats to participants who know that their responses will be interpreted by computer software
4. Potential for violation of privacy when test results are stored in computer files

10. (obj. 6) One of the steps required to protect the rights of research participants is to give each participant a letter of informed consent. Briefly describe three types of information that such a letter should cover.

Answer (any 3 OK):

1. Participants are informed of the information that will be disclosed to the researchers.
2. The tests and experimental procedures to be used are described.
3. Participants are informed that they may withdraw from participation at any time.
4. Participants are informed that any incentives promised for participation will be received even if they withdraw from the study.
5. Participants are informed of the purpose of the research by the end of the study, if not sooner.
6. Participants are given their own copy of the informed consent letter to keep, and they are asked to return a signed copy to the researcher to signify their informed consent.

11. (obj. 6) Name one approach researchers can take to ensure that their research is well designed and thus sensitive to the needs of the research participants.

Answer (any 1 OK):

1. Study only problems with which they are competent to deal.
2. Ask colleagues for feedback on their competence to conduct a given study.
3. Determine whether they have any values or biases that might compromise the integrity of the research design of the welfare of research participants.

12. (obj. 7) Describe three steps that can be taken to protect the privacy of individuals who are to serve as participants in a research project.

Answer: (any 3 OK):

1. Get written consent from the participants or their guardians before accessing school records.
2. Use codes instead of names on measures.
3. Set up procedures to limit access to the data.
4. Do not use the data for purposes other than those originally intended without the prior consent of the participants.
5. Do not share information about specific research participants with teachers or others involved in the research.
6. Do not include the research participants' names in research reports or other documents, except with their prior consent.

13. (obj. 7) Briefly describe three strategies that can be used to maintain the confidentiality of information gathered on research participants.

Answer (any 3 OK):

1. Have research participants furnish all information anonymously.
2. Use a third party to select the sample and collect the data.
3. Use an identifier that is destroyed as soon as the individual's response is received.
4. Have research participants make up their own code numbers or aliases.
5. Dispose of sensitive data after a designated time.

14. (obj. 8) Describe one advantage and one disadvantage of conducting one's dissertation research project at the institution where one is employed.

Answer (any 1 from each set OK):

Advantages

1. Ease of obtaining approval because of access to institutional decision makers
2. Familiarity with the institution's routines
3. The logistical convenience in conducting the study where one already is located

Disadvantages

1. Less sensitivity to other members' perspectives because of one's position in the institution
2. Vulnerability to certain sanctions because of one's employment or relationship with particular individuals
3. Conflict between being a researcher and one's normal institutional role

15. (obj. 8) If members of the community protest a research study, what are three things the researcher can communicate publicly to reduce possible resistance to the study?

Answer (any 3 OK):

1. Point out the procedures that were used to obtain the informed consent of research participants.
2. Explain the steps being taken to protect the safety and confidentiality of research participants.
3. Emphasize the benefits that research participants will derive from being involved in the study.
4. Describe the positive outcomes of past studies related to your research.

APPLICATION PROBLEMS

Problem 1

"Many educational practitioners do not understand the nature of educational research. Therefore, the researcher only needs to inform administrators and teachers about the general purpose of his research project. They need not be informed of specifics, such as tests to be administered, number of students to be involved, how the results will be reported, etc." Is this a sound position to take? Support your answer.

Sample Answer:

No. Educatiors usually want detailed information about details of any research project that will affect them. For example, they will want to know who is to be involved, whether the tests are controversial, how the participants' right to privacy is to be protected, and whether the findings might reflect unfavorably on the school district.

Problem 2

You are meeting with the district superintendent to explain a research project you wish to conduct that involves giving personality tests to high school students and teachers. The superintendent asks, "What steps are you taking to protect the rights of the teachers and students who will be in your experiment?" Describe the steps that you could mention.

Sample Answer:

a. Each individual's consent will be obtained prior to the start of the project.
b. The test data will be kept confidential; participants' names will be removed from the tests as soon as possible.
c. When the research design permits, tests will be anonymous.
d. All participants will be fully informed in advance of the conditions of their participation.

Problem 3

The text describes three criteria that educators should consider in deciding whether to agree to have their institution participate in a research study. The criteria are (a) the conceptual soundness of the research, (b) the feasibility of the research, and (c) whether the research is ethically designed. Say that a high school has been asked to participate in research comparing a standard, in-class career education unit with an innovative program in which students are placed in work sites for part of the school day. Give an example of a concern that might arise in relation to each criterion.

Sample Answer:

a. Will the work sites enable students to learn skills and concepts of value rather than simply putting in time?
b. Will it be possible for students to satisfy course requirements for graduation while also working during the day?
c. Will employers provide training, pay, or other incentives instead of simply leaving students on their own?

Problem 4

In a study of truthfulness, you set up research conditions that make it possible to detect certain lies that research participants are likely to make, which could not be detected under normal conditions. At the end of the study, several participants appear to be very upset when they discover that they have been caught in lies. As the investigator, suggest the steps you could take to meet your responsibility to the research participants.

Sample Answer:

The investigator should take steps to ensure the adequate desensitization of research participants, including the following:

a. Do not conduct the study until you have planned a desensitization procedure and tried it out in a small-scale pilot study.
b. Point out that most people tell a great many small lies in situations in which they believe there is no chance to be caught.
c. Provide evidence to support the statement in (b) above, if possible. This could include data from previous research as well as the research in question.
d. Check on whether all participants have accepted your arguments. If not, arrange individual conferences and, if necessary, counseling, for participants who still appear to be troubled.

Problem 5

Suppose you have carried out a study in which you gave students incorrect scores on a test of algebra aptitude (some higher and some lower than the correct scores) to see how this information affects responses on a vocational interest test to vocations that require mathematics (e.g., electrical engineering and computer programming). Describe the procedure you would use to debrief students at the completion of the study.

Sample Answer:

Incorrect scores on this test could lead students to develop incorrect self perceptions and aspirations. Therefore, the investigator should use a procedure to dehoax students at the end of the study. This procedure could include the following steps:

a. Describe the purpose of the study and explain why the deception was necessary.
b. Hold individual conferences with the students to show them their test papers, point out their correct score, and discuss how this score was changed.
c. Give students a questionnaire to determine if they are dehoaxed, i.e., do they believe your explanation and accept their actual score on the test?
d. Offer to give students another algebra aptitude test so they can be sure of their actual performance.

TEACHING ACTIVITIES

Activity 1

Obtain a research proposal and copies of comments made by the institutional review board that reviewed it. Ask your students to review the ethical strengths and weaknesses of the proposal. Compare the students' comments with those of the IRB.

Activity 2

Identify a real or simulated proposal for a research study. Ask students to generate a list of points that should be included in a letter of informed consent to potential participants in this study.

Activity 3

Invite someone who is serving on an institutional review board to your class. The discussion can focus on ethical issues that have come up before the board. Also, students can ask the board member questions about potential ethical problems in the research studies that they are planning to do.

Activity 4

Invite to class a researcher who is conducting an ongoing study in a field setting. Ask the researcher to speak about the procedures that she used to protect human subjects, her experiences with an institutional review board, and any human relations issues that arose in the field setting and their resolution.

Activity 5

Ask students to bring to class a list of one ethical standard, one legal requirement, and one human relations principle that is particularly relevant to the research they propose to do for their master's thesis or doctoral dissertation. Discuss examples of each.

CHAPTER 4
REVIEWING THE LITERATURE

Note: The phrase in parentheses following the item number for both closed-form and open-form items, for example, "(obj. 3)", refers to the textbook chapter objective to which the item is keyed.

CLOSED-FORM ITEMS

1. (obj. 1) A researcher wishes to explore whether children's conceptions of learning vary depending on their gender and social class. In what situation should the researcher collect data *before* reviewing the literature?
   a. The researcher intends to develop grounded theory about how social class and gender affect children's conceptions of learning.
   b. The researcher intends to develop a new measure of conceptions of learning.
   c. The researcher plans to study a population of children that he thinks has not been studied previously.
   d. The researcher plans to test hypotheses derived from a theory of intellectual development.

Answer: a

2. (obj. 1) Match the following purposes of a literature review with the example that illustrates that purpose.
   __ 1. Delimiting the research problem
   __ 2. Seeking new lines of inquiry
   __ 3. Avoiding fruitless approaches
   __ 4. Gaining methodological insights
   __ 5. Identifying recommendations for further research
   __ 6. Seeking support for grounded theory
   a. A researcher identifies attempted programs that were unsuccessful in reducing dropout rates.
   b. A researcher explores suggestions that other researchers have posed to determine the best ways to keep students in school until graduation.
   c. A researcher identifies all the major lines of inquiry that have been pursued in the field of dropout prevention.
   d. A researcher develops a conceptual model to explain his discovery that dropouts tend to leave school because they had a compelling, time-intensive interest in some out-of-school activity.
   e. A researcher speculates about the possible value of an approach to dropout prevention that has not been previously tried.
   f. A researcher examines the literature on dropout prevention programs to determine how student satisfaction with such programs was measured.

Answers: 1 = c 2 = e 3 = a 4 = f 5 = b 6 = d

3. (obj. 1) It is important to conduct a review of literature before starting a research project in order to
   a. gain insight into the research methods used by other investigators.
   b. select tried-and-true approaches.
   c. broaden the research problem.
   d. compare preliminary sources.

Answer: a

4 (obj. 1) In general, research articles
a. do not include recommendations for further research.
b. do include recommendations for further research.
c. do not include recommendations for further research, but do include contact information for the authors, so that the reader can ask them directly for such recommendations.
d. only include a report of the study's findings and refer the reader to other sources for a critique of the findings.

Answer: b

5. (obj. 2) A good first step in conducting a literature review for a research study is to
a. finalize your problem statement before reading any primary sources.
b. do a thorough search of each preliminary source that indexes the literature relevant to your problem.
c. read selected secondary sources to get an overview of the literature relevant to your problem.
d. read the references in various primary sources to generate a list of other primary sources.

Answer: c

6. (obj. 3) A drawback of using secondary sources in reviews of the research literature is that
a. for many topics in education, primary sources are more accessible.
b. changes and omissions may have been made in the description of the original studies.
c. it takes longer to obtain an overview of a topic when using secondary sources.
d. the number of secondary sources in education and the social sciences is very limited.

Answer: b

7. (obj. 3) Mark a *P* in front of the sources listed below that most likely are primary sources and an *S* in front of those that most likely are secondary sources.
__ a. A textbook on educational research
__ b. An annual review of the literature on various topics of current interest
__ c. An article describing the author's dissertation investigation
__ d. A final report of the results of an evaluation study
__ e. An encyclopedia article summarizing theories of school organization
__ f. A summary of the findings of several experiments that the author helped conduct.

Answer: a = S b = S c = P d = P e = S f = P

8. (obj. 3) In educational research, the review of the literature should concentrate on presenting information from ___________ sources.
a. primary
b. secondary
c. preliminary
d. theoretical

Answer: a

9. (obj. 3) If you are interested in identifying all studies conducted by a particular researcher, it would be easiest to start by
a. consulting a secondary source.
b. consulting a primary-source document written by the researcher.
c. consulting a preliminary source.
d. contacting the researcher directly.

Answer: c

10. (obj. 4) In a preliminary source such as *Education Abstracts*, the collection of records is called a
    a. search engine.
    b. citation list.
    c. database.
    d. secondary database.

Answer: c

11. (obj. 4) Boolean operators are designed to
    a. facilitate the selection of relevant descriptors for searching a preliminary source.
    b. produce an automatic, detailed record of search procedures that one has used during an online session with a preliminary source.
    c. expand or limit the number of citations retrieved when searching a preliminary source.
    d. link citations in a preliminary source to hard copies of the citations in the Library of Congress and Google Scholar.

Answer: c

12. (obj. 4) In a search of a preliminary source, use of an *or* connector between two terms will most likely
    a. increase the number of citations retrieved.
    b. decrease the number of citations retrieved.
    c. produce only citations that are highly relevant to your topic.
    d. produce only citations that are coded by both the terms you specified.

Answer: a

13. (obj. 4) In a search of a preliminary source, truncation makes it possible to
    a. limit the number of retrieved records.
    b. identify all records that contain any keyword having a common root.
    c. rank keywords in their order of relevance to a specified topic.
    d. all of the above.

Answer: b

14. (obj. 4) Downloading your citations with bibliographic software like Endnote or ProCite
    a. allows you to put each citation into a standard format.
    b. provides fields in which you can type notes about each citation.
    c. allows you to import citations directly into your research report.
    d. all of the above.

Answer: d

15. (obj. 5) The available preliminary sources in education provide an index to
    a. bibliographies.
    b. book reviews.
    c. journal articles, paper, and reports.
    d. all of the above.

Answer: d

16. (obj. 5) Web of Science indexes
    a. documents that cite a particular document.
    b. fugitive literature.
    c. journal articles in the physical sciences that are relevant to education.
    d. journal articles in all countries that conduct educational research.

Answer: a

17. (obj. 5) The most used preliminary source indexing the literature on education is
   a. *Education Abstracts.*
   b. *Dissertation Abstracts.*
   c. ERIC.
   d. Google Scholar.

Answer: c

18. (obj. 6) Reading a secondary source on the topic of research about class size is of particular benefit to a researcher planning to carry out a study involving this variable because
   a. it provides the direct perspective of the individuals who conducted the research.
   b. it combines knowledge from many primary sources into a single publication.
   c. it provides an exhaustive list of preliminary sources relevant to the topic of class size.
   d. it eliminates the need to do one's own synthesis of the primary source literature.

Answer: b

19. (obj. 6) An example of a secondary source of literature on education is
   a. *Education Abstracts.*
   b. *Dissertation Abstracts.*
   c. *Web of Science.*
   d. *Review of Educational Research.*

Answer: d

20. (obj. 7) The best basis for classifying primary source documents in preparation for writing a literature review usually is by
   a. the questions, objectives, or hypotheses in one's study to which the document pertains.
   b. a code classifying each document as primarily concerned with research, theory, or opinion.
   c. the year of publication.
   d. the quality of the study's methodology.

Answer: a

21. (obj. 8) A presentation of the use of appropriate statistical techniques in a correct fashion should be included in the _________________ section of a research report.
   a. Introduction
   b. Research Procedures
   c. Research Results
   d. Discussion of Results

Answer: c

22. (obj. 8) Studies of the quality of published reports of educational research studies found that
   a. about half the studies should not have been published or should have been extensively revised.
   b. most of the studies were of high quality.
   b. about half of the studies were literal replications of previous research.
   c. nearly all the studies incorporated too few variables in the research design.

Answer: a

23. (obj. 8) Which of the following questions is most relevant to judging the quality of any published study?
   a. Were the researchers' measures developed within the past five years?
   b. Were the researchers' measures sufficiently valid and reliable for their intended purpose?
   c. Did the sample include at least 50 research participants?
   d. Did the literature review include at least 20 citations?

Answer: b

24. (obj. 9) In writing a literature review, the researchers devote a paragraph to each study, listing the authors, the measures and treatments used, and the statistical significance of the findings. This type of literature review has the following flaw(s):
   a. Failing to describe the search procedure by which they identified the reviewed studies.
   b. Not considering the soundness of the methodology used to generate the findings.
   c. Not fitting the findings into a conceptual or theoretical framework.
   d. all of the above.

Answer: d

25. (obj. 10) Match each of the following methods for synthesizing the findings of quantitative studies included in a literature review with its distinctive features.
   __ 1. Narrative review
   __ 2. Vote-counting
   __ 3. Chi-square method
   __ 4. Meta-analysis
   a. Calculates a statistic called *effect size* to assess the overall magnitude of the differences between groups of research participants on each variable of interest.
   b. Focuses on the sample size and magnitude of the effects in each study.
   c. Provides a subjective summary of selected research, theory, and opinion on a particular topic.
   d. Classifies studies included in the review into categories based on the direction and statistical significance of the findings.

Answers: 1 = c 2 = d 3 = b 4 = a

26. (obj. 10) The most serious shortcoming of traditional narrative reviews of the education literature is that they
   a. paid insufficient attention to the better studies.
   b. relied too much on the reviewer's subjective judgment.
   c. ignored the statistical significance of the results of quantitative analyses.
   d. ignored the expertise and reputation of the researchers whose studies were reviewed.

Answer: b

27. (obj. 10) A shortcoming of the vote-counting method of synthesizing research studies on a particular topic is that it ignores
   a. the statistical significance of the findings.
   b. the hypotheses that were tested.
   c. whether the experimental or the control group was more effective.
   d. the magnitude of the difference between the experimental and control group on each outcome measure..

Answer: d

28. (obj. 10) A major advantage of meta-analysis as an approach to synthesizing research studies on a particular topic is that it
   a. is equally applicable to quantitative and qualitative research studies.
   b. focuses primarily on the statistical significance of the effects found in each study.
   c. focuses primarily on the magnitude of the effects found in each study.
   d. excludes studies that have serious methodological limitations.

Answer: c

29. (obj. 11) In a meta-analysis of experiments on a particular instructional method, an effect size would provide information about
    a. the amount by which the experimental group falls above or below the mean score of the control group.
    b. which experiments produced results that were not statistically significant.
    c. the reliability and validity of each measure on which the experimental and control group differed.
    d. all of the above.

Answer: a

30. (obj. 12) In using the principles and procedures of the exploratory case study method for synthesizing the findings of qualitative research studies, reviewers should
    a. focus on identifying common constructs across the studies, but avoid drawing conclusions about causal linkages among the constructs.
    b. focus both on identifying common constructs and causal linkages among them across the studies.
    c. avoid using their own judgment to classify the total set of studies into categories.
    d. avoid using their own judgment to define constructs that will determine whether a particular study is relevant or irrelevant to the literature review.

Answer: b

31. (obj. 12) In the use of the exploratory case study method for reviewing qualitative research on a particular topic, audit trails
    a. involve the participation of a senior researcher who oversees the work of the review team.
    b. are conducted at the conclusion of the review process by an oversight committee.
    c. require the reviewers to record their key activities, problems, and decisions throughout the review process.
    d. focus on the number of preliminary sources that were examined, the number of studies actually included in the review, and other quantitative information.

Answer: c

OPEN-FORM ITEMS

1. (obj. 1) Suppose that you plan to do research that involves designing and evaluating a high school course about career planning. Describe two purposes of doing a literature review concerning your topic.

Answer (any 2 OK):

1. To determine the various types of programs that have been designed to teach students about careers
2. To identify promising new ways in which students can be helped to explore possible careers
3. To choose teaching strategies for the course that have been successful and avoid those that have been unsuccessful
4. To design an evaluation of the course that will allows its effectiveness to be tested in a sound manner
5. To build on the experiences of other researchers who have taught or evaluated similar courses
6. To build grounded theory about how students develop their conceptions of their own and others' potential careers

2. (obj. 2) Describe two of the steps that should be included in a thorough review of the literature after you have defined your research problem and identified key terms related to the problem.

Answer (any 2 OK):

1. Search preliminary sources that index the literature relevant to your problem.
2. Identify and read secondary sources that review the literature relevant to your problem.
3. Obtain and read the primary sources that bear most closely on your research problem.
4. Write a synthesis of what you have learned from the secondary and primary sources you have read.

3. (obj. 3) Define the terms (a) *preliminary source*, (b) *secondary source*, and (c) *primary source*.
Answer:
  a. A preliminary source indexes particular bodies of literature relevant to various topics.
  b. A secondary source is written by someone who did not actually do the research, develop the theories, or express the opinions that are presented, but that reviews and summarizes the research, theories, or opinions of others.
  c. A primary source is an original report written by the individuals who actually conducted the research, developed the theory, or formulated the opinions that are described.

4. (obj. 4) What is the effect of using (a) *or* connectors and (b) *and* connectors on the number of citations retrieved by a computer search?
Answer:
  a. *Or* connectors tend to increase the number of citations selected, because any citation is selected that has either of the descriptors that are connected by *or*.
  b. *And* connectors tend to decrease the number of citations selected, because any reference selected must include both of the descriptors that are connected by *and*.

5. (obj. 5) State four types of documents that are likely to be included in a preliminary source.
Answer (any 3 OK):
  1. Bibliographies
  2. Book reviews
  3. Books in education and related fields
  4. Curriculum materials
  5. Directories
  6. Dissertations and theses
  7. Journal articles
  8. Technical reports of funded studies
  9. Conference papers
  10. Magazines and newspapers
  11. Tests and self-report measures

6. (obj. 5) State the name of one preliminary source, and describe its purpose.
Answer:
  (Any of the preliminary sources listed in Table 4.1 are acceptable.). For example: ERIC. Its purpose is to index documents in all areas of education.

7. (obj. 6) Name one standard secondary source that is a good source of reviews on a variety of current topics of interest to many educational researchers.
Answer
  (Any of the secondary sources listed in Table 4.2 in the textbook are acceptable.)

8. (obj. 7) Describe one advantage of using a coding system to classify the primary sources you identify in your literature search.
Answer (any 1 OK):
  1. The necessity of coding each source motivates you to read it thoroughly.
  2. The necessity of coding each source stimulates you to assess its relevance to the major topics that underlie your research problem.
  3. Checking the codes that you have assigned helps you quickly identify the sources that are relevant to the particular topic you are addressing in each section of your literature review.

9. (obj. 8) State one question that you can pose in evaluating the quality of each of the following sections of a research report: the introduction, the research procedures, the research results, and the discussion of results.

Answer:

(See Figure 4.2 in the textbook for appropriate answers to this question; any one question from each section of Figure 4.2 is OK. Also see Appendix A and Appendix B for other relevant questions.)

10. (obj. 9) Describe one of the flaws that are commonly found in the literature review section of a primary source.

Answer (any 1 OK):

1. It stands alone from other parts of the source, with no explanation of how others' work relates to the present study.
2. It focuses on the size and direction of research findings, without consideration of the soundness of the methodology used to generate the findings.
3. It does not describe the search procedures used to identify relevant literature.
4. It lists isolated findings, opinions, and ideas without fitting them into a conceptual or theoretical framework.

11. (obj. 9) Describe one of the flaws that are commonly found in the literature review section of a primary source.

Answer (any 1 OK):

1. It stands alone from other parts of the source, with no explanation of how others' work relates to the present study.
2. It focuses on the size and direction of research findings, without consideration of the soundness of the methodology used to generate the findings.
3. It does not describe the search procedures used to identify relevant literature.
4. It lists isolated findings, opinions, and ideas without fitting them into a conceptual or theoretical framework.

12. (obj. 10) Describe one desirable feature of meta-analysis as an approach to reviewing the literature on a particular topic.

Answer (any 1 OK):

1. It provides information about the magnitude of the effects found in each study included in the review.
2. Its metric, effect size, can be applied to any statistic and any measure.
3. It enables the reviewer to determine whether the effect sizes across studies are affected by particular variables, such as the quality of a study's research design.

13. (obj. 12)

a. Define the term *audit trail* as used in a review of qualitative research literature.
b. Describe the purpose of creating an audit trail.

Answer

a. An audit trail describes all the procedures and decision rules that were used by the reviewer in reviewing the literature.
b. The purpose of creating an audit trail is to help readers to understand how the review was designed and carried out, and to replicate it if they desire to do so.

APPLICATION PROBLEMS

Problem 1

Suppose that you have identified the following research study as a useful foundation on which to build your own study: Scott, T. J., & O'Sullivan, M. (2000). The Internet and information literacy: Taking the first step toward technology education in the social studies. *The Social Studies*, May/June, 121-125.

How can you find other published studies that refer to or build on this study?

Sample Answers:

a. List key terms in the abstract or introduction section of the article. Then use each of these key terms as keywords in searching a preliminary source such as ERIC or *Education Abstracts*
b. Using *Web of Science*, enter the article by Scott and O'Sullivan, and determine what other subsequent articles cited it.

Problem 2

Suppose you have collected and read a substantial number of journal articles, dissertation abstracts, conference papers, and books relating to your research problem. What would be the next reasonable step as you proceed to write a literature review synthesizing this literature?

Sample answer:

Develop a classification scheme to determine the different approaches that have been used to understand and collect data about the research problem. For example, some documents might focus on theoretical approaches to understanding the phenomena of interest. Others might be descriptive studies, which might be further classified into quantitative descriptions or qualitative case studies. Still others might be experiments to determine whether certain variables of interest can be changed through intervention.

Problem 3

Suppose you have collected and read a substantial number of journal articles, dissertation abstracts, conference papers, and books relating to your research problem. What would be the next reasonable step as you proceed to write a literature review synthesizing this literature?

Sample answer:

Develop a classification scheme to determine the different approaches that have been used to understand and collect data about the research problem. For example, some documents might focus on theoretical approaches to understanding the phenomena of interest. Others might be descriptive studies, which might be further classified into quantitative descriptions or qualitative case studies. Still others might be experiments to determine whether certain variables of interest can be changed through intervention.

Problem 4

Explain why it is often useful to consult more than one preliminary source as part of the process of doing a literature review.

Sample answer:

Different preliminary sources index different types of documents. For example, *Dissertation Abstracts* is an index whose exclusive focus is doctoral dissertations, whereas *Educational Administration Abstracts* focuses on indexing journal articles. If someone was interested in the literature on a particular topic in educational administration, *Educational Administration Abstracts* would be a good preliminary source for identifying journal articles on this topic, but it would not indicate whether relevant research in the form of doctoral dissertations had been completed. To answer this question, it would be necessary to search *Dissertation Abstracts.*

TEACHING ACTIVITIES

Activity 1

Arrange a field trip to your institution's library, or an in-class presentation, to demonstrate your university library's resources for doing a literature search and retrieving documents. These resources might include online and hard-copy preliminary sources, encyclopedias and handbooks of educational research, curriculum materials collections, online library catalogs, and library machines for copying and printing. If your university has a librarian who specializes in education, you might draw on this person's expertise by asking him or her to make a presentation and provide handouts, if available, describing the library's resources.

Activity 2

You can ask students to select and read an article in a major secondary source such as the *Encyclopedia of Educational Research* or the *International Encyclopedia of Education*, on a topic of their choice. The students can be asked to give brief oral reports in class about their articles. They might focus their oral reports on how the article would be of help to them if they were to plan a research study on the topic that they chose.

Activity 3

Because meta-analysis has become a major method for synthesizing research literature, you might assign a published meta-analysis for the class to read. Class time can be used to explain the technical aspects of the meta-analysis, such as the procedures used to identify and delimit the studies selected for the meta-analysis and the types of calculations used to compute effect sizes.

CHAPTER 5
STATISTICAL TECHNIQUES

Note: The phrase in parentheses following the item number for both closed-form and open-form items, for example, "(obj. 3)", refers to the textbook chapter objective to which the item is keyed.

CLOSED-FORM ITEMS

1. (obj. 1) Qualitative researchers differ from quantitative researchers in that they
   a. collect quantitative data, but do not analyze it statistically.
   b. do not use descriptive statistics to represent what is happening in a situation.
   c. use statistical analysis as a supplement to interpretive analysis.
   d. avoid collection of any quantitative data.

Answer: c

2. (obj. 2) Match each type of score named below with the appropriate example.
   __ 1. High-anxiety, moderate anxiety, and low-anxiety students
   __ 2. High school graduation standing
   __ 3. Verbal IQ = 120
   __ 4. Grade equivalent for scores on a reading test
   __ 5. Stanine scores for a reading test
   a. Derived score
   b. Categories
   c. Rank score
   d. Continuous score
   e. Standard score

Answer: 1 = b 2 = c 3 = d 4 = a 5 = e

3. (obj. 2) The assignment of a score of 1 to male students and a score of 2 to female students is an example of a(n)
   a. nominal scale.
   b. ordinal scale.
   c. interval scale.
   d. ratio scale.

Answer: a

4. (obj. 2) Age equivalents, grade equivalents, and normal curve equivalent scores are all
   a. test statistics.
   b. standard scores.
   c. derived scores.
   d. all of the above.

Answer: c

5. (obj. 2) The difference between continuous scores and discrete scores is that
   a. continuous scores are derived from interval scales, whereas discrete scores are derived from ratio scales.
   b. continuous scores are derived from ratio scales, whereas discrete scores are derived from interval scales.
   c. continuous scores, but not discrete scores, can be converted to percentiles.
   d. continuous scores, but not discrete scores, can have fractional values.

Answer: d

6. (obj. 3) Match each statistic named below with the type of descriptive statistic under which it is classified.
   __ 1. Standard deviation
   __ 2. Bivariate coefficient
   __ 3. Median
   __ 4. Variance
   a. Measures of central tendency
   b. Measures of variability
   c. Correlational statistics

Answer: 1 = b 2 = c 3 = a 4 = b

7. (obj. 3) Correlational statistics serve the purpose of determining
   a. the degree of relationship between two or more variables.
   b. the degree to which the distribution of scores on a variable follow the normal probability curve.
   c. whether the mean or median is the more appropriate descriptive statistic.
   d. the magnitude of the difference in the standard deviations of two or more variables.

Answer: a

8. (obj. 4) The median of a group of scores
   a. is a measure of variability.
   b. reflects average performance less accurately than the mean when the distribution of scores is skewed.
   c. is the middle score in the distribution of scores.
   d. is an inferential statistic.

Answer: c

9. (obj. 4) Compared to the median, the mean
   a. is less stable across samples drawn from the same population.
   b. is more useful in analyses involving inferential statistics.
   c. provides a more accurate representation of average performance.
   d. is easier to compute.

Answer: b

10. (obj. 5) The mean and the ___________, taken together, give a good description of the nature of the group being studied.
   a. percentile distribution
   b. median
   c. standard deviation
   d. score range

Answer: c

11. (obj. 5) If a score distribution forms a normal curve,
   a. each standard deviation above or below the mean will include a fixed percentage of scores.
   b. the standard deviation can be calculated from the mean alone.
   c. the median is a better measure of central tendency than the mean.
   d. the mode is a better measure of central tendency than the mean.

Answer: a

12. (obj. 5) Skewness means that
   a. the distribution of scores on a measure is not symmetrical.
   b. the mean will be in the direction of the more extreme scores in the score distribution.
   c. the median and mean will differ.
   d. all of the above.

Answer: d

13. (obj. 6) Compared with the use of a *p* value of .05, use of a *p* value of .01
    a. provides a more stringent test of the research hypothesis.
    b. makes a Type 1 error less likely.
    c. increases the likelihood of accepting the null hypothesis when there is a real population difference.
    d. all of the above.

Answer: d

14 . (obj. 6) A significance level of .05 means that there is one chance out of ___ that the researcher will reject the null hypothesis when it is true.
    a. 100
    b. 50
    c. 10
    d. 20

Answer: d

15. (obj. 6) A test of the statistical significance of the difference between two sample means results in a *t* value that is significant at the .01 level. Which of the following is *not* a correct interpretation of this finding?
    a. The probability is 99 percent that the samples were not drawn from the same population.
    b. The mean difference exceeds the mean difference we would find once in 100 samples if the population mean difference was zero.
    c The null hypothesis can be rejected at the .01 alpha level.
    d. It is probable that the difference between the sample means reflects a true difference between the population means.

Answer: a

16. (obj. 6) When we plan a research project, we decide on the level of statistical significance we will use to reject the null hypothesis. This level is called the
    a. probability value.
    b. *t* level.
    c. alpha level.
    d. Type I value.

Answer: c

17. (obj. 7) One way to increase statistical power is to
    a. select a *p* value of .01 instead of .05.
    b. select a larger sample.
    c. decrease the risk of making a Type 1 error.
    d. use a two-tailed test of statistical significance rather than a one-tailed test.

Answer: b

18. (obj. 7) Statistical power is
    a. the power of a particular statistical test to detect a significant difference or other effect.
    b. the ratio between the significance level and the effect size.
    c. equivalent to the number of research participants included in the study.
    d. the probability that a particular statistical test will lead to rejection of a false null hypothesis.

Answer: d

19. (obj. 7) The only factor that a researcher cannot manipulate in order to increase statistical power is
    a. effect size.
    b. sample size.
    c. the *p* value for rejecting the null hypothesis.
    d. the specification of directionality in the research hypothesis.

Answer: a

20. (obj. 8) The mean and standard deviation of a sample's distribution of scores on a measure can be used to estimate
    a. a range of values that is likely to include the true population mean.
    b. the probability that the sample and population means truly differ.
    c. the probable margin of error in an individual's obtained score on a measure used in the study.
    d. statistical power.

Answer: a

21. (obj. 8) The fifth edition of the *Publication Manual of the American Psychological Association* states that the best statistics to use in reporting the results of quantitative analyses are
    a. tests of statistical significance.
    b. confidence intervals.
    c. effect sizes.
    d. means and standard deviations..

Answer: b

22. (obj. 8) The replication of a finding from one study by a subsequent study is generally considered to be
    a. more supportive of a knowledge claim than a finding from one study that has strong statistical power.
    b. less supportive of a knowledge claim than a finding from one study that has strong statistical power.
    c. unnecessary because of the development of confidence-limit methodology.
    d. unnecessary because of the development of effect-size methodology.

Answer: a

23. (obj. 8) A comparison of the mean scores of two groups on a test yields an effect size (ES) of 1.41. An ES of this magnitude means that
    a. the difference between the mean scores of the two groups is trivial.
    b. the difference between the mean scores of the two groups is large.
    c. the difference between the standard deviations of the two groups is trivial.
    d. both a and c above are correct.

Answer: b

24. (obj. 8) The practical significance of a research finding usually is best determined by
    a. tests of statistical significance.
    b. tests of statistical power.
    c. confidence intervals.
    d. effect sizes.

Answer: d

25. (obj. 9) One of the advantages of stem-and-leaf displays of data is that they facilitate the detection of outliers. What is an outlier?
    a. An individual whose score differs markedly from the other scores in the display.
    b. An individual whose score differs substantially from the other scores on any of the leaves of the display.
    c. An individual whose score is either at the top or at the bottom of the display's stem.
    d. An individual who is outside of the target population.

Answer: a

26. (obj. 9) Stem-and-leaf displays are useful because they make it easy to
    a. see the distribution of scores on a measure.
    b. detect outliers.
    c. see unexpected patterns in the data.
    d. all of the above.

Answer: d

27. (obj. 9) A diagram that shows the relationship between scores on two measures of continuous variables is called a
    a. bar graph.
    b. histogram.
    c. stem and leaf display.
    d. pictogram.

Answer: b

28. (obj. 9) The difference between histograms and bar graphs is that
    a. only histograms show the relationship between two variables.
    b. only bar graphs show the relationship between two variables.
    c. only bar graphs include categorical scores.
    d. only bar graphs can have bars that touch each other.

Answer: c

29. (obj. 10) The best approach for dealing with the problem of missing data is to
    a. have the same person carry out all aspects of the data analysis.
    b. increase the number of required data collection sessions.
    c. eliminate incomplete cases from the statistical analysis.
    d. take extra care beforehand to ensure that all required data are collected.

Answer: d

30. (obj. 11) Multilevel analysis refers to a procedure in which
    a. students at different grade levels are compared.
    b. the analysis of data is carried out at several levels, such as individual students, classrooms, and schools.
    c. the statistical analysis begins with simple statistical tests, such as chi-square, and progresses to more sophisticated tests, such as ANOVA.
    d. the appropriate probability level for statistical analysis is determined in advance.

Answer: b

31. (obj. 12) In statistical analyses made with a computer, a command file is
    a. the raw data entered into the computer program.
    b. a list of the statistical procedures from which one can choose in analyzing the data.
    c. a summary of the results of the statistical analysis.
    d. a list of the computer instructions that were used to analyze a data set.

Answer: d

OPEN-FORM ITEMS

1. (obj. 1) Why are quantitative researchers more likely than qualitative researchers to use statistics in their investigations?

Answer:

Quantitative researchers collect numerical data, and statistics are needed to analyze the data. Qualitative researchers are less likely to collect numerical data, and therefore they are less likely to use statistics in their data analyses.

2. (obj. 2) A researcher collects data from a sample of school principals on the following variables: (a) age; (b) gender; (c) whether the principal's school is at the elementary, middle, or high school level; and (d) their standing relative to each other on a measure of effectiveness. Identify the type of score that would be yielded by a measure of each of these variables.

Answer:
   a. Continuous score
   b. Category
   c. Category
   d. Rank

3. (obj. 3) If researchers want to know whether boys are more homogeneous in visual-spatial ability than girls, would they use a measure of central tendency, a measure of variability, or a correlational method?

Answer:
A measure of variability

4. (obj. 4) State one advantage and one disadvantage of the median as a measure of central tendency.

Answer:
An advantage is that the median is not affected by extreme scores. A disadvantage is that the median is less stable than the mean, especially with a small number of cases.

5. (obj. 5) If a sample's scores on a test form a normal curve, what is one piece of information that the standard deviation provides?

Answer (any 1 OK):
   1. The standard deviation tells the percentage of individuals in the sample who earned scores within a given range of standard deviation units.
   2. An individual's standard deviation score indicates his percentile in the distribution of scores for the sample.

6. (obj. 6) What does a test of statistical significance of the difference between the mean scores of two groups tell researchers about their null hypothesis?

Answer:
If the difference is statistically significant, the null hypothesis is rejected and the researcher concludes that the difference between the sample means probably reflects a true difference between the population means.

7. (obj. 7) (a) What is statistical power? (b). Briefly describe two factors that increase statistical power.

Answer:
   a. Statistical power is the probability that a particular test of statistical significance will lead to the rejection of the null hypothesis.
   b. *Factors that increase statistical power* (any 2 OK):
      1. Increasing the sample size
      2. Lowering the alpha level used to reject the null hypothesis (e.g., from .01 to .05)
      3. Stating a directional hypothesis
      4. Studying variables that yield a larger effect size

8. (obj. 8) A researcher compares the scores of 1,000 randomly selected urban eighth grade students with 1,000 randomly selected rural eighth grade students on a 30-item test of mathematical understanding. The urban sample obtains a mean raw score of 12.6, while the rural sample obtains a mean raw score of 13.2. The standard deviation is 5.1. The difference between the mean scores is significant at the .05 level. Would you consider this difference to be of practical significance? Why or why not?

Answer:

No. Statistical significance was reached mainly because of the large sample size. The difference amounts to only .6 points on a 30-item test; it would be difficult to argue that a difference this small has any practical significance for policy or classroom instruction.

9. (obj. 8) Explain what confidence limits reveal about the population values based on the findings for a research sample.

Answer:

Confidence limits define the upper and lower value of a range of values for a sample statistic that is likley to contain a population parameter, that is, the actual value that would be obtained if the entire population were measured.

10. (obj. 9) What are two advantages of organizing data into a stem-and-leaf display for exploratory data analysis?

Answer (any 2 OK):

1. The researcher can see the shape of the score distribution.
2. The display provokes questions about the data by revealing patterns not shown in a conventional listing of scores.
3. The display facilitates the detection of outliers.

11. (obj. 10) Several students in a researcher's sample take a test administered at the start of the study but do not take the test administered at the end of the study. Give one reason why this creates a problem for the research procedure.

Answer (any 1 OK):

1. The missing data make the statistical analysis more complicated.
2. The missing data make it more difficult to interpret the statistical results.

12. (obj. 11) A researcher administers a test of musical knowledge to all students in 30 classrooms and then compares the performance of the boys and girls on this test. If the unit of statistical analysis is the classroom, how would the comparison be made?

Answer:

The mean score of boys and the mean score of girls in each of the 30 classrooms would be computed. Then the average of the 30 mean scores for the boys would be compared with the average of the 30 mean scores for the girls.

13. (obj. 12) State one reason why it is desirable to retain one's raw research data for a period of time after a study has been completed.

Answer (any 1 OK):

1. The data could be reanalyzed later to yield additional insights.
2. If anyone questions the accuracy of the statistical results, they can be checked by reanalyzing the research data.

APPLICATION PROBLEMS

Problem 1
You want to know the average gain in reading speed that is made by students who take a speed-reading course. A reading test was given to 250 students before and after they took the course. In looking over the scores, you notice that most students gained 100 to 300 words per minute. However, there are about 20 students who made outstanding gains, ranging from 600 to 1,000 words per minute. Would the mean or the median be a more accurate measure of central tendency, and why?

Sample Answer:

The median would be more accurate than the mean, because it would not be affected as much by the 40 extreme scores.

Problem 2
A researcher finds that the mean score of scholarship students on a final exam in a university history course is 89.7, and the mean score of other students is 85.3. A *t* test of this difference yields a *p* value of .01. What does the *p* value tell us about the null hypothesis? Also, what generalization does the *p* value allow us to make?

Sample Answer:

A *p* value of .01 usually is considered sufficient to reject the null hypothesis. Therefore, we can generalize beyond this sample and conclude that there is a real difference in performance on the exam in the total population of foster-care students and other students that this sample represents.

Problem 3
A researcher has completed a study in which an experimental group of 60 college students was formed into pairs and was requested to ask each other questions in preparation for an examination. A control group of 60 students was requested to quiz themselves in preparation for the same examination. Students' scores on the examination formed the dependent variable. What is the appropriate unit of statistical analysis for determining whether the examination performance of the experimental group differed from that of the control group?

Sample Answer:

The researcher should use each pair of students in the experimental group as the unit of analysis, because the learning of each student probably was affected by her partner. The scores of each pair would be averaged to yield a mean score. Because there are 60 experimental group students, there will be 30 mean scores in the statistical analysis. The unit of analysis for the control group should be the individual, because each student engaged in the learning activity independently of the other students. Thus there will be 60 control group scores in the statistical analysis.

TEACHING ACTIVITIES

Activity 1

Have your students read a research article that contains descriptive and inferential statistics. In class, review with the students each statistic that was used and its purpose in the study. Although some students take a statistics course prior to a course in research methods, they may not have learned how statistics actually are used in research. Activity 1 is helpful because it gives students an opportunity to see statistics in a relevant research context.

Activity 2

Have each of your students collect data about two variables and bring the data to class. (A simple alternative to this procedure is to ask each student in class to write down the heights of their father and mother or of a married couple whom they know.) You can list the data for these two variables on the blackboard and show students how you can compute various descriptive statistics about them (e.g., mean, median, mode, range, standard deviation, and effect size). You also can generate a null hypothesis (e.g., there is no significant difference between the height of males and females), and show students how this hypothesis can be accepted or rejected by a *t* test.

Activity 3

Invite to class a researcher who used computer software in carrying out statistical analyses for a recent study. Ask the researcher to explain how the data were entered into the computer file, how the statistical analyses were done, the kinds of computer printouts that were generated, how to interpret the results, and any problems that arose in the use of the computer.

CHAPTER 6
SELECTING A SAMPLE

Note: The phrase in parentheses following the item number for both closed-form and open-form items, for example, "(obj. 3)", refers to the textbook chapter objective to which the item is keyed.

CLOSED-FORM ITEMS

1. (obj. 1) In sampling a phenomenon to investigate in a research study, quantitative researchers need to
   a. select individuals for study who are familiar with the phenomenon.
   b. study the entire population that represents instances of the phenomenon.
   c. apply replication logic.
   d. systematically select instances of the phenomenon for the sample.

Answer: d

2. (obj. 1) Unlike quantitative researchers, qualitative researchers select their samples to
   a. satisfy the requirements of grounded theory.
   b. test theories about the phenomenon being studied.
   c. accurately represent a defined population.
   d. study cases that are information-rich with respect to their research questions.

Answer: d

3. (obj. 1) The most important requirement for being able to generalize the results of a quantitative research study is to
   a. minimize sample attrition and missing data.
   b. formulate a theory and use it to interpret the study's findings.
   c. define a population in advance of data collection and sample from it.
   d. use measures for which population norms are available.

Answer: c

4. (obj. 2) All the members of a set of persons to whom a researcher wishes to generalize the results of a study are referred to as
   a. the defined population.
   b. the accessible population.
   c. the target population.
   d. the sampling distribution.

Answer: c

5. (obj. 2) Another term corresponding to *target population* in quantitative research is
   a. accessible population.
   b. universe.
   c. defined population.
   d. cohort.

Answer: b

6. (obj. 3) For a study to have population validity,
   a. the study must employ an experimental research design.
   b. the sample must be randomly selected from the defined population.
   c. the study must replicate a previous study involving the same population.
   d. research participants must be randomly assigned to the experimental and control groups.

Answer: b

7. (obj. 3) The deviation of a sample statistic from the actual parameter for the population from which the sample was randomly drawn is a measure of
   a. population validity.
   b. sampling error.
   c. statistical significance.
   d. variability.

Answer: b

8. (obj. 3) A researcher plans a study in a school district to compare method A and method B of teaching reading. Which of the following approaches would be most likely to ensure a representative sample?
   a. Obtain permission from a cooperative principal to nominate students in his school to experience each teaching method.
   b. Require all students enrolled in English literature classes to serve as research participants.
   c. Use students from one school as research participants to receive method A and students from a comparable school to receive method B.
   d. Define the population as all students in the district receiving reading instruction, select a random sample, and randomly assign students to methods A or B.

Answer: d

9. (obj. 3) Replication logic refers to
   a. the conduct of replications of a study with samples from different populations to determine the stability of the findings.
   b. the use of theory to determine the other types of cases to which the findings of one case study can be generalized.
   c. the cross-validation of research hypotheses through repeated replications of the original study.
   d. precise specification of a population so that subsequent researchers can draw equivalent samples in an effort to replicate the original study's findings.

Answer: b

10. (obj. 3) If a qualitative researcher is doing a theoretical replication, the next case to be studied should
   a. differ from the first case in ways that allow a further test of the theory.
   b. be similar to the first case.
   c. yield similar results to the findings obtained from the first case.
   d. be selected to test alternate interpretations of the findings from the first case.

Answer: a

11. (obj. 3) Population validity is achieved only if
   a. the researcher limits generalizations of the study's findings to the accessible population.
   b. a test effectively predicts a relevant variable within the target population.
   c. the accessible population is randomly selected from the target population.
   d. the accessible population is reasonably representative of the target population.

Answer: d

12. (obj. 3) Which of the following is an important criterion for determining whether an experiment has population validity?
   a. A clear description of the target population
   b. A detailed description of the sampling procedure
   c. Identification and description of the sampling frame
   d. all of the above

Answer: d

13. (obj. 4) Picking names out of a hat is an example of
    a. simple random sampling.
    b. systematic sampling.
    c. cluster sampling.
    d. sampling error.

Answer: a

14. (obj. 4) An investigator wants to compare the reading comprehension of first-grade students who are taught reading by treatment A versus first-grade students taught reading by treatment B. He selects all first graders in Washington Elementary School (6 classes, $N = 200$) and places their names in a hat. The first 60 names taken from the hat are placed in treatment A, and the next 60 names are placed in treatment B. What procedure has the researcher used?
    a. Simple random sampling
    b. Random assignment
    c. Cluster sampling
    d. Stratified random sampling

Answer: b

15. (obj. 4) Stratified random sampling is usually a better approach than random sampling if the researcher
    a. wants to avoid sampling bias.
    b. is studying a target population that is highly homogeneous.
    c. expects small differences between the groups being compared.
    d. wants to study the performance of different subgroups within the sample.

Answer: d

16. (obj. 4) In doing a survey of Chicago residents' evaluation of their schools, the researcher divides the city into 9 square-block areas and randomly selects 20 areas for study. This is an example of
    a. stratified random sampling.
    b. cluster sampling.
    c. subgroup analysis.
    d. use of a large sample.

Answer: b.

17. (obj. 4) A disadvantage of cluster sampling compared to other sampling techniques is that
    a. one cannot use conventional formulas for computing statistics on the data.
    b. it requires including research participants in the sample from every sampling unit.
    c. this technique is more expensive than other sampling techniques.
    d. it rejects randomization as a basis for sample selection.

Answer: a

18. (obj. 4) The main reason that most educational research involves non-probability sampling is researchers' concern for
    a. convenience in obtaining the sample.
    b. generalizability of the findings.
    c. fairness to all research participants.
    d. statistical significance.

Answer: a

19. (obj. 5) A researcher wants to analyze the match between state science standards and what is taught in the high school science curriculum. He selects the five most frequently-adopted high school science textbooks as his sample. This is an example of:
    a. systematic sampling.
    b. sampling of a phenomenon.
    c. convenience sampling.
    d. studying the entire population.

Answer: b

20. (obj. 6) The problem of attrition (loss of research participants) is best reduced by
    a. the use of systematic sampling techniques.
    b. the use of volunteers as research participants.
    c. fostering research participants' commitment to the study and maintaining rapport with them.
    d. including subgroups of research participants proportional to their numbers in the population.

Answer: c

21. (obj. 6) Put an *L* before the following research situations that require a large sample and an *S* before those situations in which a small sample is acceptable.

__ a. Many uncontrolled variables are present.
__ b. Large relationships are anticipated between the variables to be correlated.
__ c. Subgroup analyses are to be performed.
__ d. The research participants have been closely matched on the critical variables.
__ e. Small differences are expected between the scores of the experimental and control groups on the dependent variable.

Answer: a = L b = S c = L d = S e = L

22. (obj. 6) A small sample is most appropriate when
    a. small differences are anticipated between the experimental and control groups.
    b. subgroup analyses are planned.
    c. the population is highly heterogeneous on the variables being studied.
    d. close matching of the comparison groups is possible.

Answer: d

23. (obj. 6) The first step in estimating needed sample size is to
    a. determine the size of the target population.
    b. determine the size of the accessible population.
    c. study the findings of related research using similar variables.
    d. determine the population mean and standard deviation for each variable of concern.

Answer: c

24. (obj. 7) Sampling techniques are more flexible in qualitative research than in quantitative research mainly because qualitative researchers
    a. need only one or a few cases.
    b. are interested in typical cases.
    c. prefer emergent research designs.
    a. have no interest in generalizing study results.

25. (obj. 7) The primary goal of purposeful sampling is to
    a. enable researchers to test theories.
    b. select cases that are information rich with respect to the study's purpose.
    c. replicate the result of previous research.
    d. select cases that are convenient for researchers to study.

Answer: b

26. (obj. 8) Replication logic is used in case study research primarily to
    a. enable researchers to develop or test a theory.
    b. generate research findings that can be generalized to a defined population.
    c. duplicate the findings of previous research.
    d. all of the above.

Answer: a

27. (obj. 9) In a study of teachers' use of power, selecting as a case a teacher who is known throughout the country as an exceptionally active opinion maker would be an example of
    a. typical case sampling.
    b. intensity sampling.
    c. deviant case sampling.
    d. convenience sampling.

Answer: c

28. (obj. 9) Random sampling in qualitative research is sometimes used in order to
    a. ensure that the cases studied are representative.
    b. establish that the sampling procedure is not biased.
    c. confirm the findings of previous case studies.
    d. select cases that illustrate the full range of variation in the phenomenon being studied.

Answer: b

29. (obj. 10) A qualitative researcher who is interested in the study of a phenomenon in depth would be well advised to
    a. study a wide range of experiences for a small number of people.
    b. study a narrow set of experiences for a large number of people.
    c. document the naturally occurring diversity and variation of the phenomenon.
    d. use stratified purposeful sampling to select the cases.

Answer: a

30. (obj. 10) Study of a large number of cases in a qualitative research study is particularly desirable for
    a. avoiding redundancy in the information provided by different cases.
    b. conducting critical case sampling.
    c. understanding the range of diversity or variation in the phenomenon being studied.
    d. doing a theoretical replication.

Answer: c

31. (obj. 11) Volunteers are likely to constitute a biased sample because they
    a. have been found to differ from nonvolunteers on numerous characteristics.
    b. are less responsive to experimental interventions than individuals who are required to participate.
    c. are more susceptible to the Hawthorne effect than nonvolunteers.
    d. tend to have more conservative attitudes than nonvolunteers.

Answer: a

32. (obj. 11) Comparing the characteristics of volunteers and nonvolunteers for a research study best helps a researcher to
    a. increase the response rate.
    b. determine how well the findings can be generalized to the population.
    c. determine the best method to recruit participants.
    d. obtain statistically significant findings.

Answer: b

33. (obj. 11) Compared to nonvolunteers for participation in a research study, volunteers tend to be
    a. more introverted.
    b. lower in need for achievement.
    c. better educated.
    d. more conforming.

Answer: c

34. (obj. 11) If it is necessary to use only volunteers in a research study, the best precaution is for the researcher to
    a. consider whether volunteers are likely to differ from nonvolunteers on critical variables.
    b. increase the sample size.
    c. require a public commitment to participate.
    d. keep the description of the study's purpose brief and matter-of-fact.

Answer: a

35. (obj. 12) Which of the following is an effective method for recruiting individuals to participate in a research study?
    a. Make the study sound appealing.
    b. Offer gifts and other benefits to prospective participants.
    c. Have the request for volunteers made by a person of high status.
    d. all of the above.

Answer: d

36. (obj. 12) In situations where volunteering is regarded by the target population as the normal thing to do, a recommended way to increase the rate of volunteering is to
    a. create a situation where each individual can volunteer in private.
    b. emphasize that volunteering represents a tremendous contribution to society.
    c. ask each individual to make a public commitment to volunteer.
    d. post a description of the study in a public place.

Answer: c

OPEN-FORM ITEMS

1. (obj. 1) A qualitative researcher who is interested in studying school teachers who moonlight in other jobs decides to select cases who have only one extra job, at which they spend no more than 10 hours a week.
    a. What type of purposeful sample does the researcher appear to be seeking?
    b. What is the researcher's probable rationale for limiting the study to such cases?

Answer:

   a. This appears to be an typical-case sample, in which the researcher wishes to study cases who represent the majority of moonlighting teachers rather than intense or extreme cases who moonlight far less or far more than 10 hours a week.
   b. By studying less extreme cases the researcher is more likely to obtain findings that will deepen the understanding of the general effects of moonlighting on teachers and their students.

2. (obj. 2) What is the difference between a target population and an accessible population?

Answer:

The target population is the population to which you want to generalize your results, and the accessible population is the population from which you draw your sample.

3. (obj. 2) Define *sampling* as this term is used in quantitative research.

Answer:

In quantitative research, sampling is the process of selecting members of a research sample from a defined population with the intent that the sample accurately represents the population.

4. (obj. 3) How does an educational researcher establish the population validity of his research study?

Answer:

Population validity is established by demonstrating that the sample is representative of the target population to which the researcher wishes to generalize his findings. It can be established by showing that the sample was randomly selected from the accessible population and that the accessible population in turn represents the target population.

5. (obj. 3) A researcher randomly selects a sample of 100 teachers from inner-city schools in a large U.S. city. She views her sample as representative of the defined population of all inner-city school teachers in the United States. The researcher measures the teachers' attitudes toward site-based management of schools. If her study has population validity, what can she conclude from the results of the study?

Answer:

The researcher can conclude that the results she obtained for this sample of inner-city school teachers would be similar if she had measured the attitudes of the entire population of inner-city school teachers in the U.S., that is, she can generalize her findings from the sample to the defined population.

6. (obj. 3) Describe one criterion that should be satisfied in order to determine that a research study has high population validity.

Answer (any 1 OK):

1. The researcher should provide a clear description of the target population to which she intends to generalize the results.
2. The researcher should describe the sampling procedure to be used, including type of sampling technique, sample size, and geographic area in which the accessible population is located.
3. The researcher should describe the sampling frame, that is, the list or source from which the sample was selected.
4. The researcher should include information about the completion rate, that is, the proportion of the original sample for whom complete data were obtained.

7. (obj. 4) Explain the difference between random sampling and random assignment in experimental research.

Answer:

Random sampling means that every individual in the accessible population has an equal chance of being selected for the sample. Random assignment involves the use of randomization procedures to ensure that each individual in the sample has an equal chance of being in the experimental or control group.

8. (obj. 4) State one reason why, if all other things are equal, randomly selected samples are preferable for research purposes in quantitative research.

Answer (any 1 OK):

1. Random samples yield research data that can be generalized to a larger population within margins of error that can be estimated by statistical techniques.
2. Random sampling satisfies the logic by which a null hypothesis is tested with inferential statistics.

9. (obj. 4) Name one condition under which it would be appropriate to use nonproportional stratified sampling, that is, to select an equal number of research participants from each stratum rather than selecting from each stratum the same proportion that exists in the target population.

Answer (any 1 OK):
1. You are concerned primarily with the performance of research participants in each of the strata rather than with comparing the performance of research participants in different strata.
2. You want to be sure you have enough cases in each of the strata for your analysis.
3. You do not intend to compute means or other statistics for the entire sample.

10. (obj. 4) You wish to obtain a simple random sample of 1,000 members of the American Psychological Association to whom you will send a questionnaire about their views concerning the appropriate preparation of clinical psychologists. List the steps you would take in selecting your sample.

Answer:
a. Obtain a list of members and number the names on the list.
b. Using a table of random numbers to at least four digits, select 1,000 numbers.
c. Identify those 1,000 members on the member list who have the selected numbers.

11. (obj. 4) Suppose that you are planning a study on the relationship between teachers' use of six verbal behaviors (specific praise, prompting, etc.) and student achievement. Your accessible population includes all fourth-, fifth-, and sixth-grade teachers in the Chicago public schools, who previously have been classified as either bilingual or English-speaking-only. Your sample will include a total of 120 teachers.
a. What sampling procedure should you use to ensure that you have an adequate sample of teachers at each grade level, including both bilingual and English-speaking-only teachers?
b. How would you carry out the sampling procedure?

Answer:
a. You should use stratified random sampling.
b. Divide the accessible population into six groups: fourth-grade bilingual, fourth grade English-speaking-only, fifth-grade bilingual, fifth-grade English-speaking-only, sixth-grade bilingual, and sixth-grade English speaking-only. Then randomly select 20 teachers from each group.

12. (obj. 4) Define probability sampling, and give an example of a sampling method that involves this sampling approach.

Answer:
Probability sampling is an approach to selecting a sample in which each individual in the population has a known chance of being selected.

Methods that involve this approach (any 1 OK):
1. Simple random sampling
2. Systematic random sampling
3. Stratified random sampling
4. Cluster sampling

13. (obj. 5) Explain how in sampling a phenomenon rather than individuals it might be feasible to study the entire accessible population or target population.

Answer:
The research might involve a fairly specific phenomenon, such that it is possible to identify and study the total number of available or existing instances of the phenomenon. For example, say that the research concerns comparing the educational achievement standards set by states in response to the No Child Left Behind legislation. If the researchers could obtain the standards set by all 50 states, in the United States, their sample would be the entire target population

14. (obj. 6) Briefly describe three types of research situations that require a fairly large sample size.
Answer (any 3 OK):
1. Many uncontrolled variables are present.
2. Small changes or small differences between the comparison groups are expected on the dependent variables.
3. The research design calls for breaking the sample into subgroups.
4. The population is highly heterogeneous on the variables being studied.
5. Reliable measures are not available.
6. High attrition is expected.
7. A high level of statistical significance or statistical power is required.

15. (obj. 7) When using purposeful sampling, what does the researcher strive to accomplish in selecting the sample?
Answer:
The selection of cases that are likely to be information-rich in relation to the specific phenomena being studied

16. (obj. 7) Describe one rationale that a qualitative researcher can use to justify her selection of a particular case to study.
Answer (any 1 OK):
1. The particular case will enable her to develop a deeper understanding of the phenomenon being studied.
2. The particular case will enable her to discover or test theories about the phenomenon.
3. The particular case will enable her to generalize the findings to other, similar cases.

17. (obj. 8) Describe one type of replication that a qualitative researcher might carry out.
Answer (any 1 OK):
1. The researcher can do a literal replication, in which she selects a case for whom she predicts similar results to those for the case or cases previously studied.
2. The researcher can do a theoretical replication, in which she selects a case for whom she predicts the results will differ from those for the case or cases previously studied in ways consistent with the theory underlying the research.

18. (obj. 9) Briefly name and describe three purposeful sampling strategies.
Answer:
(Note: See pages 180-185 in the textbook, which describes 14 types of purposeful sampling strategies plus opportunistic sampling; any 3 of the 14 purposeful sampling strategies are acceptable.)

19. (obj. 10) Give one reason why a qualitative researcher might find it desirable to study more than one case in a research study.
Answer (any 1 OK):
1. The researcher wishes to document the diversity or variations in a phenomenon that are reflected in different individuals' experience.
2. The researcher wishes to conduct a literal replication to increase the certainty of the findings for one case.
3. The researcher wishes to conduct a theoretical replication in order to determine if the results for the next case are different from those for the previous case in a theoretically consistent way.

20. (obj. 11) List three characteristics that researchers have found to differ for volunteer and non-volunteer research participants.
Answer:
(Note: See Table 6.3 on page 187 in the textbook, which lists 11 characteristics of research volunteers; any 3 of these characteristics are acceptable.)

21. (obj. 12) State three suggestions for increasing the proportion of volunteers and thus reducing volunteer bias.
Answer:

(Note: See Table 6.4 on page 189 in the textbook, which lists 11 suggestions for improving the rate of volunteering to participate in a research study; any 3 of these suggestions are acceptable.)

APPLICATION PROBLEMS

Problem 1
A researcher wants to do a case study of the emotional reactions and motivational states of a child while the child is playing computer games.

a. What rationale can he use to justify generalizing about the results of the case study?
b. How could he increase the generalizability of his case study findings?

Sample Answer:

a. If the researcher describes the student's characteristics to demonstrate that the student is typical of a larger group of students, he is justified in generalizing the findings to that larger group.
b. The researcher can increase the generalizability of his findings by using literal or theoretical replication and doing multiple case studies.

Problem 2
An investigator wishes to study the oral reading performance of second-grade students in a large school district. A total of 3,172 second-grade students are enrolled in 104 classrooms in the district. The investigator wishes to obtain a total group of 100 research participants using a two-stage cluster sampling technique. Describe the steps she would take in selecting her sample.
Sample Answer:

a. Identify the 104 second-grade classrooms and assign each classroom a number.
b. Randomly select 10 classrooms using a table of random numbers, or by drawing numbers from a container.
c. Obtain the names of all students in the selected classrooms, and assign each student a number.
d. Randomly select 10 students from each of the 10 classrooms using a table of random numbers.

Problem 3
A researcher is studying the effects of learning a problem-solving strategy upon the mathematics achievement of sixth-grade students. He selects a sample of students in one school and randomly assigns half of them to the experimental group and half to the control group. All students will be given a pretest of mathematics achievement. The experimental group then will receive a one-hour lesson that teaches a problem-solving strategy for students to use in solving word problems in mathematics. The control group receives conventional instruction. Because he expects the problem-solving training to work best with the brighter students, the researcher divides both groups into two subgroups based on their IQ scores, using the following categories: below 90, 90-110, 111-130, and above 130. He administers a mathematics achievement posttest to all research participants two months after the treatment ends. Explain why a fairly large sample size is required for this project.
Sample Answer:

a. Because the treatment lasts only one hour and involves only word problems, the researcher might well expect only a small difference in the groups' posttest mathematics achievement.
b. In an average school population, only a very small percentage of the students are likely to have IQ scores above 130. Because the researcher has broken his sample into subgroups based on IQ level, he must obtain a large enough sample to ensure that he has enough research participants in this category.

Problem 4
Identify the procedures in the following research description that are likely to cause sampling bias: A researcher teaches three sections of a remedial English class for freshmen in a large state university. A colleague teaches three sections of regular freshman English. The researcher has developed a special 20-hour program to teach rules of spelling. She gives a spelling test in her sections and in her colleague's sections. She identifies 63 students from her sections and 36 from her colleague's sections who scored below 50 percent on the test. She then describes the special program to her sections and asks the 63 low scorers to take the program by attending special sessions one hour per day for four weeks. Fifty-one agree to do so. The 36 students in her colleague's sections are used as a control group and receive no special treatment. At the end of four weeks, 26 of her students have completed the spelling program, while the remainder have missed between 1 and 18 of the sessions. She administers a spelling posttest to the 26 treatment participants and the 36 control participants and compares their gains since the pretest.
Sample Answer:

a. The research participants were a sample of convenience, rather than being drawn systematically from a defined population.
b. The treatment group consisted entirely of volunteers.
c. The treatment group suffered a large loss of research participants, and the participants who completed the program probably were highly motivated by comparison. No control-group participants were lost, because they were not required to do anything.
d. Research participants were not drawn from the same participant pool. That is, the experimental group was drawn from the remedial course, whereas the control group was drawn from the regular course. Because research participants were drawn from different populations, they probably differed in ways that affected the study results, e.g., their overall mastery of English.

Problem 5
Describe a qualitative research problem for which intensity sampling would be a good purposeful sampling strategy.
Sample Answer:

a. The researcher wishes to do an in-depth study in which he asks a small number of students to reflect freely on their feelings and thoughts related to a specific phenomenon, e.g., their experiences with loneliness in school or their jealousy about another student's success. The researcher would not seek extreme manifestations of the phenomena of interest because they might not lend themselves to the reflective process, but would seek intense manifestations of the phenomena so that there are enough to study.
b. In evaluating an instructional program that has been implemented in many schools, the researcher might want to avoid selecting either extreme successes or unusual failures, that might be discredited as being too extreme or unusual for providing trustworthy information. Therefore, the evaluator would select cases that manifest sufficient success or failure to illuminate the nature of the phenomenon but do not fall at the extremes.

TEACHING ACTIVITIES

Activity 1

Ask students to identify a quantitative research problem they are studying or might want to study. Ask each student to describe a relevant target population to whom they wish to generalize the results of their study, an accessible population from which they could draw a sample, and the sampling technique described in the textbook that appears most appropriate for selecting the sample.

Activity 2

Have students identify an educational phenomenon on which they would like to shed light by doing a case study. Have them describe some of the characteristics they would look for in the case selected for study if they were to use (a) extreme or deviant case sampling, (b) intensity sampling, or (c) typical case sampling.

Activity 3

Have all students read the same qualitative case study. During class time, have students (a) identify the purposeful sampling strategy that was used, (b) discuss what this strategy enabled the researcher to learn about the phenomena of interest, and (c) whether another sampling strategy might have been more appropriate.

CHAPTER 7
COLLECTING RESEARCH DATA WITH TESTS AND SELF-REPORT MEASURES

Note: The phrase in parentheses following the item number for both closed-form and open-form items, for example, "(obj. 3)", refers to the textbook chapter objective to which the item is keyed.

CLOSED-FORM ITEMS

1. (obj. 1) The objectivity of a standardized test refers to its
   a. degree of relationship to a criterion variable.
   b. freedom from tester bias.
   c. accuracy of prediction.
   d. provision of normative data.

Answer: b

2. (obj. 1) In contrast to the use of performance tests in research, the use of self-report measures generally
   a. is directed at measurement of personality characteristics.
   b. is meant to demonstrate each respondent's level of a characteristic that is typical for her.
   c. is subject to distortion due to response sets.
   d. all of the above.

Answer: d

3. (obj. 1) The tendency to present oneself in a favorable light when responding to a self-report measure is known as a(n) ______________ response set.
   a. social desirability
   b. acquiescence
   c. deviance
   d. carelessness

Answer: a

4. (obj. 2) To standardize a test, the developer must establish
   a. agreement between researchers and practitioners about test content.
   b. the test's reliability.
   c. procedures that ensure consistency in how the test is administered and scored.
   d. all of the above.

Answer: c

5. (obj. 2) In test development, *differential item functioning* refers to the tendency for
   a. some test items to relate more closely with the total test score than other items.
   b. individual scorer bias to affect how test items are scored.
   c. individuals of equal ability but from different subgroups not to have the same probability of earning a given score.
   d. individuals to score differently on each administration of the test.

Answer: c

6. (obj. 3) Match each example of evidence about a test below with the type of evidence of test validity that it represents.

__ 1. The test was found to include 32 of the 47 topics covered in a textbook.
__ 2. The test was found to lead to a higher rate of referral for boys than for girls to a treatment program for attention deficit disorder.
__ 3. Students' rank order of performance on the test was found to correspond well to the students' rank order of performance on an established longer test of the same ability.
__ 4. The test was found to be a good measure of students' ability to learn independently.

a. Evidence from relationship to other variables
b. Evidence from consequences of testing
c. Evidence from response processes
d. Evidence from test content

Answer: 1 = d 2 = b 3 = a 4 = c

7. (obj. 3) Test validity is
a. not a unitary concept.
b. an intrinsic property of the test.
c. an intrinsic property of the test scores.
d. associated with inferences that are made from test scores.

Answer: d

8. (obj. 3) Recent research on the effects of standards-based instruction has shown that test data collected in school settings generally show
a. high evidence of content-related validity.
b. low evidence of content-related validity.
c. high alignment between curriculum content, teachers' instruction, and assessment by standardized tests.
d. teachers' ability to judge evidence of a test's content-related validity by brief inspection of the items.

Answer: b

9. (obj. 3) If a test is used to make decisions that are found to be harmful to certain groups, this represents evidence of the test's
a. lack of validity.
b. misuse.
c. low objectivity.
d. lack of reliability.

Answer: b

10. (obj. 4) Match each example of test reliability below with the type of reliability coefficient that is used to calculate it.

__ 1. After the test is administered, it is split into two halves and the scores on one half are correlated with those on the other half.
__ 2. Two parallel forms of the test are administered, and scores on one form are correlated with those on the other form.
__ 3. The test is administered and then readministered after a time delay, and scores from the first administration are correlated with those from the second administration.
__ 4. Individual test items are analyzed with the use of standard formulas.

a. Coefficient of equivalence
b. Coefficient alpha
c. Coefficient of internal consistency
d. Coefficient of stability

Answer: 1 = c 2 = a 3 = d 4 = b

11. (obj. 4) A test is reliable to the extent that it
  a. yields scores that are interpreted the same way by different raters.
  b. measures a known construct.
  c. contains nonrandom measurement error.
  d. minimizes measurement error.

Answer: d

12. (obj. 5) The various sources of measurement error in a test can be estimated by
  a. classical test theory.
  b. generalizability theory.
  c. the standard error of measurement.
  d. coefficient alpha

Answer: b

13. (obj. 5) Calculation of the standard error of measurement allows researchers to determine
  a. the combined measurement error due to all sources of error that were investigated.
  b. the probable range within which individuals' true scores fall.
  c. the likelihood that that test was too easy or too difficult for most testees.
  d. the reliability of each test item.

Answer: b

14. (obj. 6) Item response theory allows researchers to develop tests having all the following advantages over traditional tests *except that*
  a. the test can be customized to students at different ability levels.
  b. it is possible to construct many parallel tests of equivalent difficulty.
  c. measurement error can be reduced by administering items geared to each individual's ability level.
  d. each individual can take a test containing just a few items at an appropriate difficulty level.

Answer: d

15. (obj. 7) When the researcher has the choice of using a standardized test or an achievement test constructed by the teachers who are being studied, the researcher
  a. should use the teacher-constructed test, because such tests generally are freer of measurement error.
  b. should use the teacher-constructed test, because such tests generally have better concurrent validity.
  c. should use the standardized test, because such tests generally are better written.
  d. can use either test, because both types of test have similar strengths and weaknesses.

Answer: c

16. (obj. 8) The interpretation of an individual's test score by comparing it to the scores earned by other individuals is referred to as
  a. norm-referenced measurement.
  b. individual-referenced measurement.
  c. domain-referenced measurement.
  d. objectives-referenced measurement.

Answer: a

17. (obj. 8) A prespecified standard of performance is most important in
  a. norm-referenced measurement.
  b. individual-referenced measurement.
  c. criterion-referenced measurement.
  d. objectives-referenced measurement.

Answer: c

18. (obj. 9) In computer-adaptive testing, the test-taker
   a. responds only to items that are at a moderate level of difficulty.
   b. is allowed as much time as he wishes to respond to each item.
   c. responds to items that are matched to his ability level.
   d. is allowed to choose the items to which he will respond.

Answer: c

19. (obj. 9) The process by which items are placed on a scale in order of relative difficulty in computer-adaptive testing is based on
   a. item response theory.
   b. generalizability theory.
   c. classical test theory.
   d. grounded theory.

Answer: a

20. (obj. 10) It is usually better to administer an individual test than a group test when
   a. it is necessary to ensure standard conditions of administration.
   b. a high degree of objectivity in scoring is desired.
   c. it is necessary to obtain data on all research participants within a short period of time.
   d. the researcher is interested in the process by which the overall score is obtained.

Answer: d

21. (obj. 11) Match each of the following types of test with the appropriate definition.
   __ 1. Intelligence tests
   __ 2. Aptitude tests
   __ 3. Achievement test batteries
   __ 4. Diagnostic tests
   a. Estimate general intellectual level by sampling performance on various tasks.
   b. Aim at predicting performance on future tasks.
   c. Provide scores indicating individuals' strengths and weaknesses in a given area of the curriculum.
   d. Measure knowledge or mastery of a variety of content areas.

Answer: 1 = a 2 = b 3 = d 4 = c

22. (obj. 12) Which of the following is *not* an appropriate criterion for judging the validity of inferences drawn from a performance assessment?
   a. Whether all students had an equal opportunity to acquire the expertise measured by the test
   b. The extent to which the test scores correlate with the test-takers' scores on a well-established standardized test
   c. The extent to which the test's content represents the content domain covered during instruction
   d. The cost of administering the test

Answer: b

23. (obj. 13) The hermeneutic approach to test reliability
   a. requires test scorers to reach a consensus about the score or rating that each test-taker will receive.
   b. requires administration of parallel forms of a test.
   c. involves identifying experts with a consistent perspective to score the tests.
   d. involves the calculation of a standard error of measurement.

Answer: a

24. (obj. 13) To determine an individual's unique structuring of reality, the researcher is advised to administer a
    a. variety of attitude scales.
    b. personality inventory.
    c. combination of attitude scales and a personality inventory.
    d. projective test.

Answer: d

25. (obj. 14) The *Mental Measurement Yearbooks* are particularly helpful for
    a. determining the latest trends in assessment methodology.
    b. identifying procedures that can be used to establish a test's validity and reliability.
    c. obtaining a list of tests that are available for measuring a particular variable.
    d. obtaining a statistical summary of the test scores of students with different demographic characteristics.

Answer c

26. (obj. 14) The best source of information about tests that are not commercially available is
    a. Test Reviews Online.
    b. Test Collection.
    c. Tests in Microfiche.
    d. *Standards for Educational and Psychological Testing.*

Answer: c

27. (obj. 15) Contacting the test developer directly is particularly useful when you wish to obtain
    a. tables of norms for the test.
    b. recent information about the test that has not yet been published.
    c. reliability and validity information about the test.
    d. information about how to administer and score the test.

Answer: b

28. (obj. 16) In test development, the purpose of item analysis is to determine
    a. the difficulty level of each test item.
    b. the reliability of each test item.
    c. the validity of each test item.
    d. all of the above.

Answer: d

29. (obj. 16) Put the following steps of test development in the order that they usually occur.
    a. Developing a prototype
    b. Defining the constructs to be measured
    c. Reviewing related tests that have been developed
    d. Collecting data on the test's validity and reliability

Answer: b, c, a, d

30. (obj. 16) Item analysis is a set of procedures used to
    a. develop items for a parallel form of a standardized test.
    b. revise the wording of test items to eliminate bias toward certain groups.
    c. assess the validity, reliability, and difficulty of each item on a test.
    d. all of the above.

Answer: c

31. (obj. 17) Which of the following actions by the researcher is least likely to be helpful if protestors question the administration of a certain test in a research study?

a. Defending the test by reviewing with the protestors the merits of each item on the test
b. Demonstrating how the test as a whole is valid and reliable
c. Demonstrating that the test follows the guidelines in the *Standards for Educational and Psychological Testing*
d. Offering to withdraw individuals from the study if they do not wish to take the test

Answer: a

32. (obj. 18) Match each testing procedure below with the outcome for which it is intended.

__ 1. Have the teacher tell the students (the research participants) that the test is important and that they should try to do their best.
__ 2. Remind the research participants that data collected on any particular individual will not be revealed.
__ 3. Emphasize the official nature of the testing session.

a. You want to ensure that the research participants depict themselves in a typical, honest manner.
b. You want to obtain the research participants' maximal performance.
c. You want to enhance the research participants' cooperation.

Answer: 1 = b 2 = a 3 = c

OPEN-FORM ITEMS

1. (obj. 1) Name four types of performance tests that are commonly used in educational research.

Answer:

1. Intelligence tests
2. Aptitude tests
3. Achievement tests
4. Diagnostic tests

2. (obj. 1) Name five types of personality measures that are commonly used in educational research.

Answer:

Measures of

1. personality traits
2. creativity
3. self-concept
4. attitudes
5. interests

3. (obj. 2) Describe three criteria for judging the quality of a test.

Answer (any 3 OK):

1. Objectivity, that is, the extent to which the test's scores are free from bias by the individuals who administer and score it
2. Standard conditions for administering and scoring the test
3. Whether the test scores can be interpreted by using a set of norms derived from a large sample representing a defined population
4. The extent to which inferences from the test's scores are valid, that is, appropriate, meaningful, and useful
5. The extent to which the test scores are reliable, that is, free of measurement error

4. (obj. 3) A researcher uses a theory of academic self-esteem to identify five behavior patterns that are indicative of students' level of academic self-esteem, such as the frequency of positive statements students make about themselves. The researcher next observes 50 students for one month and records the frequency of these behavior patterns for each student. Finally, the researcher develops a paper-and-pencil test of academic self esteem and correlates the students' scores with their level of academic self-esteem based on the observations. What type of evidence of test validity has the researcher established?

Answer:

Evidence from relationship to other variables

5. (obj. 4) A researcher has developed a new test designed to measure musical aptitude. She selects a random sample of 200 college freshmen and administers the test to them. One month later she again administers the test to the same students and computes a correlation coefficient between the two sets of scores. What type of reliability does this coefficient indicate?

Answer (any 1 OK):

1. Test-retest reliability
2. Coefficient of stability

6. (obj. 5) An investigator administers a reading achievement test that has a mean of 220, a standard deviation of 20, and a standard error of measurement of 5. Mary obtains a score of 235. Using the standard error of measurement (sm), what estimate can we make of her true score?

Answer (any 1 OK):

1. There are about two chances in three that Mary's true score is 235 $\pm$ 1 sm, that is, between 230 and 240.
2. There is a 95 percent chance that her true score is 235 $\pm$ 2 sm, that is, between 225 and 245.

7. (obj. 6) What is one advantage of using item response theory to develop an achievement test?

Answer (any 1 OK):

1. Test administration is more efficient.
2. Test takers are not frustrated by test items that are too difficult or easy for them.
3. The testing time necessary to obtain valid estimates of test-takers' ability is shortened.

8. (obj. 6. Describe four problems to which tests developed within the classical test theory framework are susceptible.

Answer:

1. If the test is used with a sample representing a different population from the one used in test development, reliability estimates and item statistics for the test may be incorrect.
2. If the test is too easy or difficult for some individuals in the sample, it will provide a poor estimate of their true scores.
3. A test might be less reliable for individuals at one level of ability than for those at a different level of ability.
4. Because development of alternate parallel forms of a test is difficult, a reliability check of the measurement error due to test items might not be possible.

9. (obj. 6) Describe three assumptions on which the item-response-theory approach to test construction is based.

Answer:

1. An individual's performance on any single test item reflects a single ability.
2. Individuals with different amounts of a given ability will perform differently on an item reflecting that ability.
3. The relationship between the variables of ability and item performance can be represented by a mathematical function.

10. (obj. 7) The superintendent tells a researcher who is conducting a study in her district that he should use achievement tests constructed by the teachers to measure student learning rather than a standardized achievement test. How can the researcher defend the decision to use a standardized test?

Answer:

The researcher can note that teacher-constructed tests are useful for certain purposes but not for research. Research requires tests that have standard conditions of administration and scoring, as well as tables of norms. Only standardized tests satisfy these requirements.

11. (obj. 7) Name three factors that can distort the scores on a standardized test.

Answer:

1. Guessing
2. Response sets
3. Random or careless answers

12. (obj. 7) Describe three limitations of standardized achievement tests.

Answer:

1. Scores on such tests correlate poorly with indicators of the instruction students have received.
2. Such tests tend to perpetuate bias against ethnic minorities and other groups.
3. Such tests fail to measure many personal and intellectual qualities that are not easily assessed in an objective, paper-and-pencil test format.

13. (obj. 8) A student earns a score of 85 on a 100-item achievement test. How would this score be interpreted if the test was criterion-referenced?

Answer:

The score would be compared to a prespecified standard of performance. For example, if the standard is a score of 90, we would conclude that the student did not achieve the criterion level of performance.

14. (obj. 9) State two advantages of administering a test in computer format.

Answer (any 2 OK):

1. The order in which the test items are presented can be varied for each individual who takes the test.
2. The amount of time that each item is exposed to the test taker can be controlled.
3. The opportunity for test-takers to look back or ahead to other sections of the test can be controlled.
4. Scoring of the test is easier and more accurate.
5. The test can be administered by using the principles of item response theory.

15. (obj. 10) Describe one situation in which an individually administered test would be preferable to a group-administered test.

Answer (any 1 OK):

1. When the researcher wishes to study the process by which individuals arrive at their responses to test items
2. When the individuals to be tested have a limited attention span or other condition that would impair their performance if tested in a group situation
3. When the individuals to be tested cannot read the test directions and items

16. (obj. 10) Name one drawback of administering a standardized test individually as opposed to administering it to an entire group at once.

Answer (any 1 OK):

1. It takes more time to administer tests individually.
2. Individual tests typically require more training to administer correctly.
3. Individual tests require more skill to interpret scores properly.

17. (obj. 11) Give one reason why the test ceiling is an important factor to consider in selecting an achievement test to use in a research study.

Answer (any 1 OK):

1. If the test is too easy or difficult, it will not reflect how much students know.
2. If the test is too easy or difficult, it will not reflect how their learning has improved as a result of an experimental intervention.

18. (obj. 12) Some school districts require candidates for a teaching position to teach an actual lesson, which is rated for quality. The district also may require candidates to submit a collection of curriculum materials and lesson plans that they have prepared in their previous teaching positions.

a. What is this approach to measurement called?
b. What is the technical name for the collection of completed work?

Answer:

a. This approach is called *performance assessment*.
b. The technical name is *portfolio*.

19. (obj. 12) Describe four criteria recommended for judging the validity of performance assessments.

Answer

(Note: See the eight criteria in Table 7.2 on page 217 of the text; any four of these criteria are acceptable.)

20. (obj. 13) Describe at least one advantage and one disadvantage of self-report personality measures.

Answer:

Advantages (any 1 OK):

1. These measures are inexpensive and easy to administer.
2. They often can be scored by machine.
3. Norms often are available for these measures.

Disadvantages (any 1 OK):

1. These measures are based on self-report and thus a respondent can lie or mislead the investigator if he wants to. Also, the responses are subject to distortion due to inaccurate self-perceptions.
2. They can be attacked as an invasion of privacy.
3. They are subject to faking.
4. They are subject to response sets.

21. (obj. 14) How do the *Mental Measurement Yearbooks* contribute to the use of tests in research?

Answer:

The *Mental Measurement Yearbooks* provide a comprehensive list of tests, information about each test, and a critique of many of them.

22. (obj. 15) State one reason why it is important for a researcher to examine an actual copy of an achievement test before deciding to use it in a study.

Answer (any 1 OK):

1. To decide whether there is content-related evidence of the test's validity for the situation in which the researcher plans to use it
2. To determine whether the test's reading level for the research sample is appropriate
3. To determine whether there might be problems in administering or scoring the test

23. (obj. 15) State two questions that can guide a search for relevant information to help you select among the range of tests that appear related to one's sample and research problem.

Answer (any 2 OK):

1. Is there evidence that the test is valid and reliable for the uses to which you wish to put it?
2. Is the test's reading level or task level appropriate to your sample?
3. Can the test be administered within the time constraints of your data-collection situation?
4. If the test measures achievement or aptitude, are the items at an appropriate difficulty level for your sample?
5. Are the test's norms and validity and reliability evidence based on a population that is similar to the population from which your sample is drawn?

24. (obj. 16) Describe one procedure that customarily is used as part of an item analysis of a test under development.

Answer (any 1 OK):

1. An item validity coefficient is computed to determine how well individuals' scores on each item correlate with their scores on a criterion measure.
2. An item reliability coefficient is computed to determine how well individuals' scores on each item correlate with their total test scores.
3. If it is a performance test, a difficulty index is computed to determine the percentage of individuals who answer each item correctly.

25. (obj. 17) How can the publication *Standards for Educational and Psychological Testing* help if a test to be administered as part of a research study comes under attack?

Answer:

The researcher can use it to demonstrate that professional standards for testing exist and that her test and procedures for administering it meet those standards.

26. (obj. 17) Describe three actions you could take if you encounter public or professional resistance to the tests that you wish to administer for a research study.

Answer:

1. Make efforts to convince test-takers or other concerned individuals of the value of the study.
2. Cooperate with news reporters or other media representatives and explain to them the purpose and potential value of the study.
3. Allow individuals to withdraw from a study at any point that they or their care-givers express a desire for withdrawal.

27. (obj. 18) A researcher plans to administer a personality measure and wants to ensure that the research sample gives honest responses to its items. What is one procedure that the researcher can use to accomplish this goal?

Answer (any 1 OK):

1. Assure the research participants that their responses will be kept confidential.
2. Have individuals write a code number on the measure rather than their names.
3. Inform the research participants that the research results will be presented in group form only.

28. (obj. 18) Describe three procedures that might help obtain individuals' maximal effort on a performance test.

Answer:

1. Make the testing a positive experience by emphasizing the importance of the test.
2. Promise to reveal the purpose and findings of the research study after testing is completed.
3. Emphasize the official nature of the test by such strategies as the use of a stopwatch and reading directions from a test manual.

29. (obj. 18) Describe four procedures that might help obtain individuals' honest responses on a personality measure.

Answer:

1. Create an atmosphere in which test takers feel comfortable about giving an honest response by assuring them that individual test data will not be revealed and that scores will be reported only in group form.
2. Assign code numbers to all test takers and make sure that individuals understand that their identities will be kept confidential.
3. Provide a comfortable physical environment in which individuals respond to the measure.
4. Train testers beforehand to ensure that they are able to administer the test accurately.

APPLICATION PROBLEMS

Problem 1

Describe a procedure for handling each of these testing problems.

a. A researcher is planning to administer several aptitude tests to groups of college students as part of a research project. What can he do to increase the likelihood that students will give their maximum performance?
b. A researcher wants to administer a measure of sexual attitudes to high school and college students. What can she do to increase the likelihood that students will give frank, honest responses?

Sample Answer:

a. Make the testing appear to be important. Tell the students you will reveal the purpose of the research after the testing is completed.
b. Before administering the measure, tell students that the individuals' responses will not be revealed to anyone and that results will be reported in group form only. It is also desirable not to oblige research participants to write their names on the measure; if later identification is needed, code numbers can be used.

Problem 2

An investigator has developed a new technique to teach eighth-grade students the characteristics of positive and negative numbers. She wishes to evaluate the technique by using it to teach group A. Group B, which receives conventional instruction on positive and negative numbers, serves as a control. She needs a mathematics achievement test to measure the post-training performance of the two groups. She considers the XYZ Test of Mathematics Achievement. In checking the test manual, she finds that when this test was administered to a sample of eighth-grade students at the end of the academic year, the test scores correlated .72 with their end-of-year grades in mathematics. No other validity evidence was given in the test manual.

a. What type of validity evidence was given in the test manual?
b. What type of validity evidence is most relevant to the proposed study, and why?

Sample Answer:

a. Evidence of concurrent validity was given, because the test scores and grades both measure the same construct and were obtained at the same time.
b. Evidence of content-related validity is most relevant, because the training was concerned with a limited content area. Most regular achievement tests would be inappropriate because they deal mainly with content not covered in the new instructional technique. What is needed is a measure that deals only with positive and negative numbers. This can be determined only by comparing the test content with the training content.

Problem 3
A researcher is asked by school district personnel to collect data for a period of three years to determine whether their plans to improve third-grade reading skills are successful. The researcher decides to administer the same reading achievement test at the end of each school year for the next three years. List the aspects of their content that she should judge carefully as she examines various achievement tests for possible use in the study.
Sample Answer:

a. The degree of similarity between the content of the achievement test and the content of the district's third-grade reading curriculum
b. The extent to which the content of the achievement test is up to date and reflects the students' culture
c. The extent to which the test is appropriate for testing fourth-, fifth-, and sixth-grade students
d. Whether the test ceiling is sufficiently high

Problem 4
(Note to the instructor: This is a complex problem that might be assigned as a long homework assignment. See also problem 5 below, which is a simpler version of problem 4.)

a. Select one standardized test. If your thesis or dissertation will involve the use of standardized tests, select a measure relevant to that study. Otherwise, select a measure that relates to your major professional interests.
b. Obtain a specimen set for your measure. Most departments of psychology, university libraries, or counseling centers have a file of standardized tests. A copy of the test, the test manual, and the scoring key are included for most measures. Your instructor will give you the information you need to obtain a specimen set.
   (Note to the instructor: If specimen sets are not available, you should make a collection of standard test catalogs and have students order the tests they will evaluate. These orders should be sent during the *first* week of the class so that they will arrive by the time they are needed. Some tests are restricted, and the student order will have to be endorsed by you.)
c. Sources of Information
   (1) Look up the selected measure in the most recent edition of the *Mental Measurements Yearbook* available in your institution's library. If your measure is not reviewed, select another measure.
   (2) Check the name of the measure you have selected in the most recent three annual volumes of *Psychological Abstracts* and ERIC. Also check key words related to the topic of the measure. For example, if your measure were the *IPAT Anxiety Scale Questionnaire*, you would check the key word *anxiety* in the subject index. Locate one study in which the measure was used. Read the study, giving particular attention to data related to the questions below. Prepare a note card on the article and submit it as part of this assignment.
d. Answer the following questions based on your study of the sources mentioned above.
   (1) Objectivity
      (a) Is the measure subject to administrator bias? Discuss.
      (b) Is the measure subject to scoring bias? Discuss.
   (2) Normative Data
      (a) Are normative data provided? Describe.
      (b) Are the samples used in establishing the norms satisfactory? Describe.
      (c) How comparable are norm groups to the sample in your study (if this measure is being considered for your thesis or dissertation project)?
   (3) Validity
      (a) What type of validity evidence is most appropriate for this measure? Why?
      (b) What validity evidence is given in your sources? Describe.
      (c) Write a brief evaluation of the validity evidence available on this measure.
   (4) Reliability
      (a) What type of reliability data are available for this measure? Describe.
      (b) What are the reliability coefficients?

(c) Write a brief evaluation of the reliability data available for this measure.

e. Submit a typed, double-spaced paper giving the name and a brief description of the measure, including the publisher's name, publication data, administration time, age levels if appropriate, and the types of scores that it yields. Answer the four questions listed in "d" above. Be sure to include your note card with your paper [see (c-2)]. Be prepared to report on your standardized test evaluation in class.

Sample Answer:

Because each student is likely to select a different test to evaluate, it is not meaningful to provide a sample answer. You can award or deduct points for each part of the answer depending on its completeness and accuracy.

Problem 5

(Note to the instructor: This is a simpler version of problem 4.)

Find a test that pertains to a research problem or topic of interest to you. Indicate in writing:

a. how the test possibly is relevant to your research problem.
b. the reference source in which you identified the information.
c. something interesting you learned about the test from the reference source. (Write just two sentences.)

Attach a copy of the page(s) in the reference source that reviews the test. (If the review is more than two pages, just copy the first two pages.) Write a complete, standard citation for the source on the first page of your copy.

Sample Answer:

Because each student is likely to select a different test to evaluate, it is not meaningful to provide a sample answer. You can award or deduct points for each part of the answer depending on its completeness and accuracy.

TEACHING ACTIVITIES

Activity 1

If you require students to do Application Problems 4 or 5, have them share their experiences in class. Ask them, What did you learn from doing this exercise? What problems did you encounter? What are the strengths and weaknesses of the test that you described?

Activity 2

Engage students in a discussion of this issue: Many educators believe that the most important things in education cannot be measured. Drawing on what you have read in chapter 7, create a case supporting or challenging this position.

Activity 3

Have students take all or part of an achievement test, attitude scale, or personality measure in class. Ask students to describe their experience in taking the test and what they learned from this experience that might affect the way they would administer the same or a similar test to a research sample.

Activity 4

Of the various standardized tests, projective techniques such as the *Rorschach* or the *Thematic Apperception Test* probably are most applicable to qualitative research because they assess how individuals view reality. If you can obtain a few cards from one of these tests, you can have students generate their own responses to them. You then can ask students to reflect on this experience and to consider how such tests might be used in educational research.

Activity 5

Before class, have students read a research article in which the study being reported used standardized tests. In class, have students discuss the tests and the types of information about the tests that were included in the report. Ask them to consider whether the tests were appropriate and whether adequate validity and reliability evidence was presented.

CHAPTER 8
COLLECTING RESEARCH DATA WITH QUESTIONNAIRES AND INTERVIEWS

Note: The phrase in parentheses following the item number for both closed-form and open-form items, for example, "(obj. 3)", refers to the textbook chapter objective to which the item is keyed.

CLOSED-FORM ITEMS

1. (obj. 1) Questionnaires and interviews have in common the feature that
   a. they are both suitable for collecting highly personal information.
   b. it is convenient to record the responses to either method of data collection.
   c. both are less convenient than direct observation to collect data about observable phenomena.
   d. both can be used to collect data about nonobservable phenomena.

Answer: d

2. (obj. 1) In this text the term *survey research* is used to refer to
   a. quantitative research studies that rely on questionnaires or interviews for data collection.
   b. research in which questionnaire or interview data are used to study cause-and-effect relationships.
   c. qualitative research using questionnaires or interviews to provide thick descriptions of phenomena.
   d. the use of telephones or computers to collect questionnaire or interview data.

Answer: a

3. (obj. 1) The interview technique is better than a questionnaire when
   a. a small sample is adequate.
   b. in-depth responses are desired.
   c. factual information must be obtained.
   d. cost is a major consideration.

Answer: b

4. (obj. 1) An advantage of questionnaires over interviews is that questionnaires
   a. allow more flexibility in administration and in response.
   b. can be designed to require less subjective responses, thus minimizing bias.
   c. permit greater depth of response.
   d. are likely to yield more data on negative aspects of the respondents.

Answer: b

5. (obj. 2) Research has shown that when respondents receive questionnaires dealing with topics of great concern to them,
   a. respondents provide more biased data.
   b. more follow-ups are necessary to obtain a satisfactory response rate.
   c. respondents are less responsive to personal appeals to participate.
   d. the response rate is higher.

Answer: d

6. (obj. 2) All the following statements are to be answered on a scale measuring degree of agreement or disagreement. Which statement is best constructed according to common guidelines for constructing questionnaire items?
   a. Every teacher should have several well-defined interests.
   b. Although unions are important in industry, they are inappropriate in education.
   c. Grouping students on the basis of ability provides for maximum attention to individual needs.
   d. Forcing students to take driver education is contrary to individual freedom.

Answer: c

7. (obj. 2) A guideline that should be observed in constructing questionnaire items is to
   a. avoid predetermining how you will report the results of an item.
   b. be sure to use precise, technical language.
   c. avoid questions that require research participants to respond to two separate ideas in a single answer.
   d. use open-form items whenever possible.

Answer: c

8. (obj. 2) An important guideline in designing a questionnaire is to
   a. use black ink on white paper.
   b. randomize item order.
   c. provide examples to explain potentially confusing items.
   d. put important items near the end of the questionnaire.

Answer: c

9. (obj. 2) An important benefit of doing a pilot test of a questionnaire is that it
   a. encourages respondents to be more truthful in answering questionnaire items.
   b. permits respondents to decline to participate.
   c. increases the proportion of questionnaire recipients who complete the questionnaire.
   d. allows the researcher to revise and retest the questions until most respondents understand them.

Answer: d

10. (obj. 3) Which of the following is a serious problem in using an anonymous questionnaire?
   a. Follow-ups are difficult and inefficient.
   b. No subgroup analyses can be performed.
   c. Respondents answer less thoughtfully and completely than on signed questionnaires.
   d. Respondents do not make a serious effort to answer accurately.

Answer: a

11. (obj. 3) The researcher provides a prepaid postcard with an individualized code on it, along with a copy of the questionnaire that contains no code, to each respondent, and requests that they be returned separately. This procedure
   a. enables the researcher to match each questionnaire with the correct respondent.
   b. enables the researcher to provide complete anonymity to respondents.
   c. makes it impossible to follow up with nonrespondents to increase the rate of response.
   d. is recommended for any questionnaire to be mailed to a sample that is widely distributed geographically.

Answer: b

12. (obj. 4) The major advantage of closed-form questionnaire items over open-form questionnaire items is that closed form items
    a. yield data that are more easily analyzed.
    b. are easier to design.
    c. are more valid.
    d. are less threatening.

Answer: a

13. (obj. 5) When attitude or opinion questions are asked on a questionnaire, it has been found that
    a. some respondents give opinions on topics about which they know nothing.
    b. uninformed responses can be eliminated by adding a "no opinion" choice.
    c. most attitudes can be satisfactorily measured with one well-phrased item.
    d. open-form attitude items usually provide more valid data.

Answer: a

14. (obj. 5) Research has shown that individuals who express a favorable or unfavorable attitude toward fictitious organizations tend to ____________________ than other respondents.
    a. have more formal education
    b. express less favorable attitudes
    c. use a "don't know" or neutral response choice more often
    d. express more favorable attitudes

Answer: d

15. (obj. 6) Precontacting the members of a sample to whom a questionnaire will be sent generally
    a. reduces the problem of individuals with little knowledge of the topic responding to questions.
    b. eliminates the problem of missing data.
    c. improves the response rate.
    d. increases the honesty of individual responses.

Answer: c

16. (obj. 6) The form of precontact that evidence suggests has been found most effective in eliciting a response to a mailed questionnaire is
    a. a postcard.
    b. a letter.
    c. a telephone call.
    d. an email.

Answer: c

17. (obj. 7) It is essential that the cover letter for a questionnaire survey
    a. be individually typed.
    b. not refer to the respondent's institutional affiliation.
    c. specify when the questionnaire needs to be returned.
    d. include an explicit payment for the respondent's time.

Answer: c

18. (obj. 7) Which of the following guidelines should be followed in preparing the cover letter for a mailed questionnaire?
    a. Refer to the respondent's affiliation with a group relevant to the questionnaire's topic.
    b. Avoid the use of appeals to the respondent's interest in doing good.
    c. Explain why the results of the questionnaire study cannot be made available to the respondents.
    d. Provide a summary of the literature that supports the study's objectives.

Answer: a

19. (obj. 7) When accompanying a questionnaire that includes sensitive or potentially threatening questions, the cover letter should
    a. provide a specific description of how confidentiality will be maintained.
    b. emphasize the importance of respondents answering sensitive questions honestly.
    c. indicate that respondents can request an analysis of how their responses compared to those of other respondents.
    d. all of the above.

Answer: a

20. (obj. 8) If more than 20 percent of the questionnaires are not returned after several follow-up attempts, the researcher should
    a. send another copy of the questionnaire to the nonrespondents.
    b. select an additional sample and mail them the questionnaire.
    c. administer the questionnaire by telephone or in person to a random sample of the nonrespondents.
    d. discontinue attempts to contact nonrespondents.

Answer: c

21. (obj. 8) Research studies suggest that, on average, three follow-up contacts with nonrespondents increases the response rate to a questionnaire by about _____ percent.
    a. 10
    b. 25
    c. 40
    d. 50

Answer: c

22. (obj. 9) The first step in conducting a study that will employ interviews to collect research data is to
    a. specify how the data will be analyzed.
    b. train interviewers.
    c. select a sample.
    d. define the purpose of the interview.

Answer: d

23. (obj. 10) Key informants tend to differ from other members of the defined population in all but which one of the following ways?
    a. Possession of a unique perspective on the phenomenon of interest to the researcher
    b. Greater knowledge about the phenomenon being investigated
    c. Better ability to communicate with the researcher about the phenomenon
    d. Possession of the emic perspective concerning the phenomenon

Answer: d

24. (obj. 10) An interview that seeks to learn how informants structure their social or physical world is called
    a. a confirmation survey interview.
    b. a participant construct interview.
    c. a projective technique interview.
    d. a key informant interview.

Answer: b

25. (obj. 10) An important characteristic of focus group interviews is that
   a. interviewees are selected to have a wide range in their level of knowledge about the research topic.
   b. the research topic is explored through a relaxed, free-flowing discussion among the participants.
   c. it saves time because up to 30 individuals can be interviewed at once.
   d. the interviewer takes major responsibility for structuring the discussion.

Answer: b

26. (obj. 11) The first question that the interviewer asks each respondent is, "Do you think parents should be able to send their child to any school in the city, should only send their child to the school nearest their home, or should pay a special fee if they wish their child to attend a school other than the one in their neighborhood?" This question is typical of those asked in
   a. an unstructured interview.
   b. a structured interview.
   c. a standardized open-ended interview.
   d. an informal conversational interview.

Answer: b

27. (obj. 11) In an unstructured interview, the interviewer tends to
   a. follow a general plan that allows the individual to respond freely.
   b not have predetermined objectives.
   c. not take notes or record the interview.
   d. use structured questions to probe more deeply.

Answer: a

28. (obj. 12) A major advantage of conducting telephone interviews with the aid of a computer is that
   a. it prevents the interviewer from rephrasing questions.
   b. a live interviewer is not needed to ask the questions.
   c. the computer can be programmed to detect when a respondent is lying.
   d. the computer indicates the next appropriate question based on the previous response.

Answer: d

29. (obj. 12) A significant disadvantage of telephone interviewing as compared with face-to-face interviewing is that
   a. telephone interviewing is more costly.
   b. there is more likelihood that the interviewer will fake data in telephone interviews.
   c. frequent call-backs become very expensive if no one answers the phone.
   d. only persons with telephones can be reached.

Answer: d

30. (obj. 12) Research comparisons of telephone and face-to-face interviews show that
   a. telephone interviews cannot be used to collect sensitive data.
   b. about twice as many face-to-face interviews are completed.
   c. telephone interviews are much easier to monitor and supervise.
   d. about 20 percent of U.S. households do not have telephones, thus leading to biased samples.

Answer: c

31. (obj. 13) An essential criterion for selecting individuals to conduct research interviews is to select
   a. males to interview male respondents and females to interview female respondents.
   b. interviewers who are older than the respondents.
   c. interviewers who are members of the respondent target population.
   d. interviewers who are able to relate to the respondents positively.

Answer: d

32. (obj. 14) A major purpose of the interview guide in a study involving several interviewers is to
    a. train interviewers in question wording, format, recording procedures, and allowable probes.
    b. serve as a script from which interviewers should read when conducting the interview.
    c. provide information for answering any queries from respondents about the research hypotheses.
    d. all of the above.

Answer: a

33. (obj. 14) In preparing interviewers to use an interview guide, the researcher should
    a. avoid informing the interviewers about the study's hypotheses and research questions.
    b. inform the interviewers about the study's hypotheses and research questions, and provide the rationale for each one.
    c. allow the interviewers to use their natural interviewing style rather than training them to standardize their use of the interview guide.
    d. focus on general principles of interviewing rather than on the specific aspects of the interview guide.

Answer: a

34. (obj. 15) In her interview notes the interviewer comments on the respondent's speech pacing and pauses during the interview. These notes reflect the interviewer's attention to the task of
    a. understanding the respondent's language and culture.
    b. being sensitive to nonverbal information.
    c. gaining the respondent's trust.
    d. appearing competent in the eyes of the respondent.

Answer: b

35. (obj. 15) An essential task of the interviewer during a research interview is to
    a. record word-for-word each of the respondent's comments.
    b. help the respondent feel comfortable in the interview situation.
    c. clarify the interviewer's own experiences and beliefs concerning the research topic.
    d. avoid taking notes so as not to distract the respondent.

Answer: b

36. (obj. 16) The chief advantage of note taking during an interview is that it
    a. provides the most accurate possible record of the subject's responses.
    b. speeds up the interview process.
    c. enhances the respondents' concentration.
    d. provides readily accessible data for analysis.

Answer: d

37. (obj. 16) Tape recording an interview generally
    a. requires the interviewer himself to evaluate and classify the responses.
    b. reduces the tendency of the interviewer to bias the data.
    c puts respondents on the defensive.
    d. eliminates the option of anonymity.

Answer: b

38. (obj. 17) To analyze responses to open-form interview questions, quantitative researchers typically
    a. calculate the number of times that particular words are uttered by each respondent.
    b. replay a tape recording of the interview.
    c. develop a category system to code the responses.
    d. have two or more raters rate the responses of each respondent.

Answer: c

OPEN-FORM ITEMS

1. (obj. 1) Give at least two advantages and two disadvantages of the use of interviews compared to the use of questionnaires in a research study.

Answer (any 2 from each set OK):

Advantages
1. The interview is more flexible and adaptable; the interviewer can follow up leads.
2. The interview permits greater depth of response.
3. The interview yields more complete data.
4. The interview yields more data on negative aspects of the respondents.
5. The interview provides data more appropriate for qualitative analysis.

Disadvantages
1. The interview is more costly and time-consuming to administer.
2. The interview is more subjective and thus subject to bias.
3. The interview cannot provide anonymity for the respondents.
4. Respondents may become embarrassed in a face-to-face situation.
5. It is difficult to sample respondents from a widely distributed geographic area.

2. (obj. 2) Describe one desirable procedure for pretesting a questionnaire for use in a research study.

Answer (any 1 OK):
1. Leave space on the questionnaire for respondents to state what they think each question means.
2. Do in-depth interviews with a sample of respondents to solicit their interpretations of the questions.
3. Try different versions of specific questions on different subgroups of the pretest sample.
4. Revise the items based on the above steps and then submit the revised questionnaire to another pretest sample to test the response rate.

3. (obj. 2) Briefly identify four of the major steps involved in carrying out a research study based on a questionnaire.

Answer (any 4 OK):
1. Defining objectives for the questionnaire
2. Selecting the sample
3. Designing the questionnaire format
4. Pretesting the questionnaire
5. Precontacting the sample
6. Writing a cover letter and distributing the questionnaire
7. Following up with nonrespondents
8. Analyzing questionnaire data

4. (obj. 2) Describe two advantages to design and administration of a questionnaire on the World Wide Web as opposed to mailing a written questionnaire to respondents.

Answer (any 2 OK):
1. It eliminates postal costs.
2. The possibility of missing data is reduced because a reminder can be sent automatically to respondents who did not respond to some questions.
3. The raw data are already in electronic format, which makes scoring and computer analysis convenient.
4. Items can be tailored to individual respondents.
5. Respondents can be given feedback as they complete the items.

5. (obj. 3) Describe one procedure that can be used to provide anonymity to questionnaire respondents.

Answer (any 1 OK):

1. Create a master code sheet that contains a code for each individual in the sample; put the codes on the questionnaires; and when a questionnaire is returned, check off the name of the person having that code on the master code sheet.
2. Send each individual a prepaid postcard with the code on it, and a questionnaire that contains no code; ask the individual to return the questionnaire and the postcard separately.

6. (obj. 4) Describe the difference between an open-form and a closed-form question, and identify which form usually is preferable for collecting qualitative information and why.

Answer:

An open-form question permits the respondent to respond in his own words; for example, essay questions are open-form. A closed form-question permits only certain responses, for example, a multiple-choice item. An open-form format is preferable for collecting qualitative information because it permits respondents to respond at any length and in their own terms, consistent with the principles of qualitative research.

7. (obj. 4) Describe two important skills needed to write good questionnaire items.

Answer (any 2 OK):

1. Ability to write succinctly and clearly
2. Ability to use language that respondents will understand
3. Ability to generate items that will engage respondents' interest and willingness to respond honestly
4. Ability to generate a mix of items that will provide all the needed information without exhausting respondents' patience

8. (obj. 5) Describe one strategy that can be used to reduce the tendency for questionnaire respondents to give opinions about attitude objects with which they are unfamiliar.

Answer (any 1 OK):

1. Include a "no opinion" response option for each item.
2. Include several information questions at the beginning of the questionnaire to screen out respondents who lack knowledge about the attitude object.
3. Select your sample from a population of individuals who are likely to have a sufficient level of knowledge about the attitude object, e.g., college-educated people.

9. obj. 6) Describe one advantage of precontacting the sample to whom you plan to send a questionnaire.

Answer (any 1 OK):

1. A precontact alerts respondents to expect the questionnaire, so they are less likely to disregard it by mistake.
2. A precontact puts a more personal, human face on the research study, which might make participants more comfortable and also more willing to reveal personal information honestly.
3. If the precontact obtains respondents' commitment to participate, they are likely to feel obligated to keep their commitment when the questionnaire arrives.

10. (obj. 7) Describe four features that can be incorporated in a cover letter for a mailed questionnaire to make it effective.

Answer (any 4 OK):
1. The use of mail-merge on a word processor to personalize the addresses
2. Duplication of the letter by using a word processor or offset process so that the letter appears individually typed
3. A brief description of the study's purpose
4. Emphasis on the study's importance
5. Mention of the value of obtaining this respondent's views
6. A reasonable, but specific, time within which to return the questionnaire
7. Enclosing a self-addressed, stamped envelope (SASE) to make the return convenient
8. Assurance of the confidentiality of the information to be obtained
9. An offer to share a summary of the results if the respondent is interested
10. Expression of appreciation for the respondent's cooperation, time, etc.
11. Personal signing of the letter or printing of the signature in a different colo
12. Sending the letter from an individual whose endorsement represents a favorable symbol of authority

11. (obj. 8) A researcher received 72 percent of the questionnaires that were sent to a sample of high school counselors. Describe one method the researcher could use to increase the response rate.

Answer (any 1 OK):
1. Send a different follow-up letter with another copy of the questionnaire.
2. Telephone nonrespondents and ask them to return the questionnaire.
3. Send a telegram to nonrespondents, asking them to return the questionnaire.
4. Send a postcard reminder asking nonrespondents to return the questionnaire.

12. (obj. 9) Briefly list three steps involved in doing a research project with interviews as the means of collecting data.

Answer (any 3 OK):
1. Defining the purpose of the study
2. Selecting a sample
3. Designing the interview format
4. Developing questions
5. Selecting and training interviewers
6. Pilot-testing the interview procedures
7. Conducting the interviews
8. Analyzing the interview data

13. (obj. 9) Place the following eight steps of a research study involving use of a questionnaire in the order in which they typically are carried out, from 1 to 8:

___ a. Writing a cover letter
___ b. Pilot-testing the questionnaire
___ c. Defining research objectives
___ d. Selecting a sample
___ e. Following up with nonrespondents
___ f. Designing the questionnaire
___ g. Precontacting the sample
___ h. Analyzing questionnaire data

Answer: 1. c 2. d 3. f 4. b 5. g 6. a 7. e 8. h

14. (obj. 10) What is a key informant interview?

Answer:

An interview in which the interviewer collects data from individuals who have special knowledge or perceptions that would not be available to the researcher from other individuals in the defined population or in the field setting

15. (obj. 10) Describe one of the defining characteristics of a focus group as used in educational research.
Answer (any 1 OK):
1. It involves group discussion of a defined topic.
2. It provides a permissive, nonthreatening environment in which informants can express their views.
3. It is conducted by a skilled interviewer with a group of about 7-10 respondents.
4. Group members may influence one another by responding to others' ideas and comments.

16. (obj. 11) Describe the format of each of the following types of interview used in qualitative research: (a) the informal conversational interview, (b) the general interview guide approach, and (c) the standardized open-ended interview.
Answer:
a. The informal conversational interview relies entirely on the spontaneous generation of questions in a natural interaction; a participant may not even realize that she is being interviewed, because the interviewer engages in a seemingly casual conversation with her.
b. In the general interview guide approach, the interviewer has a standard outline of a set of topics to be explored with each respondent; topics can be explored in varied order and questions can be worded differently depending on how the interview evolves.
c. In the standardized open-ended interview, the interviewer asks a predetermined set of questions of each respondent in the same sequence and with the same wording.

17. (obj. 12) Describe two advantages of conducting interviews by telephone rather than in person.
Answer (any 2 OK):
1. Respondents can be selected from a much broader accessible population because there is no need for the interviewers to travel to the location of each respondent.
2. Because all interviewers can work from a central location, monitoring of interviews and quality control are much easier.
3. In telephone interviewing little cost is incurred when no one answers, making frequent callbacks feasible.
4. Many groups such as business people, school personnel, and parents are easier to reach by telephone than by personal visits.
5. Telephone interviewing provides safe access to dangerous locations, and access to restricted locations where interviewers might not be admitted.
6. Telephone interviews are less expensive than face-to-face interviews, especially when the sample is geographically dispersed.

18. (obj. 12) Describe one common problem in interview research that computer-assisted telephone interviewing virtually eliminates.
Answer (any 1 OK):
1. Data can be recorded in the wrong place on the interview response form.
2. The interviewer can ask the wrong question after a given response.
3. It may take a long time to transfer the interview data to a form in which they can be statistically analyzed.

19. (obj. 13) Describe one selection criterion that researchers often establish in selecting the interviewers for a research study.
Answer (any 1 OK):
1. Matching interviewers and respondents on critical variables (e.g., social class, race, age, or gender)
2. Selecting interviewers who are members of the respondent's target population
3. Retaining only interviewers who during training meet criterion standards of performance

20. (obj. 14) Briefly describe the two phases in the training of research interviewers.
Answer:
1. The trainees study the interview guide to learn about question wording, format, recording procedures, and allowable probes, and they are also informed about the interview conditions (e.g., logistics, necessary controls and safeguards, and topics being investigated).
2. The trainees conduct practice interviews and receive corrective feedback until their performance becomes polished and reaches the desired level of structure, objectivity, and reliability.

21. (obj. 15) State one circumstance in which superficial rapport with the interview respondent is sufficient and one circumstance in which the interviewer needs to develop stronger rapport.
Answer:
Superficial rapport is sufficient when the respondent already appears very comfortable with the interview process. Stronger rapport is needed when the interviewer intends to ask the respondent to reveal sensitive or deeply personal information.

22. (obj. 16) List one advantage and one disadvantage of note taking as a method of recording interview responses as compared to audio recording the interview.
Answer (any 1 from each set OK):
Advantages
1. When notes are taken during or immediately after the interview, it is not necessary for anyone to listen to an audio recording and transcribe the interview before beginning the data analysis.
2. The presence of an audio recorder may distract or upset some respondents.

Disadvantages
1. The interviewer cannot simply listen but must pause to take notes, which can disrupt communication.
2. The interviewer may forget to make a record of some important information.
3. There is no opportunity to check the accuracy of the record of the respondent's answers or to reanalyze the raw data at a later time.

23. (obj. 17) How does a researcher typically analyze the responses to closed-form interview or questionnaire items?
Answer:
The researcher calculates the percentage of respondents who indicated each response option for each item.

APPLICATION PROBLEMS

Problem 1
A researcher is studying the unique needs of physically challenged students during the school day. Name two types of individual who could serve as a key informants for the researcher.
Sample Answer:
Key informants would include: teachers who have one or more severely physically challenged students in their classes, students who have physical handicaps but who are not handicapped verbally or socially; and the parents of students with physical handicaps.

Problem 2
Give an example of the type of information for which using only one item on a questionnaire would be suitable and an example of a type of information for which using only one item on a questionnaire would not be suitable.
Sample Answer:

One item on a questionnaire is suitable for seeking the answer to a specific fact, e.g., asking a teacher how many students in her first-period class have been absent ten days or more so far during the school year. To collect information about attitudes--for example, to learn how students feel about their school's policy for handling incidents of violence--the researcher needs to use an attitude scale that includes several items in order to obtain a reliable assessment of their attitudes.

Problem 3
A researcher wants to learn the factors that determine where college students decide to live while attending a university. State one question that typifies what a quantitative researcher might ask in interviewing students on this topic and one that typifies what a qualitative researcher might ask.
Sample Answer:

Quantitative researchers generally prespecify the variables of interest in the research and thus ask specific questions, e.g., "Did your parents influence your decision as to where to live this year while at the university?"
Qualitative researchers typically do not prespecify the aspects of the phenomena that interest them and so ask broad questions, e.g., "How did you decide where to live this year while at the university?"

TEACHING ACTIVITIES

Activity 1

Have students select a topic on which to collect information by interviewing or giving a brief questionnaire to several individuals. Provide class time to assist students in designing their questionnaires or interview guides. (If desired, students can work in groups.) You also can ask the students to design a procedure for obtaining feedback to be collected from the respondents about the effectiveness of the questionnaire or interview guides. Specify a date by which the data need to be collected. Give students the assignment of writing a brief report on the procedures used in, and the results obtained from, their questionnaires or interviews. Discuss some of the reports in class.

Activity 2

Locate a research report in which the researcher used either questionnaires or interviews as the method of collecting data. Have students use the guidelines for designing a questionnaire in Table 8.1 on page 233 in the textbook, or for conducting a research interview in Table 8.3 on page 254 in the textbook, to evaluate the information in the research report.

Activity 3

Bring to class a few cover letters that were used in questionnaire or interview studies conducted by you or your colleagues. Ask students to note which features of the sample cover letter in Figure 8.1 on page 239 in the textbook were addressed by each of the cover letters, and to evaluate the overall effectiveness of each.

CHAPTER 9

COLLECTING RESEARCH DATA THROUGH OBSERVATION AND CONTENT ANALYSIS

Note: The phrase in parentheses following the item number for both closed-form and open-form items, for example, "(obj. 3)", refers to the textbook chapter objective to which the item is keyed.

CLOSED-FORM ITEMS

1. (obj. 1) A major advantage of observation over questionnaires is that observation
   a. is not susceptible to the self-report bias of questionnaires.
   b. requires less time for data collection and analysis.
   c. is not susceptible to theoretical saturation.
   d. needs to be employed only at one point in time in order to obtain reliable data.

Answer: a

2. (obj. 2) The number of students who enter a classroom after the lesson has started is an example of
   a. an inferential observational variable.
   b. an evaluative observational variable.
   c. a descriptive observational variable.
   d. a duration observational variable.

Answer: c

3. (obj. 2) Which of the following is an example of an inferential observational variable?
   a. The number of times the audience applauds during a lecture
   b. The lecturer's empathy with the audience
   c. The amount of time that the lecturer used an overhead projector
   d. The quality of the examples provided by the lecturer

Answer: b

4. (obj. 3) A researcher records whether a particular student is on-task or off-task when the lesson begins, five minutes later, and every five minutes thereafter until the lesson is over. This procedure for recording observations is called
   a. continuous recording.
   b. frequency-count recording.
   c. duration recording.
   d. interval recording.

Answer: d

5. (obj. 3) Measuring the elapsed time that target behaviors occur is referred to as
   a. duration recording.
   b. time sampling.
   c. interval recording.
   d. continuous recording.

Answer: d

6. (obj. 4) One disadvantage of using standard observation forms to collect data is that
   a. they tend to have low reliability.
   b. typically it is not possible to find a schedule that includes all the variables that the researcher wishes to measure.
   c. they generally require a high level of inference.
   d. they are limited to frequency-count recording.

Answer: b

7. (obj. 5) Audio or video recording is especially useful in observational research when
   a. teacher-student interaction occurs with low frequency.
   b. descriptive variables are to be recorded.
   c. inter-rater reliability must be calculated.
   d. untrained observers are used.

Answer: c

8. (obj. 6) In the training of observers, it is desirable to
   a. show video recordings of events similar to those that will be observed during actual data collection.
   b. avoid the use of video recordings, because they do not provide the context needed for reliable observation.
   c. train each observer independently so that the observers do not bias one another.
   d. allow the observers to develop their own rules for resolving disagreements in recording events.

Answer: a

9. (obj. 7) The extent to which a trained observer's scores agree with those of an expert observer is a measure of
   a. intra-observer reliability.
   b. inter-observer reliability.
   c. criterion-related reliability.
   d. test-retest reliability.

Answer: c

10. (obj. 7) Intra-observer reliability is a measure of the extent to which
    a. observers agree with each other during data collection.
    b. each observer is consistent in her observational codings.
    c. observers' codings agree with those of an expert observer.
    d. observations of all relevant variables are recorded on the observation form.

Answer: b

11. (obj. 8) The term *observer drift* refers to the tendency for observers to
    a. stop attending to the situation during long periods of recording observational data.
    b. decline in inter-rater reliability over time.
    c. use different standards for making ratings of groups toward whom they have a bias.
    d. deviate from the standard definitions of observational variables they learned during training.

Answer: d

12. (obj. 8) Observers who tend to rate most individuals at the high end of a scale are exhibiting
    a. observer drift.
    b. the error of leniency.
    c. acquiescence.
    d. contamination.

Answer: b

13. (obj. 9) Which one of the following is *not* a characteristic of qualitative observation?
   a. The observer looks at events from a holistic perspective.
   b. The observer attempts to remain neutral during data collection.
   c. The observer may change the focus of observation as data collection proceeds.
   d. The observer is not constrained by prespecified hypotheses and variables.

Answer: b

14. (obj. 9) The main difference between reactive observation and nonreactive observation involves whether
   a. individuals know they are being observed
   b. efforts have been made to control observer bias.
   c. data are analyzed with quantitative or qualitative methods.
   d. observers use an observation form in coding data.

Answer: a

15. (obj. 10) A researcher who becomes a substitute teacher in order to collect qualitative data about the culture of substitute teaching has assumed the role of
   a. an observer participant.
   b. a participant observer.
   c. a complete participant.
   d. an unobtrusive participant.

Answer: c

16. (obj. 11) In qualitative observation, the point at which the researcher decides that new observational findings are replicating earlier findings is called
   a. the focused stage.
   b. the reflective stage.
   c. grounded-theory replication.
   d. theoretical saturation.

Answer: d

17. (obj. 11) In observation at the ______________ stage, observers seek to refine and deepen their understanding of the specific elements most essential to the study's purposes.
   a. theoretical
   b. descriptive
   c. focused
   d. selective

Answer: d

18. (obj. 11) As data collection proceeds in qualitative observation, the researcher's observations are likely to become more
   a. focused.
   b. objective.
   c. reflective of the observer's role as complete participant.
   d. oriented to the study of material culture.

Answer: a

19. (obj. 12) To prepare for making field observations, a qualitative researcher would find it most helpful to
   a. use the same training procedures as those used in quantitative observation.
   b. serve an apprenticeship with an experienced qualitative researcher.
   c. attempt to reduce his level of observer personal bias.
   d. focus on learning procedures to avoid reliability decay.

Answer: b

20. (obj. 13) Field notes in qualitative research should
    a. focus on theoretical constructs rather than on concrete details of the events being observed.
    b. focus on duration and frequency variables.
    c. be made only after the observer leaves the research site.
    d. include both descriptive details and the observer's reflections.

Answer: d

21. (obj. 14) In qualitative research, observer bias
    a. is best avoided by making video recordings of the events being studied.
    b. is best avoided by having someone other than the researcher who designed the study collect the data.
    c. can be reduced by using both quantitative and qualitative methods of data collection.
    d. is usually an issue at the descriptive stage of data collection.

Answer: c

22. (obj. 15) A limitation of unobtrusive measures is that they
    a. alter the meaning of the variable that is being studied.
    b. are susceptible to response sets.
    c. are influenced by the observer's presence.
    d. have uncertain reliability.

Answer: d

23. (obj. 15) Unobtrusive measures have the advantage of
    a. requiring less time for data collection.
    b. not being susceptible to observer effects.
    c. permitting the researcher to study a total behavior pattern.
    d. not requiring the use of sampling techniques.

Answer: b

24. (obj. 15) Qualitative researchers tend to study physical objects
    a. when they want to understand how groups construct social reality.
    b. very rarely, because they are decontextualized.
    c. when they can interview the individuals who constructed or used them.
    d. when the objects have a communication function.

Answer: a

25. (obj. 16) The categories used to code documents in a quantitative content analysis
    a. should be based on a consistent unit of analysis, such as a sentence or a paragraph.
    b. should be developed by the researcher during the content analysis.
    c. should be checked to determine whether raters can use them to code documents reliably.
    d. all of the above.

Answer: c

26. (obj. 17) As a criterion for confirming interpretations based on qualitative analysis of documents and records, *external coherence* refers to
    a. the compatibility between different parts of the researcher's theoretical arguments and conclusions.
    b. the match between the researcher's interpretations and accepted theory inside and outside the discipline.
    c. how many new lines of inquiry are opened up by the researcher's theoretical position.
    d. the degree of correspondence between the data and the researcher's coding categories.

Answer: b

OPEN-FORM ITEMS

1. (obj. 1) State one advantage and one disadvantage of observation as a data-collection method in research.

Answer (any 1 from each set OK):

Advantages

1. Observation avoids the bias often found in self-report data.
2. Observation does not depend on the verbal fluency of the research participants.

Disadvantages

1. It can be expensive to obtain reliable data through observation.
2. Observational data tend to be expensive and time-consuming to collect.

2. (obj. 2) An observer collects quantitative data about (a) the number of meetings that an administrator attends during one work week, (b) how effective the administrator is in each meeting, and (c) the extent to which the administrator employs participatory decision making. Classify each of these observational variables using the three classification categories presented in the textbook.

Answer:

a. Descriptive observational variable
b. Evaluative observational variable
c. Inferential observational variable

3. (obj. 3) In recording observational variables in quantitative research, the researcher must decide whether to make a continuous recording or to use some other type of recording procedure. Name and briefly describe two other possible types of recording procedure.

Answer (any 2 OK):

1. Duration recording, which involves measuring the amount of time that each observational variable occurs
2. Frequency recording, which involves counting each instance of the observational variable
3. Interval recording, which involves checking for the occurrence of the observational variable at a regular interval

4. (obj. 4) State one advantage and one disadvantage of using a standard observation form in a research project.

Answer (any 1 from each set OK):

Advantages

1. Usually well developed, yielding valid and reliable data
2. Saves the investigator all the time and effort required to develop her own schedule
3. Permits comparing the findings with those of other researchers who used the same schedule

Disadvantages

1. The items may address some topics in which you are not interested.
2. The form may not cover all the areas about which you want information.

5. (obj. 5) State two tasks that a computer can perform when a researcher includes observational data in a research study.

Answer (any 2 OK):

1. Record and time events.
2. Transfer observational data into a computer file.
3. Detect coding errors.
4. Create graphic data displays of observational results.

6. (obj. 6) If observers disagree with one another's ratings while being trained to use an observational schedule, what is one procedure that the researcher can use to resolve the disagreement?

Answer (any 1 OK):

1. Review the event that the disagreement involved and explain how it should be recorded.
2. Revise the definition of variables on the observation form to remove ambiguities that may have caused the disagreement.
3. Write data-recording rules to handle the situation that caused the disagreement.

7. (obj. 6) Name three steps recommended for training observers for a quantitative research study.

Answer (any 3 OK):

1. Discuss the observation form with the observers.
2. Make video recordings of situations similar to those to be observed in the study.
3. Set up practice observations in which all observer trainees participate.
4. Reconcile any disagreements among observers or with the criterion.
5. Revise the observers' instruction sheet to include any necessary clarifications that arose during training.

8. (obj. 7) Describe a procedure that a researcher could use to check the inter-rater reliability of three observers who will collect data on 20 meetings of a university faculty senate.

Answer:

Have all three observers together attend a certain number of the meetings and collect data on the same observational variables. Determine the extent to which the observers' ratings agree by calculating the appropriate inter-rater reliability statistic.

9. (obj. 8) Describe one type of rating error that occurs in quantitative observation.

Answer (any 1 OK):

1. The error of central tendency, which occurs when the observer rates most of the research participants near the middle of the rating scale. This error occurs because the observer is unable to discriminate between the behavior of different participants.
2. The halo effect, which occurs when the observer forms an opinion of a research participant based on information about the participant on one variable and then allows this information to influence her ratings of the participant on other variables
3. **The error of leniency, which is the tendency to assign high ratings to the majority of research participants even when they differ markedly on the variable being measured**

10. (obj. 8) Describe two characteristics of research participants that have been found to be associated with biased observations by observers.

Answer (any 2 OK):

1. Research participants are described by the researchers by such labels as *emotionally disturbed* or *mentally retarded.*
2. Research participants are particularly high or low in physical attractiveness.
3. Research participants have certain ethnic or socioeconomic backgrounds.

11. (obj. 9) Explain one major difference between observation in quantitative research and observation in qualitative research.

Answer (any 1 OK):

1. In quantitative research, observers attempt to remain objective (i.e., neutral) about the phenomenon being studied. In qualitative research, observers consider their personal reactions and reflections to be part of the phenomenon being studied.
2. In quantitative research, observers collect data about prespecified variables. In qualitative research, observers can change the aspect of the phenomenon about which data are to be collected as the study proceeds.
3. The focus of observation in qualitative research typically is much wider and includes more aspects of context than in quantitative research.

12. (obj. 10) A qualitative researcher who is studying a private Christian school participates in many of its activities as a volunteer, for example, by serving as a teacher aide, driving the school bus, and cleaning up after church services. The observer is of a different faith from those in the school community. What type of observational role is the researcher performing?

Answer:

The researcher is a participant observer.

13. (obj. 10) Describe two advantages of using multiple observers who are diverse in factors relevant to the phenomenon being studied in a qualitative observation study.

Answer (any 2 OK):

1. The burden on each observer is lower.
2. More observation time is possible overall.
3. **The validity of observations can be enhanced by observers cross checking each others' findings and eliminating inaccurate interpretations.**

14. (obj. 11) What typically occurs during the focused stage of observation in a qualitative research study?

Answer:

The observer collects more intensive data about the features of the phenomenon that proved to be of most interest during the descriptive stage.

15. (obj. 12) While a qualitative researcher is in the process of collecting observational data, a more experienced researcher advises him to change his data-collection procedures. Is it acceptable for the researcher to make the recommended changes, and why?

Answer:

Yes, in qualitative research, observational methods can be changed as the researcher develops new insights.

16. (obj. 13) A qualitative researcher wishes to make notes about what she is observing in a field situation but does not wish to be seen doing so. How can the researcher deal with this situation?

Answer:

The researcher may be able to make a few notes surreptitiously in the field setting and then write a longer summary of what she observed immediately upon leaving the setting. These records can be expanded into a more complete set of field notes at a later time.

17. (obj. 13) Descibe two desirable characteristics that qualitative researchers should aim to achieve in preparing field notes of their observations.

Answer (any 2 OK):

1. The field notes should include both descriptive and reflective information.

2. The field notes should be detailed and concrete rather than vague and overgeneralized.
3. The field notes should include visual details, such as sketches, photographs, or video recordings.

18. (obj. 14) Suppose the individuals being observed appear to be affected by the observer's presence. Compare how a qualitative researcher and a quantitative researcher would handle this situation.

Answer:

The qualitative researcher would collect and analyze data about the individuals' reactions to his presence. In contrast, the quantitative researcher would not collect any data until the individuals had appeared to have adjusted to his presence.

19. (obj. 14) Name and briefly explain four types of observer effects in qualitative research.

Answer (any 4 OK):

1. Effect of the observer on the observed: Individuals being observed are distracted by the observers' presence or influenced by the observers' intentions.
2. Observer personal bias: Observers code data in erroneous ways that are traceable to specific characteristics of the observers.
3. Rating errors: Observers' ratings reflect one or more response sets.
4. Observer contamination: Observers' knowledge of certain data in a study influences the data that they record about other variables.
5. Observer omissions: Observers fail to record the occurrence of certain behaviors that fit categories on the observation form.
6. Observer drift: Observers' skills or discipline decline over time such that the data collected no longer reflect the coding categories that they were trained to identify.
7. Reliability decay: Data recorded during later phases of data collection are less reliable, particularly when selected observations are not checked for accuracy.

20. (obj. 15) How might computer printouts generated by trainees in an architectural drafting firm be studied (a) by a quantitative researcher as unobtrusive measures and (b) by a qualitative researcher as objects of material culture?

Answer:

a. The quantitative researcher would obtain permission to collect the printouts without the knowledge of the trainees or their supervisor. The printouts would be analyzed by using prespecified variables.
b. The qualitative researcher would study the printouts as expressions of how individuals and groups construct a material culture that has certain purposes, including the communication of information. The qualitative researcher would also be interested in the symbolic meanings of the computer printouts and the contexts in which they are used.

21. (objs. 16-17) How would a quantitative researcher and a qualitative researcher differ in their approach to analyzing the content of a textbook?

Answer:

The quantitative researcher would code the content by using categories that reflect prespecified variables. The frequency of occurrence of each category most likely would be determined. In contrast, a qualitative researcher would study the meaning of the text for the author and for different audiences with no preconceived variables in mind. Also a qualitative researcher would be more likely to study contextual features relating to the textbook (e.g., the situations in which students read it) than would a quantitative researcher.

22. (objs. 16-17) Name three types of communication media that quantitative or qualitative researchers might study through nonreactive observational research methods.

Answer:

1. Written documents
2. Visual media

3. Audio media

23. (obj. 17) Explain the distinction typically made between documents and records in qualitative observation research.

Answer:

Documents are written communications that are prepared for personal rather than official reasons, while records are written communications that have an official purpose.

APPLICATION PROBLEMS

Problem 1

A researcher is interested in testing the theory that children learn by imitating the behavior of others. To test the theory, she asks one group of teachers to be exceptionally neat in their classrooms for a period of several weeks, for example, conspicuously taking time to arrange their desks (i.e., the teacher's own desk in the classroom) neatly. She asks another group of teachers to be sloppy for a similar period of time. The researcher's prediction is that children whose teachers are neat will themselves be neater by the end of the experiment than will children whose teachers are sloppy. Give examples of unobtrusive measures of the children's degree of neatness that could be used in this experiment.

Sample Answer:

a. The extent to which the objects on the children's desks are organized in an orderly manner
b. The amount of litter on the floor at the end of the school day
c. The neatness of the children's paperwork
d. If there is an area for storing clothing during the school day, the neatness with which the children's clothes are arranged in it
e. The alignment of the students' desks in an orderly pattern at the end of the school day

Problem 2

A researcher wants to determine whether the cognitive level of students' essays improves from the first to the fourth year of college. She has a collection of essays written by the same students over a four-year period of college attendance. What are three aspects of essay-writing style that could be content-analyzed to yield a measure of cognitive level?

Sample Answer:

a. Frequency of the use of low-frequency words
b. Frequency of words denoting abstract concepts, e.g., *nationalism*, *logic*, *symbolism*
c. Frequency of connectives such as *if*, *but*, *therefore*, and *whereas*
d. Average length of sentences
e. Frequency of cited evidence in support of a position

Problem 3
A quantitative researcher and a qualitative researcher want to use observational methods to study the phenomenon of collegiality among the counselors and other service staff in a high school. How are the two researchers likely to differ in (a) their approach to conceptualizing collegiality and (b) the types of data that they would collect?
Sample Answer:

a. The quantitative researcher would identify observable aspects of collegiality, would conceptualize each aspect as a separate variable, and would develop an observation form for recording data on each variable. The qualitative researcher would do less conceptualization prior to collecting data in the field. His emerging conceptualization would focus on the different meanings of collegiality for individuals in different roles (e.g., counselors, speech therapists, and nurses) and on the context in which collegiality is manifested.
b. The quantitative researcher would collect numerical data on variables that are descriptive, inferential, or evaluative. The qualitative researcher would collect verbal data, and perhaps visual data as well, about collegiality and the context in which it occurs and does not occur. The qualitative researcher's data would be rather general at the descriptive stage of data collection, and in the focused and selected stages it would narrow to fewer elements in the situation with more intensive data being collected about each element.

Problem 4
A quantitative researcher and a qualitative researcher are working as members of a team project whose goal is to study how journeyman contractors work with apprentice construction workers to guide their learning of their trades. While training observers, the quantitative researcher finds out that some of them bias their observational ratings in favor of contractors who were originally trained as carpenters. Upon hearing of this bias, the qualitative researcher realizes that she, too, shares their bias that contractors with a carpentry background are more effective than those with another construction specialization (e.g., electricians, cabinet makers, or painters). How would each researcher be likely to deal with this bias?
Sample Answer:

a. The quantitative researcher would eliminate observers from the study if their bias continues to affect their ratings despite training in use of the observation form. Also, the researcher would take care not to reveal to the observers whether the contractors to be observed were originally trained as carpenters or in some other construction specialization.
b. The qualitative researcher would check whether her bias affected her findings by making active efforts to test rival explanations for the findings, using both qualitative and quantitative research methods, using multiple observers, and examining the findings from various theoretical perspectives.

TEACHING ACTIVITIES

Activity 1
Assign students to read a quantitative research study and a qualitative research study that involves the use of observational methods. In class, have students compare how the observational data were collected, analyzed, and reported in the two studies.

Activity 2
If you know a researcher who is doing or has done a quantitative or a qualitative research study involving extensive observation, invite this person to be a guest presenter. Ask the researcher to discuss why he chose to

collect observational data, how he prepared to collect such data, any problems he experienced while collecting the data, and how the data were analyzed.

Activity 3

You can demonstrate the complexity of making field notes or doing continuous recording by showing a few minutes of a video recording of a classroom lesson or other educational event. As the event is being shown, ask students to write down everything that they observe. You can ask some of the students to write their notes on a transparency, so that they can be shared with others in the class by showing them on an overhead projector. Ask students what they learned about collecting observational data from this experience.

Activity 4

Mention a complex construct such as enthusiasm, attentiveness, or empathy. Ask students to identify observable indicators of the construct and how these indicators might be recorded in a quantitative research study.

CHAPTER 10
NONEXPERIMENTAL RESEARCH:
DESCRIPTIVE AND CAUSAL-COMPARATIVE DESIGNS

Note: The phrase in parentheses following the item number for both closed-form and open-form items, for example, "(obj. 3)", refers to the textbook chapter objective to which the item is keyed.

CLOSED-FORM ITEMS

1. (obj. 1) In educational research, description
   a. is a major goal of both quantitative and qualitative research.
   b. rarely is the focus of data-collection efforts.
   c. is associated with nonparametric tests of statistical significance.
   d. focuses on demonstrating cause-effect connections.

Answer: a

2. (obj. 1) Causal-comparative research differs most distinctly from descriptive research in its
   a. use of measures of central tendency and measures of variability.
   b. appropriateness for exploring how variables are related to each other.
   c. potential for impact on educational practice.
   d. study of the same population at different times.

Answer: b

3. (obj. 1) Descriptive research can focus on depicting
   a. educators' attitudes.
   b. educators' professional behavior.
   c. educators' beliefs.
   d. all of the above.

Answer: d

4. (obj. 2) A descriptive research study would be likely to report all but which of the following types of scores or statistics?
   a. Standard deviation
   b. Mean
   c. Percentiles
   d. Analysis of variance

Answer: d

5. (obj. 2) Derived scores are useful in descriptive research because they
   a. identify the amount of discrepancy between actual and ideal behavior or values.
   b. show how an individual's performance compares with that of a comparison group.
   c. explain how test scores are generated by individuals' performance on the test.
   d. do not require an understanding of the normal probability curve.

Answer: b

6. (obj. 3) An opinion poll is an example of which type of descriptive research?
   a. Description of a sample at one point in time
   b. Cross-sectional research
   c. Longitudinal research
   d. Case study research

Answer: a

7. (obj. 4) Longitudinal research designs are particularly useful for studying
   a. processes involved in human development.
   b. cross-cultural differences in beliefs and values.
   c. possible causal relationships between different variables.
   d. differences in the views of various members of a defined population at a given time.

Answer: a

8. (obj. 4) If a researcher studies the same population over time by repeatedly contacting the same sample of individuals, the researcher is conducting a _________ study.
   a. trend
   b. cohort
   c. panel
   d. cross-sectional

Answer: c

9. (obj. 4) Match each of the following types of longitudinal research study with the appropriate description of what audience is studied at each data-collection point.
   __ 1. Trend study
   __ 2. Cohort study
   __ 3. Panel study
   a. A different sample from a population that changes over time
   b. A different sample from the same population
   c. The entire population
   d. The same sample from the same population

Answer: 1 = a 2 = b 3 = d

10. (obj. 5) Compared with a longitudinal study, an important advantage of a cross-sectional study is that
   a. information is collected at several points in time.
   b. the data can be obtained more rapidly.
   c. developmental changes can be detected more accurately.
   d. the data are not distorted by faulty recall.

Answer: b

11. (obj. 5) Suppose you wish to examine the changes in attitudes toward school that occur as students mature. You select a sample of elementary, middle, and high school students and measure their attitudes toward school. A weakness of your cross-sectional design for studying this research problem is that
   a. this method cannot be used to explore relationships between variables.
   b. this method cannot be used to explore developmental changes.
   c. the sample of elementary, middle, and high school students may differ on other characteristics besides grade level.
   d. data must be collected over an extended time period.

Answer: c

12. (obj. 6) Match each of the following research results with the type of interpretation of it that a researcher is likely to make about the relationship among females' athletic participation (*X*), engaging in irresponsible sexual activity (*Y*), and receiving supportive parenting (*Z*).
    __ 1. Female students who participate in school athletic events are less likely to engage in irresponsible sexual activity.
    __ 2. Females with supportive parents are more likely to participate in athletic events while in school and to make responsible decisions about sexual activity.
    __ 3. Females who engage in irresponsible sexual activity have less time and interest for athletic participation while in school.
    a. *Z* causes both *X* and *Y*.
    b. *Y* causes *X*.
    c. *X* causes *Y*.
    Answers: 1 = c 2 = a 3 = b

13. (obj. 6) In causal-comparative research, matching is used to
    a. equate two groups on one or more extraneous variables.
    b. identify groups that represent the extremes of a phenomenon.
    c. predict the direction of a presumed causal relationship.
    d. ensure that groups with different characteristics are selected randomly.

Answer: a

14. (obj. 7) The best way to select two groups for comparison in a causal-comparative research study so that they are highly different on the presumed causal variable is
    a. through the use of matching.
    b. by random selection of the groups from the defined population.
    c. by determining the range of scores of the defined population on a measure of the variable and then selecting individuals whose scores are at the extreme of the range.
    d. by using theory to determine the hypothetically extreme ranges of the presumed causal variable and then recruit volunteers who satisfy the requirements of the these ranges.

Answer: c

15. (obj. 8) After the researchers have selected a group having the characteristic they wish to study in a causal comparative design, the next logical step is to
    a. randomly form subgroups from the selected group.
    b. identify a comparable group without the selected characteristic.
    c. collect biographical data on this group.
    d. choose the statistical analyses to be performed.

Answer: b

16. (obj. 9) The *t* test should be used instead of the *z* distribution to test the difference between two means when
    a. the size of the population is difficult to estimate.
    b. the scores of the two samples are correlated.
    c. *N* is less than 30.
    d. very large samples are studied.

Answer: c

17. (obj. 9) For which of the following hypotheses is a one-tailed test of significance appropriate?
    a. Teaching method A and teaching method B will produce different student achievement gains.
    b. There is no difference in the effects of Head Start programs on the achievement gains of low-income Caucasian and African-American children.
    c. The mean IQ score of a sample is significantly different from the population mean.
    d. Children receiving a dietary supplement will show greater achievement gains than those receiving a placebo.

Answer: d

18. (obj. 9) Use of a one-tailed versus a two-tailed *t* test to test the significance of the difference between two sample means depends on whether
    a. there is expected overlap between the error curves of the two sample distributions.
    b. the difference is expected to be in one direction only.
    c. the size of the samples is proportional to their respective population sizes.
    d. research participants were matched or chosen randomly.

Answer: b

19. (obj. 9) If any of the assumptions underlying the *t* test are violated to a modest extent,
    a. the *t* test is still likely to yield an accurate estimate of statistical significance.
    b. the *t* test will yield an accurate estimate of statistical significance, but only if the test is two-tailed.
    c. a nonparametric test of statistical significance must be used instead.
    d. no test of statistical significance should be performed.

Answer: a

20. (obj. 10) The *t* test for correlated means should be used when
    a. the group possessing the characteristic of interest and the comparison group are randomly selected.
    b. subgroups are to be formed within the group possessing the characteristic of interest.
    c. the group possessing the characteristic of interest and the comparison group are matched on another variable.
    d. researchers wish to determine the magnitude of the relationship between independent and dependent variables.

Answer: c

21. (obj. 10) In comparing the mean performance of 25 delinquents and 25 matched nondelinquents, one should use the
    a. *t* test for independent means.
    b. *z* distribution.
    c. *t* test for a single mean.
    d. *t* test for correlated means.

Answer: d

22. (objs. 10-14) Match each condition below with the test most appropriate under that condition
    To determine whether:
    __ 1. the sample mean differs significantly from a specified population mean.
    __ 2. the mean achievement of a random sample of delinquents differs significantly from that of a randomly selected control group.
    __ 3. the mean anxiety scores of high, middle, and low achievers are significantly different.
    __ 4. high, middle, and low achievers have different high school dropout rates.
    __ 5. the mean achievement of two groups of students matched on aptitude differs significantly.
       a. *t* test for correlated means
       b. *t* test for a single mean
       c. chi-square test
       d. analysis of variance
       e. *t* test for independent means

Answer: 1 = b 2 = e 3 = d 4 = c 5 = a

23. (obj. 11) Use of the *t* test for a single mean requires
    a. a normal score distribution.
    b. homogeneity of variance.
    c. random selection of research participants.
    d. knowledge of the population mean.

Answer: d

24. (obj. 11) If a researcher wishes to determine whether a sample mean differs from the population mean, the appropriate statistic is the
    a. chi-square.
    b. *t* test for independent means.
    c. *t* test for a single mean.
    d. analysis of covariance.

Answer: c

25. (obj. 12) The *F* ratio is computed to determine
    a. whether the members of a sample have been randomly selected from a population.
    b. the statistical significance of the difference between the mean scores of two or more groups.
    c. whether two or more groups have different frequency distributions on a categorical variable.
    d. all of the above.

Answer: b

26. (obj. 12) Analysis of variance focuses on the
    a. between-groups variance.
    b. within-groups variance.
    c. ratio of between-groups variance to within-groups variance.
    d. mean scores of each group in the analysis.

Answer: c

27. (obj. 12) The purpose of the *t* test for multiple comparisons is to
    a. adjust for statistically significant differences that occur by chance because the comparison groups are compared on many variables.
    b. provide an alternative approach to multiple comparisons when the assumptions underlying analysis of variance are not satisfied.
    c. enable the use of analysis of variance when the number of comparison groups exceeds five.
    d. all of the above.

Answer: a

28. (obj. 12) Analysis of covariance is the preferred test rather than analysis of variance when
    a. there are initial differences between the samples on a measured variable related to the dependent variable.
    b. there are extreme differences in the sample variances.
    c. the scores of the groups being compared are in the form of categorical frequency counts.
    d. the scores of the groups being compared are in the form of ranks.

Answer: a

29. (obj. 12) In conducting a MANOVA on a cluster of five related variables, a researcher obtains an *F* value that is significant at the .01 level. What is the next step that should be taken in analyzing the data?
    a. Reexamine the cluster to see if any variables should be removed.
    b. Test for the equality of group dispersions.
    c. Compute a mean vector score for each variable.
    d. Conduct an ANOVA on each dependent variable in the cluster.

Answer: d

30. (obj. 12) The test for homogeneity of independent variances, the test for homogeneity of related variances, and the *F* maximum test for homogeneity of variance are all forms of
    a. analysis of covariance.
    b. nonparametric statistics.
    c. analysis of variance.
    d. multivariate analysis of variance.

Answer: c

31. (obj. 13) A nonparametric test of significance should be considered whenever
    a. the population scores of the comparison groups are normally distributed.
    b. group variances are equal or nearly so.
    c. scores are in the form of ranks.
    d. scores are derived from a measure with equal intervals.

Answer: c

32. (obj. 13) Compared to parametric statistics, nonparametric statistics
    a. have less statistical power.
    b. have more statistical power.
    c. involve many more assumptions about score distribution in the population being studied.
    d. cannot be used to determine whether a null hypothesis can be rejected.

Answer: a

33. (obj. 14) Chi-square should be used when data are in the form of
    a. ranks.
    b. standard scores.
    c. continuous scores.
    d. category frequencies.

Answer: d

34. (obj. 14) The Mann-Whitney *U* test, the Wilcoxon signed rank test, and the Kruskal-Wallis test
    a. all are forms of chi-square tests.
    b. are preferred when the research data are rank or interval scores that grossly violate parametric assumptions of normal distribution and homogeneity of variance.
    c. are used to compare the score distributions of three or more groups.
    d. all of the above.

Answer: b

OPEN-FORM ITEMS

1. (obj. 1) Briefly describe the different role of description in descriptive research and in causal-comparative research.

Answer:

In descriptive research, the role of description is simply to describe phenomena as they are. In causal-comparative research, the purpose is to describe phenomena as they relate to other phenomena and to infer possible cause-effect relationships among those phenomena.

2. (obj. 2) Name two descriptive statistics that often are calculated in a descriptive research study.

Answer (any 2 OK):

1. The mean
2. The median
3. The mode
4. The standard deviation
5. The variance
6. The range

3. (obj. 3) A researcher makes direct observations of the classroom question-asking behavior of third graders. What type of descriptive research does this study exemplify?

Answer:

The research involves description of a sample at one point in time.

4. (obj. 4) In longitudinal research, describe how samples are selected for (a) cohort, (b) trend and (c) panel studies, and provide an example of each sampling procedure.

Answer:

a. In *trend* studies a random sample from a general population whose members change over time (e.g., all members of the American Federation of Teachers) is selected at each data-collection point. Thus, both the population and the sample are different at each data-collection point.
b. In *cohort* studies a random sample of a fixed population whose members stay the same (e.g., the 1988 graduating class from Hoover High School) is selected at each data-collection point. Thus the population remains the same, but the sample is different at each data-collection point.
c. In *panel* studies, a sample is selected at the start of the study, and the same sample is surveyed at each data-collection point (e.g., a group of Hoover High School students who agree at the time of graduation to provide data to the researcher every 10 years). Thus both the population and the sample remains the same at each data-collection point.

5. (obj. 4) Lewis Terman's study of giftedness involved repeated measurement of a panel of children identified as geniuses at various stages in their lives. What is one weakness and one strength of this study design?

Answer (any 1 from each set OK):

Weaknesses

a. Having been given the instrument or interview before can affect individuals' responses at the next data-collection point.
b. The response rate tends to decline with repeated follow-ups.
c. Loss of research participants can reduce the representativeness of the sample.

Strengths

a. Because the same individuals are measured at each data-collection point, the panel design is sensitive to smaller changes than comparably sized samples in cohort or trend studies.
b. Because the same individuals are measured at each data-collection point, the researcher can trace the specific past experiences and characteristics of individuals that might have contributed to changes observed over time.

6. (obj. 5) Describe the major problem with the sampling procedure used in a cross-sectional research design, and provide an example that illustrates that problem.

Answer:

Over time the population that is sampled is likely to change through attrition. Thus the sample that is selected to represent the population at one stage of development may not be representative of the population at other stages of development. For example, comparing the incidence of smoking among teens, young adults, and older adults through a cross-sectional design might involve a biased sample of older adults, because some individuals who have smoked from an early age may have become ill or died by the time they would reach this age and thus are not part of the accessible population.

7. (obj. 6) A researcher finds a correlation between length of teaching experience (variable *X*) and the principal's ratings of teaching effectiveness (variable *Y*) for the teachers employed in the principal's school. Give two plausible interpretations of this finding.

Answer (any 2 OK):

1. As teachers gain more experience, they become more effective, i.e., *X* leads to *Y*.
2. The more effective teachers are more likely to survive staffing cuts and also to choose to continue teaching, i.e., *Y* leads to *X*.
3. Both teacher longevity (*X*) and rated teaching effectiveness (*Y*) are a function of some other variable, e.g., teachers' emotional stability (*Z*), i.e., *Z* leads to both *X* and *Y*.
4. The principal might hold the belief that teaching experience makes teachers more effective, and this belief (*Z*) might lead them to assign higher effectiveness ratings (*Y*) to teachers with more teaching experience (*X*).

8. (objs. 7-8) Describe two approaches to selecting a suitable comparison group for a causal-comparative research study.

Answer:

a. Draw two groups from the same population, measure whether the two groups differ on any extraneous variables that could affect the study results, and if so, match the groups on those variables.
b. Select comparison groups who are at the two extremes of the distribution on one of the variables of interest but who are similar in other respects.

9. (obj. 9) List three assumptions about the obtained scores in a causal-comparative study that should be satisfied in order to use the *t* test.

Answer:

1. The scores form an interval or ratio scale of measurement.
2. Scores in the defined populations are normally distributed.
3. Score variances for the defined populations are equal.

10. (obj. 10) Under what condition should the researcher use the *t* test for correlated means in a causal-comparative study, and what effect will use of this type of *t* test have on the likelihood of finding a significant difference between groups on the variable of interest?

Answer:

The *t* test for correlated means is appropriate when the researcher has matched the groups to be compared on an extraneous variable that is correlated with the dependent variable. Under this condition, the *t* test for correlated means is more likely to yield a statistically significant difference than a *t* test for independent means. Stated another way, the *t* test for correlated means has more statistical power.

11. (obj. 11) A researcher wishes to determine whether the sample's mean score on a standardized achievement test is different from the mean score of the norming group. What type of *t* test is most appropriate in this situation?

Answer:

The *t* test for a single mean is most appropriate, because the researcher is comparing the sample's mean score to that of the presumed mean score of the population, as estimated by the norming group's mean score.

12. (obj. 12) A researcher conducts a study in which 90 high school sophomores are randomly assigned to three algebra classes. Class A is taught by a lecture method, class B by a cooperative learning method, and class C by an individualized method. Algebra achievement, the dependent variable, is measured at the end of the course. What statistical significance test is most appropriate for comparing the mean algebra achievement scores of the three groups? If this test yields a value that is significant at the .05 level, how would you interpret this finding?

Answer:

Analysis of variance would be the appropriate statistical test. An *F* ratio that is significant at the .05 level indicates that a significant difference exists between at least one pair of the mean scores, but it does not indicate which pair were significantly different.

13. (obj. 12) What is the major difference between analysis of variance (ANOVA) and analysis of covariance (ANCOVA)?

Answer:

ANCOVA adjusts statistically for initial group differences on one or more variables (called covariates).

14. (obj. 13) Three assumptions about population parameters should be checked when deciding to use parametric statistics to analyze causal-comparative data rather than nonparametric statistics. List one of these assumptions.

Answer (any 1 OK):

1. The scores in the population are normally distributed on the variables being studied.
2. The population variances of the comparison groups are approximately equal.
3. The scores being analyzed are derived from a measure that has equal intervals.

15. (obj. 14) You have hypothesized that dogmatism is distributed among army recruits so as to approximate a normal distribution (or normal probability curve). You randomly select 1,000 recruits at a basic training center and administer the Rokeach Dogmatism Scale. Scores of the 1,000 recruits are sorted into five categories ranging from high dogmatism to low dogmatism. What statistical procedure would be most appropriate to test your hypothesis, and why?

Answer:

Chi-square is the most appropriate test, because you have categorical data that you want to check against a normal distribution.

APPLICATION PROBLEMS

Problem 1

Describe a suitable comparison group for each of the following defined groups in a causal-comparative study.

a. The discipline styles used by parents of high school students with high scores on an authoritarianism scale
b. The extent to which female college students who are in leadership roles in campus organizations report childhood experiences in which adults encouraged them to display leadership
c. The educational aspirations of fourth-grade Pueblo Indian boys who have attended school only on the reservation

Sample Answer:

a. Parents of high school students who have low scores on the authoritarianism scale
b. Female college students who are not in leadership roles in campus organizations
c. Fourth-grade Pueblo Indian boys who have attended school outside the reservation

Problem 2

Two researchers are interested in doing a study to provide descriptive information to a school district about homelessness among students attending the district's schools. One researcher is a quantitative researcher, and the other is a qualitative researcher. Assume that they are able to obtain information from school records about all the students who are categorized as homeless. Describe (a) several types of information that the quantitative researcher would be more likely to report, and (b) several types of information that the qualitative researcher would be more likely to report.

Sample Answer:

a. The quantitative researcher probably would want to report the number and proportion of students in the district who are homeless, and, perhaps, the average length of time that students have been homeless. She might be interested in classifying students by their current types of living arrangements (e.g., living in an established shelter for homeless people; living in a vehicle, tent, or other constructed personal dwelling; or not living in any permanent arrangement but being on the move); she might then calculate the percentage of homeless students in each category.
b. The qualitative researcher probably would want to report in-depth information from a purposeful sample of homeless students who are willing to be interviewed. She might explore such topics as their feelings about being homeless and the particular challenges it presents to them in relation to attending school and doing schoolwork.

Problem 3

A researcher studies the difference in reading achievement of third-grade children who learned to read by the phonics method and those who learned to read by the whole language method of teaching reading. Children in the two groups are matched on an aptitude measure that has been found to correlate with measures of reading achievement. What type of *t* test should the investigator use to analyze the results, and why? If the *t* value is significant, what interpretation can the researcher make?

Sample Answer:

The *t* test for correlated means is appropriate because children were matched for scholastic aptitude, which probably is correlated with the dependent variable, reading achievement. A significant *t* means either that students taught by the phonics method showed superior reading achievement or that students taught by the whole-language method showed superior reading achievement; this can be determined by examining the mean reading achievement scores of each group. The researcher needs to be cautious, however, in claiming that the teaching method caused the higher level of reading achievement. Even though the groups were matched on aptitude, another variable might be responsible for the differences in post-treatment reading achievement, e.g. motivation.

Problem 4

You hypothesize that low-achieving children who receive special tutoring will make significantly greater reading achievement gains than those who spend an equal amount of time engaged in solitary reading in the regular classroom. Would this hypothesis be tested with a one-tailed or a two-tailed test of significance, and why?

Sample Answer:

A one-tailed test is appropriate because you have predicted the direction of the difference that is expected between the gains of the two groups. Also, you can refer to previous research showing a relationship between tutoring and increased scholastic achievement. Thus, if a difference is found, it probably will favor the group that received special tutoring.

Problem 5

You hypothesize that low-achieving children who receive special tutoring in reading skills will make significantly greater gains than low-achieving children who do not receive the special tutoring on a measure of reading achievement and also on measures of three types of academic achievement (mathematics, social studies, and physical science). What test of statistical significance would you use in this situation?

Sample Answer:

Multivariate analysis (MANOVA) would be appropriate, because the sample has been measured on four dependent variables (reading, mathematics, social studies, and physical science). Also, these variables are related to each other in a conceptually meaningful manner, that is, they are all aspects of the over-arching construct of "academic achievement."

Problem 6

A researcher is interested in learning whether attendance at a high school with strict rules of discipline and conduct tends to produce authoritarian students. He locates two high schools that are located in very similar neighborhoods serving similar racial and socioeconomic groups. School A promotes strict rules of discipline and conduct, and most of its teachers and administrators have higher than average scores on a measure of authoritarianism. School B employs flexible rules of discipline and conduct, has a high level of student involvement in formulating school rules, and primarily employs teachers and administrators with lower than average scores on a test of authoritarianism.

a. In a pilot study the researcher randomly selects 25 students from each school and administers a 40-item scale of authoritarianism. What statistical technique should be used to analyze these data?
b. Each high school has 12 extracurricular programs that are classified by a group of independent judges as either high, average, or low in terms of authoritarian structure and activities. The researcher wishes to compare the proportion of students in each school who participated in each of the three types of programs. What statistical technique should be used to make this comparison?
c. In checking school records, the researcher found that most seniors in the two high schools had been administered the California F scale (a measure of authoritarianism) during their last year of junior high school. He decides to administer a different but similar authoritarianism measure to seniors who had taken the earlier test, and then see how the senior-level authoritarianism scores differed between students in the two schools when their earlier scores were taken into consideration. What statistical technique should be used?

Sample Answer:

a. A *t* test for uncorrelated means would be used to compare the authoritarianism scores of the two samples.
b. A chi-square test would be conducted on the percentage of students in each cell of the following table:

	High Authoritarianism	Average Authoritarianism	Low Authoritarianism
School A			
School B			

c. Analysis of covariance should be used, because it permits adjusting the senior high school authoritarianism scores for differences found in the junior high school authoritarianism scores.

TEACHING ACTIVITIES

Activity 1

Have students read an educational research study that involved describing the characteristics of a sample at one point in time. (The study by Glesne and Webb discussed in chapter 8 of the text, involving a questionnaire survey, is an example.) Ask the students to write a brief paper in which they specify how a longitudinal study could be carried out with the same target population, measures, and procedures. Tell students to be sure to specify whether the longitudinal research design would involve a trend study, a cohort study, or a panel study, and why they chose that study design.

Activity 2

Identify a research report that describes a causal-comparative study involving two groups, and have students read it as a homework assignment. Discuss in class the following features of the study: statement of the research problem, selection of the defined group and the comparison group, the measures and procedures used to measure the dependent variable, the statistical test used to test the difference between the means of the two groups, and the findings.

Activity 3

Obtain a set of approximately 100 numbers, with each number having a value between 1 and 100. (Numbers greater than 100 will complicate computations). If you wish, you can create the numbers using a random number generator. Give each student a sheet containing these numbers in columns, and tell them that the sheet represents the scores of a complete population of teachers on an achievement test. Next, have each student draw a sample of 10 teachers and calculate the mean test score of the sample. To avoid having your students draw the same sample, you can ask one student to select the first teacher in column one and then every fifth teacher after that. The next student would start by selecting the second teacher in column one and then every fifth teacher after that. The same procedure would be followed for every student in your class. For example, if your class has 30 students, the 30th student would select the 30th teacher on the list and every fifth teacher after that. Next, you would post every calculated mean score so that the entire class can see them. You can point out that the mean scores vary considerably, even though all the samples come from the same population. Next, you can state that using any two samples is similar to forming two comparison groups in a causal-comparative research study. Finally, you can note that the purpose of a *t* test is to help the researcher decide whether (a) the difference between the two sample means (it is likely that the means will differ, however slightly) were drawn from the same population or (b) the sample means are sufficiently different that they probably were drawn from different populations having different population means. You can extend this example by saying that every test of statistical significance (ANOVA, ANCOVA, MANOVA, etc.) follows the same logic as the one just illustrated.

Activity 4

Have each student make up a research problem for which chi-square would be the appropriate statistical test. Tell them to specify the purpose of the study, the variables to be measured, and the sampling procedure. You also can do this activity with other statistical tests described in chapter 10, e.g., analysis of variance and analysis of covariance.

CHAPTER 11
NONEXPERIMENTAL RESEARCH: CORRELATIONAL DESIGNS

Note: The phrase in parentheses following the item number for both closed-form and open-form items, for example, "(obj. 3)", refers to the textbook chapter objective to which the item is keyed.

CLOSED-FORM ITEMS

1. (obj. 1) An advantage of the correlational method is that
   a. it can be used to analyze the relationships among many variables within a single study.
   b. it indicates both the direction and the degree of the relationship between variables.
   c. it can be used to predict academic achievement and other outcomes.
   d. all of the above.

Answer: d

2. (obj. 1) A major advantage of correlational research designs over causal-comparative research designs is that
   a. they can examine the entire range of variation in the variables being studied.
   b. correlational statistics are easier to compute than are the statistics commonly used in causal-comparative research.
   c. they can accommodate a wider range of measurement scales.
   d. they are easier for practitioners to comprehend.

Answer: a

3. (obj. 1) One disadvantage of correlational research is that
   a. only two variables can be accommodated within a single correlational study.
   b. the results of a correlational study do not permit strong conclusions about cause-and-effect relationships.
   c. the variables in a correlational study cannot be measured reliably.
   d. it is difficult to find published measures that satisfy the assumptions of a correlational research design.

Answer: b

4. (obj. 2) A scattergram provides a visual representation of
   a. the causal relationship between two measured variables.
   b. the standard error of measurement for two measured variables.
   c. a positive or negative relationship between two measured variables.
   d. the results of a path analysis.

Answer: c

5. (obj. 2) If every point in a scattergram plotting variable *X* and variable *Y* falls on the line of best fit, we can conclude that
   a. variable *X* predicts measured variable *Y* perfectly.
   b. variable *X* explains none of the variance in variable *Y*.
   c. the relationship between variables *X* and *Y* is positive.
   d. Variable *X* causes variable *Y* , or vice versa.

Answer: a

6. (obj. 2) A scattergram can detect
   a. a positive correlation between two variables.
   b. a negative correlation between two variables.
   c the absence of correlation between two variables.
   d. all of the above.

Answer: d

7. (obj. 3) If every increase in score on a test of literary knowledge is accompanied by an increase in score on an intelligence test, one can conclude that
   a. there is a perfect negative relationship between literary knowledge and intelligence.
   b. there is no relationship between literary knowledge and intelligence.
   c. the correlation between the literary knowledge test and the intelligence test is 1.00.
   d. intelligence causes literary knowledge.

Answer: c

8. (obj. 3) A researcher who obtains a correlation of -.72 between test anxiety and college gradepoint average would be justified in concluding that
   a. scores on the two variables do not covary substantially.
   b. students who experience a great deal of test anxiety are likely to earn lower grades than students who experience minimal test anxiety.
   c. low test anxiety inhibits college achievement.
   d. high test anxiety is associated with higher grades.

Answer: b

9. (obj. 4) The purpose of a relationship study typically is to
   a. determine whether the correlation between two measured variables is caused by overlapping items.
   b. identify possible causes and effects among observed phenomena.
   c. check how well two observers agree in their ratings of the same construct.
   d. check how well a sample's scores on an individual item of a test correlate with their scores on all the other test items.

Answer: b

10. (obj. 4) A limitation of the shotgun approach to identify variables that correlate with a criterion variable is that
   a. it cannot detect whether the observed relationships are positive or negative.
   b. it cannot detect the magnitude of the observed relationships.
   c. only a few variables can be accommodated in the research design.
   d. some of the many measured variables are likely to correlate with the criterion by chance.

Answer: d

11. (obj. 4) In research investigating relationships between variables, it is best if
   a. the research sample is homogeneous with respect to major demographic variables.
   b. the number of variables is approximately the same as the number of individuals in the sample.
   c. the researcher uses the individual as the unit of statistical analysis.
   d. the researcher uses the group as the unit of statistical analysis.

Answer: a

12. (obj. 5) In a prediction study, the basic form of data analysis consists of
   a. analysis of covariance.
   b. comparing the variances of different predictor variables.
   c. correlating each moderator variable with the criterion variable.
   d. correlating each predictor variable with the criterion variable.

Answer: d

13. (obj. 5) Both multiple regression and moderator analysis can be used to
   a. determine underlying factors in a set of variables.
   b. check for item overlap as a cause of an observed correlation between two measured variables.
   c. maximize the correlation between predictor variables and a criterion.
   d. control for shrinkage in predictive validity coefficients.

Answer: c

14. (obj. 6) Prediction research can be done for the purpose of
    a. studying the validity of a new aptitude test.
    b. determining which individuals are most likely to benefit from a residential treatment program.
    c. testing a theory about the determinants of administrative effectiveness.
    d. all of the above.

Answer: d

15. (obj. 7) The effectiveness of a measure in identifying which individuals will be successful with respect to a given criterion depends upon its predictive validity, the selection ratio, and the
    a. amount of variance accounted for by the correlation coefficient.
    b. proportion of individuals who would be successful if no selection procedure was used.
    c. size of the sample.
    d. direction of the validity coefficient.

Answer: b

16. (obj. 7) Cross-validation of findings from a prediction study is particularly important for
    a. determining the stability of the base rate across replication samples.
    b. improving the selection ratio.
    c. identifying nonlinear relationships among predictor variables.
    d. checking for shrinkage when the original study is replicated.

Answer: d

17. (obj. 8) An important factor in deciding which correlational technique to use is
    a. the type of measurement scale used to collect the data.
    b. the sample size.
    c. the type of cause-effect relationship being studied.
    d. whether the relationship is hypothesized to be positive or negative.

Answer: a

18. (obj. 8) An important reason for making a scattergram is that it
    a. provides a test of the statistical significance of the obtained correlation coefficient.
    b. provides a measure of the confidence limits for the obtained correlation coefficient.
    c. is helpful for detecting nonlinear relationships.
    d. estimates the amount of shrinkage in a correlation coefficient when cross-validated.

Answer: c

19. (obj. 8) If the relationship between two variables is markedly nonlinear, the researcher should determine the degree of relationship by computing a
    a. point-serial correlation.
    b. correlation ratio.
    c. contingency coefficient.
    d. biserial coefficient.

Answer: b

20. (obj. 8) The most widely used bivariate correlation coefficient is the
    a. rank-difference coefficient, *rho*.
    b. contingency coefficient, *C*.
    c. product-moment coefficient, *r*.
    d. correlation coefficient, *eta*.

Answer: c

21. (obj. 9) The correction for attenuation estimates what the magnitude of the correlation between two measured variables would be if
    a. a cross-validation study were done.
    b. the measures were perfectly reliable.
    c. the raw scores were converted to standard scores.
    d. the influence of moderator variables were partialled out.

Answer: b

22. (obj. 9) To correct for restriction in range, the researcher must know the
    a. true correlation between the measured variables in the population.
    b. size of the population.
    c. reliability of each measured variable.
    d. variability of population scores.

Answer: d

23. (obj. 9) To hold intelligence constant when correlating scores on a Spanish achievement test and a measure of auditory acuity, a researcher should use
    a. partial correlation.
    b. correction for attenuation.
    c. the correlation ratio.
    d. factor analysis.

Answer: a

24. (obj. 10) Multiple regression involves
    a. generating a correlation matrix.
    b. determining the correlation between a criterion variable and a combination of predictor variables.
    c. testing for cause-and-effect relationships along a path of variables.
    d. identifying measured variables that correlate with each other, but not with other variables in a data set.

Answer: b

25. (obj. 10) A researcher administers 10 measures of stress and anxiety to a sample of evaluators working for state departments of education. What statistical technique can the researcher use to determine whether the information in these 10 measures can be reduced to a smaller number of variables?
    a. Factor analysis
    b. Multiple regression analysis
    c. Path analysis
    d. Discriminant analysis

Answer: a

26. (obj. 10) The multiple correlation coefficient between five predictor variables and grades is .50. This finding means that
    a. the best single predictor explains 25 percent of the variance in grades.
    b. the average correlation between each predictor variable and grades is .10.
    c. the combined set of predictor variables explains 25 percent of the variance in grades.
    d. the combined set of predictor variables explains 50 percent of the variance in grades.

Answer: c

27. (obj. 10) If a researcher wishes to determine how well a combination of predictor variables correlates with a composite of several criterion variables, the appropriate statistical technique to use is
    a. path analysis.
    b. discriminant analysis.
    c. structural equation modeling.
    d. canonical correlation.

Answer: d

28. (obj. 10) Hierarchical linear modeling is a statistical technique that can be used for understanding
    a. why linear and nonlinear relationships between two variables occur at the school level.
    b. how the relationship between two or more variables is affected by different levels of school organization.
    c. how the addition of a new predictor variable affects the magnitude of a multiple correlation coefficient.
    d. the relationship between variables within different units specified in an organization chart.

Answer: b

29. (obj. 10) Path analysis is an appropriate statistical technique when
    a. the criterion variable is a dichotomy.
    b. the criterion is a composite of variables.
    c. the researcher wishes to test a theory about the causal relationships among a set of variables.
    d. the researcher wishes to identify clusters of related variables.

Answer: c

30. (obj. 10) An advantage of structural equation modeling over path analysis is that it
    a. is much simpler to compute.
    b. requires fewer measured variables.
    c. yields more valid and reliable measures of the variables to be analyzed.
    d. can be used when some or all of the variables are measured as dichotomies or ranks.

Answer: c

31. (obj. 11) Suppose a researcher generates a correlation matrix for four variables. How many correlation coefficients would be in the matrix?
    a. 9
    b. 6
    c. 4
    d. 10

Answer: b

32. (obj. 11) A correlation matrix is used to
    a. show the extent to which each variable in a set of variables correlates with all the other variables in the set.
    b. determine which predictor variables to enter into a multiple regression equation.
    c. identify variables that have a restricted range.
    d. all of the above.

Answer: a

33. (obj. 11) In factor analysis, a factor is
    a. the variable that best correlates with all the other variables entered into the factor analysis.
    b. the set of variables, among all those measured, that best correlates with the criterion variable.
    c. a mathematical expression of the common variance in all the variables entered into the factor analysis.
    d. a mathematical expression of the common element in a subset of variables that were entered into the factor analysis and that are correlated with each other.

Answer: d

34. (obj. 12) Multiple regression, path analysis, hierarchical linear modeling, and structural equation modeling are similar in that all of them
    a. incorporate multiple criterion variables into their equations.
    b. involve the analysis of relationships among three or more variables.
    c. do not rely on theory to determine which variables should be measured.
    d. all of the above.

Answer: b

35. (obj. 12) To provide the most powerful test of the causal relationship specified by a theory, a researcher should use
    a. multiple regression.
    b. differential analysis.
    c. structural equation modeling.
    d. path analysis.

Answer: c

36. (obj. 13) Suppose that a researcher finds that aptitude test scores predict school grades better for females than for males. This finding indicates that
    a. aptitude is a moderator variable.
    b. gender is a predictor variable.
    c. gender is a moderator variable.
    d. a correction for attenuation is needed.

Answer: c

37. (obj. 14) The size of a research sample
    a. determines the type of correlation coefficient that should be calculated.
    b. affects the magnitude of an obtained correlation coefficient.
    c. has no effect on the statistical significance of a correlation coefficient.
    d. affects the statistical significance of a correlation coefficient.

Answer: d

38 (obj. 14) If the goal of a research study is to understand a complex phenomenon, such as students' motivation to learn, the researcher
    a. is likely to find a small correlation coefficient as meaningful as a large correlation coefficient.
    b. will reject correlational statistics and instead rely on descriptive statistics.
    c. will want to use moderator analysis in order to maximize the correlation between two variables.
    d. will want to use multiple regression in order the maximize prediction of the variables that represent the complex phenomenon.

Answer: a

39. (obj. 14) A correlation coefficient of .20 between two variables
    a. is too small to have practical significance for education.
    b. is sufficiently large that it might have practical significance for education.
    c. is sufficiently large to have practical significance for education if the measured variables can be linked to a proven theory.
    d. is sufficiently large to have implications for theory development, but not foreducational practice.

Answer: b

OPEN-FORM ITEMS

1. (obj. 1) State one advantage and one limitation of correlational research.

Answer:

Advantages (any 1 OK):
1. The relationships among a large number of variables can be investigated in a single study.
2. It enables the study of possible causal relationships among certain phenomena that cannot be experimentally manipulated.
3. It provides information on both the degree and the direction of the relationship between the variables being studied.
4. It can be used to identify variables that are useful in the prediction of important criterion variables.

Limitations (any 1 OK):
1. Cause-and-effect relationships cannot be established with a high level of certainty.
2. Correlational studies of a complex behavior pattern or characteristic sometimes focus on atomistic variables that do not accurately reflect the pattern or characteristic. As a result, the studies yield data that are difficult or impossible to interpret.

2. (obj. 2) Describe two types of information that can be obtained from examination of a scattergram of a group's scores on two variables.

Answer (any 2 OK):
1. The direction of the relationship between the two variables
2. The degree of the relationship between the two variables
3. Whether the relationship between the two variables is linear or nonlinear

3. (obj. 3) The correlation between variable X and variable Y is .40. What does this correlation coefficient tell us about: (a) the explained variance in the relationship between X and Y, (b) the direction of the relationship, and (c) whether the relationship is causal?

Answer:

a. Variable X explains 16 percent of the variance in variable Y.
b. The direction of the relationship is positive, meaning that higher scores on variable X tend to be associated with higher scores on variable Y.
c. The obtained correlation coefficient is consistent with a presumed causal relationship between variables X and Y, but does not prove that such a relationship exists.

4. (obj. 4) Suppose that you are interested in the nature of ability in graphic art. You identify several variables that you hypothesize to have a causal relationship to artistic ability, such as depth perception, hand-eye coordination, creative imagination, and so on.
   a. What type of correlational study would you do with these variables to explore the causes of ability in graphic art?
   b. How would this study be conducted?

Answer:

a. A relationship study
b. In a simple relationship study the artistic ability of a group of individuals would be quantified (e.g., artistic work could be rated). A measure of each of the possible causal variables also would be obtained. Correlations would be computed between the criterion and each causal variable.

5. (obj. 5) A researcher has two sets of scores for a sample of graduating seniors: their scores on a vocabulary test administered just before graduation, and their cumulative gradepoint average (GPA). The researcher finds a high positive correlation between the two sets of scores, and therefore recommends that the vocabulary test be administered to high school freshmen to identify those who are likely to experience academic difficulty during high school. What is the major flaw in this recommendation?

Answer:

The measure of the predictor variable (i.e., the vocabulary test) was administered at the same time as the measure of the criterion variable (i.e., cumulative GPA). The predictive validity of the vocabulary test needs to be established by administering it to students during their freshmen year and then determining their cumulative GPA four years later.

6. (obj. 6) Briefly describe two uses of prediction research.

Answer (any 2 OK):

1. Prediction studies can determine the extent to which some criterion behavior can be predicted. Such studies, if successful, often lead to the development of selection systems such as those employed in college, industry, and the military.
2. Prediction studies can be used in theory building. A theory can be tested by making predictions based upon the theory and then doing prediction studies to see if the theory holds up.
3. Prediction studies are employed to establish the predictive validity of tests, which can subsequently be employed in practical problems of selection and prediction.

7. (obj. 7) A researcher conducts a study of gifted children to determine which of 50 predictor variables are related to academic achievement in a summer enrichment program. They find that three of the measured variables are good predictors. Why is it important to replicate this study before using these predictor variables in selecting students for the program?

Answer:

Because so many predictor variables were measured, it is likely that some correlated significantly with the criterion by chance. To determine whether this is true, it is necessary to cross-validate the significant predictors with another sample. If the original results occurred by chance, the correlation coefficients for the significant predictor variables are likely to "shrink" in the cross-validation study.

8. (obj. 8)
   a. Under what condition would a researcher be likely to compute a correlation ratio?
   b. Why is this type of correlation coefficient superior to other types under this condition?

Answer:

a. The correlation ratio is computed when there is reason to believe that the relationship between two variables is nonlinear.
b. The correlation ratio yields a more accurate measure of the magnitude of a nonlinear relationship between two variables than other types of correlation coefficients. The other types will underestimate the magnitude of the relationship.

9. (obj. 9) You are interested in the relationship between anxiety and the willingness to take risks among cadets in training to become police officers. You select a random sample of 200 police officers in a large city and administer a standard anxiety scale with a reliability of .82 and a risk-taking test with a reliability of .68. The correlation you obtain is .42.
   a. What technique would you use to estimate what the correlation between anxiety and risk-taking would be if you had perfectly reliable measures?
   b. You believe that the sample in your study is much less variable in anxiety than the national population of police officers, having very few cases with low anxiety scores. What technique would you use to estimate what the correlation between anxiety and risk-taking would be if your sample had been as variable as the national population?

Answer:
   a. Correction for attenuation
   b. Correction for restriction in range

10. (obj. 10) A researcher is investigating the factors that underlie success or failure in high school mathematics. She measures 30 predictor variables and five criterion variables relating to mathematics learning (e.g., gradepoint average in mathematics coursework, attitudes toward mathematics, and number of mathematics courses taken). What correlation technique should be used to determine (a) which combination of predictor variables best predicts mathematics gradepoint average, (b) which combination of predictor variables best predicts whether a student takes or does not take a course on calculus (which is a dichotomous variable), (c) whether the data support a theoretical model linking some of the predictor variables to one of the criterion variables, and (d) whether there are commonalities in the 30 predictor variables such that they can be reduced to a smaller number of underlying variables?

Answer:
   a. Multiple regression
   b. Discriminant analysis
   c. Path analysis or structural equation modeling
   d. Factor analysis

11. (obj. 11) What is the purpose of a correlation matrix?

Answer:
The correlation matrix provides a visual display of the correlation coefficient for every pair of variables in a research study. By examining the correlation matrix, the researcher can determine how well a particular variable correlates with all the other variables.

12. (obj. 12) State one similarity between path analysis and structural equation modeling.
Answer: (any 1 OK):
   1. Both path analysis and structural equation modeling are used to test causal theories of relationships between variables.
   2. Both path analysis and structural equation modeling involve the formulation of a graphical display depicting the relationships between various variables.
   3. Both path analysis and structural equation modeling use a special statistic to calculate the degree and direction of the relationship between each pair of variables.

13. (obj. 13) A researcher obtains a correlation coefficient of .29 between scores on a diagnostic test and a test of first-grade reading achievement for a large sample of ethnically diverse children.
   a. Why might the researcher do a follow-up correlational analysis in which this correlation coefficient is computed separately for the major ethnic groups in the sample?
   b. What is the technical term for the variable of ethnicity in the follow-up analysis?

Answer:
   a. The correlation coefficient (.29) for the total sample might be higher or lower for certain ethnic subgroups.
   b. Ethnicity is a moderator variable in this analysis.

14. (obj. 14) What are two factors that determine whether an obtained correlation coefficient will be statistically significant?

Answer (any 2 OK):

1. The magnitude of the correlation coefficient
2. The sample size
3. Whether a one-tailed or two-tailed test of statistical significance is done

APPLICATION PROBLEMS

Problem 1

A team of researchers decide to investigate possible determinants of interest in science among elementary school children. First they develop and validate a measure of this variable. Then they locates tests that measure as many variables as possible in as short a time as possible to correlate with this interest test. Their reasoning is that they will increase the likelihood of discovering significant relationships if they maximize the number of variables in the correlational design. What is wrong with the researchers' reasoning, and how could they improve their research design?

Sample Answer:

Increasing the number of variables (an example of the shotgun approach) will not necessarily increase the likelihood of finding significant relationships. Also, some of the variables may correlate significantly with the criterion variables by chance, and these correlations probably will disappear when the study's findings are cross-validated. A better strategy is to measure variables that theory and previous research findings suggest are related to the criterion variable (i.e., interest in science).

Problem 2

Researchers intercorrelate a number of measures that they have collected on a sample of college seniors. They find a correlation of .65 between (1) the amount of time a student has been employed during his or her college years and (2) a paper-and-pencil measure of the student's personal maturity. On the basis of this finding, would they be justified in concluding that

a. the college should institute a work-study program in order to increase the maturity level of its students? Explain your answer.
b. the longer students have worked during college, the higher will be their score on the personal maturity measure? Explain your answer.
c. more mature students are better able to obtain jobs while in college than their less mature peers? Explain your answer.

Sample Answer:

a. No. This conclusion assumes that there is a causal connection between working while in college and degree of personal maturity. Causal inferences cannot be made with a high degree of assurance from correlational data.
b. Yes. The correlation of .65 means that the two variables are positively related, that is, an increment in the amount of employment is likely to be associated with an increment in personal maturity score.
c. No. As in (a) above, this conclusion makes a causal assumption that is not warranted on the basis of the correlational data obtained in this study.

Problem 3

A researcher administered a battery of 20 different tests to a group of entering medical students. She also collected their gradepoint average (GPA) at the end of their first year of medical school. What statistical technique should be used to maximize the usefulness of the 20 tests as predictors of GPA, and why?

Sample Answer:

Multiple regression, because this statistical technique yields a better prediction than could be obtained by correlating any single test with the criterion variable, that is, GPA.

Problem 4
A researcher has collected a large amount of data on a sample of college students: scores on the Stanford-Binet Intelligence Scale, scores on the Wechsler Adult Intelligence Scale, scores on the Scholastic Aptitude Test (SAT), high school class rank, scores on a test anxiety scale, and whether the students successfully completed the first year of college (pass-fail and gradepoint average). Answer the following questions about the appropriate correlational analyses to be conducted on these data:

a. What correlational technique should be used to determine whether scores on the Stanford-Binet are related to scores on the Wechsler scale? Why this technique?
b. The researcher finds that test anxiety correlates significantly with the criterion variable of gradepoint average in the first year of college. The SAT also correlates significantly with test anxiety and the criterion. What statistical technique should be used to determine the correlation between test anxiety and college gradepoint average after the influence of SAT on both variables has been removed?
c. What correlational technique should be used to determine whether all of the tests used in this study, when intercorrelated, measure a common factor?
d. What correlational technique should be used to determine whether the relationship between scores on the test anxiety scale and high school class rank is nonlinear?

Sample Answer:

a. Product-moment correlation coefficient, because both scales yield continuous scores.
b. Partial correlation, because this statistical technique is used to determine the degree of relationship between two variables after the effect of a third variable on both has been removed.
c. Factor analysis, because this technique determines the extent to which all the measures entered into a correlation matrix share a common element.
d. The correlation ratio *eta*. It also would be helpful to first prepare a scattergram of the data to check for nonlinearity in the relationship between the two sets of scores.

Problem 5
Researcher A correlates scores on a predictor variable and a criterion variable and obtains a correlation coefficient that is statistically significant but of no practical significance. Researcher B correlates scores on a different predictor variable and the same criterion variable and obtains a correlation coefficient that is not statistically significant but of practical significance.

a. How can researcher B's correlation coefficient be significant in a practical sense but not in a statistical sense?
b. How can researcher A's correlation coefficient be significant in a statistical sense but not in a practical sense?

Sample Answer:

a. Practical significance depends primarily on the magnitude of the obtained correlation coefficient. Thus, researcher B's obtained correlation coefficient must have been larger than researcher A's obtained correlation coefficient.
b. Statistical significance depends not only on the magnitude of the correlation coefficient but also on the sample size. If researcher A's sample size was much larger than that of researcher B, this would explain why researcher A's obtained correlation coefficient was statistically significant even though its magnitude was smaller.

Problem 6
A team of researchers administered a personality inventory that measures 15 personality traits to a group of entering students in a doctoral program in education. They also determined students' gradepoint average (GPA) at the end of the first year of the program. They then used multiple regression to determine which combination of personality traits best predicts GPA in this situation. The following is their table of results.

Personality Variable	Beta	Correlation Coefficient (*r*)	Multiple Correlation (*R*)	R^2	R^2 Increment
Conformity	.35	.28	.28	.08	
Independence	.04	.15	.34	.32	.12
Introversion	.21	.11	.37	.14	.02

a. What information is provided by the beta weights in the first data column?
b. What information is provided by the fact that the beta weight for conformity is .35, whereas for introversion it is .21?
c. What does the correlation coefficient of .15 for independence in the second data column mean?
d. What does the multiple correlation coefficient of .37 in the third data column mean?
e. What does the R^2 value of .08 in the fourth data column mean?
f. What does the R^2 increment of .02 in the fifth data column mean?

Sample Answer:

a. The beta weights indicate the predictive value of each personality variable in the multiple regression equation.
b. The difference in these beta weights indicates that the personality variable of conformity has more predictive value than introversion in the multiple regression equation.
c. It indicates that the measure of independence correlates .15 with GPA, meaning that there is a slight tendency for higher scores on this measure to be associated with a higher GPA.
d. It means that the combination of the measures of conformity, independence, and introversion correlate .37 with GPA.
e. It means that the measure of conformity explains 8 percent of the variance in the students' GPA.
f. It means that adding the measure of introversion to the multiple regression equation explains another two percent of the variance in the students' GPA.

TEACHING ACTIVITIES

Activity 1

Identify a research article that describes a relationship study or a prediction study employing correlational statistics. (A prediction study is described in chapter 11 of the textbook.) Have all students read the study as a homework assignment and then discuss in class the technical aspects of the study's research methodology and the study's strengths and weaknesses. This activity also can be repeated with published research studies that highlight the use of other correlational techniques, e.g., multiple regression, factor analysis, and path analysis.

Activity 2

If students have no prior experience with statistics, you can have them collect data on two variables that you are confident are correlated with each other, for example, the height and weight of people whom they know. You can prepare a transparency that contains a graph on which such data can be plotted. The students can bring their data to class, and you can show them how the data are plotted on the graph to produce a scattergram. You can use the scattergram to show students the line of best fit for the data and to discuss the concept of explained variance.

Activity 3

Multiple regression is an important correlational technique that may be unfamiliar to students, even if they have taken a statistics course. You can find a multiple regression equation in a published research study (or use the example in the textbook) and explain how it works in class.

This activity also can be done with factor analysis, another important correlational technique often not covered in elementary statistics courses. You can show students the various outputs of a factor analysis (e.g., correlation matrix, factors, and factor loadings) and explain what they mean.

CHAPTER 12
EXPERIMENTAL RESEARCH: DESIGNS, PART 1

Note: The phrase in parentheses following the item number for both closed-form and open-form items, for example, (obj. 3)", refers to the textbook chapter objective to which the item is keyed.

CLOSED-FORM ITEMS

1. (obj. 1) Match each type of extraneous variable that threatens the internal validity of an experiment (a-g) with the situation (1-6) that illustrates it.
   __ 1. A pretest similar to the posttest is administered before the experimental treatment.
   __ 2. Students below the 15th percentile in reading achievement who volunteer are placed in the experimental group, and nonvolunteers at the same reading level are placed in the control group.
   __ 3. During the experiment students are exposed to special instructional experiences that are not part of the experimental treatment.
   __ 4. Low achievers drop out at a higher rate than other students from an individualized reading program designed to improve reading achievement.
   __ 5. A group of students who fall below the 15th percentile on a reading achievement test earns higher scores on the posttest following an experimental treatment, whereas a group of students who fall above the 85th percentile earns lower scores on the same posttest following the same experimental treatment.
   __ 6. Students who attend summer camp three years in a row show annual increases on a measure of physical strength.
   a. History
   b. Maturation
   c. Testing
   d. Experimental treatment diffusion
   e. Statistical regression
   f. Differential selection
   g. Experimental mortality

Answer: 1 = c 2 = f 3 = a 4 = g 5 = e 6 = b

2. (obj. 1) An experiment is internally valid to the extent to which it
   a. yields findings that are generalizable to a defined population.
   b. uses valid measurement instruments.
   c. controls for extraneous variables.
   d. all of the above.

Answer: c

3. (obj. 1) A group of teachers receives access to the Internet as part of their participation in an experiment. The school district's administrators decide that this is a good idea, and provide Internet access for all teachers in the district, including control group teachers. The administrators' action weakens internal validity through
   a. resentful demoralization of the control group.
   b. compensatory equalization of treatments.
   c. compensatory rivalry by the control group.
   d. differential selection.

Answer: b

4. (obj. 1) If the same observers rate students' on-task behavior before and after an experimental intervention, their ratings are susceptible to an internal-validity threat known as:
   a. statistical regression.
   b. experimental treatment interaction.
   c. an instrumentation effect.
   d. a testing effect.

Answer: c

5. (obj. 2) Multiple-treatment interference refers to the situation in which
   a. research participants' performance on the dependent variable reflects the combined effect of more than one treatment.
   b. extraneous variables rather than the experimental treatment are responsible for the experimental outcome.
   c. high correlations between pretest and posttest scores reduce the chances of significant gain scores.
   d. research participants in the control group are affected by their knowledge of the experimental treatment.

Answer: a

6. (obj. 2) Students' racial attitudes are measured by a paper-and-pencil test immediately before and after viewing a film denouncing racial prejudice. What threat to the external validity of the experiment does this procedure raise?
   a. Statistical regression
   b. Attribute-treatment interaction
   c. Multiple-treatment interference
   d. Pretest sensitization

Answer: d

7. (obj. 2) In the Hawthorne effect, individuals who participate in an experiment improve their performance because
   a. they are aware that they are participating in an experiment.
   b. the experimental treatment leads to greater learning.
   c. they like the experimenter.
   d. the posttest is easier than the pretest.

Answer: a

8. (obj. 2) The external validity of an experiment refers to whether
   a. practitioners view its findings as credible.
   b. the experiment's findings generalize to individuals and settings beyond those that were studied.
   c. an independent review board approves the experiment's design and statistical procedures.
   d. the posttest measures used in the experiment have good construct validity.

Answer: b

9. (obj. 2) Which one of the following is not a threat to the external validity of an experiment?
   a. Novelty and disruption effects
   b. Pretest sensitization effects
   c. Measurement of the dependent variable
   d. Experimental treatment diffusion

Answer: d

10. (obj. 2) In determining the population validity of an experiment, one needs to know the researchers'
    a. experimentally accessible population.
    b. target population.
    c. personological characteristics of the sample that might interact with the experimental treatment.
    d. all of the above.

Answer: d

11. (obj. 3) A researcher provides an extensive orientation to introduce research participants to the experimental treatment. The purpose of this orientation is probably to
    a. control for experimental treatment diffusion.
    b. control for history.
    c. strengthen the representativeness of the experimental design with respect to real-life environments.
    d. control for the Hawthorne effect.

Answer: c

12. (obj. 3) An experiment that incorporates principles of representative design
    a. controls more rigorously for differential selection.
    b. takes more variables into account in the research design than an experiment that has a systematic design.
    c. controls more rigorously for experimenter effects.
    d. sacrifices population validity for increased internal validity.

Answer: b

13. (obj. 3) In an experiment that follows principles of representative design, it is
    a. acceptable to observe what students are doing during the experiment.
    b. not acceptable to observe what students are doing during the experiment.
    c. acceptable to observe the research participants, but not the social context in which the experiment is being conducted.
    d. not acceptable to prepare the research participants for the experiment.

Answer: a

14. (obj. 4) A useful technique to minimize the effect of experimenter bias on the outcomes of an experiment is for the researcher to
    a. fully inform the experimenters about the study's objectives and hypotheses.
    b. conduct the experiment rather than train experimenters to do so.
    c. train experimenters who are naive about the study to implement the treatments and collect the data.
    d. make the control treatment as desirable as the experimental treatment.

Answer: c

15. (obj. 4) Treatment fidelity refers to the extent to which
    a. the individuals who conduct the experimental and control interventions have been trained in the specifications of those interventions.
    b. the research participants have received training in what the interventions require them to do.
    c. the experimental and control conditions have been implemented according to the researchers' specifications.
    d. the research participants are free to adjust the experimental and control conditions to their individual learning styles.

Answer: c

16. (obj. 5) Intact groups often pose a problem when designing experiments because
    a. intact groups cannot be randomly selected from a defined population.
    b. intact groups cannot be assigned to control treatments.
    c. administrators are usually concerned that experiments may weaken the the groups' cohesiveness.
    d. individuals within an intact group cannot be randomly assigned to the experimental and control groups.

Answer: d

17. (obj. 5) One good way to avoid the internal-validity threats that might result from withholding the experimental treatment from the control group is to
    a. give the experimental treatment to a subsample of the control group chosen by public lottery.
    b. identify volunteers who do not object to being in a no-treatment control group.
    c. give the experimental treatment to the control group after the experiment is concluded.
    d. work with the control group until all necessary data have been collected, and then begin working with the experimental group.

Answer: c

18. (obj. 5) The equivalence of the experimental and control groups in an experiment
    a. is not guaranteed by the use of random assignment procedures.
    b. is guaranteed by the use of random assignment procedures.
    c. is not affected by the size of the total sample from which experimental and control groups will be formed.
    d. does not affect the internal validity of an experiment.

Answer: a

19. (obj. 6) The one-group pretest-posttest design is best used when
    a. the characteristic that constitutes the dependent variable is relatively stable.
    b. the experimental treatment extends over a relatively long period.
    c. history may function as an extraneous variable.
    d. the control group has not been randomly selected.

Answer: a

20. (obj. 6) Which of the following experimental designs has the best internal validity?
    a. The one-group pretest-posttest design.
    b. The pretest-posttest control-group design.
    c. The time series design.
    d. The one-shot case study.

Answer: b

21. (obj. 6) A researcher designs an experiment in which student teachers are randomly assigned to three treatment groups: twice-weekly supervisory visits, weekly supervisory visits, and supervisory visits every two weeks. This is an example of a
    a. pretest-posttest control-group design.
    b. one-shot case study.
    c. one-group pretest-posttest design.
    d. one-variable multiple-condition design.

Answer: d

22. (ob. 6) The posttest-only control-group design has an advantage over the pretest-posttest control-group design when
    a. the total sample that is to be assigned to the experimental and control groups is small.
    b. the researchers are interested in forming subgroups within the experimental and control groups.
    c. there is a possibility that administration of a pretest will affect the experimental treatment.
    d. there is likely to be differential attrition during the course of the experiment.

Answer: c

23. (obj. 7) Of the following experimental designs, the strongest in external validity is the
    a. one-shot case study.
    b. one-group pretest-posttest design.
    c. posttest-only control-group design.
    d. pretest-posttest control-group design.

Answer: c

24. (obj. 7) The main threat to the external validity of the pretest-posttest control-group design is the
    a. Hawthorne effect.
    b. interaction between history and the experimental treatment.
    c. interaction between time of measurement and the experimental treatment.
    d. interaction between the pretest and the experimental treatment.

Answer: d

25. (obj. 7) Of the following experimental designs, the one that is weakest in internal validity is the
    a. one-group pretest-posttest design.
    b. posttest-only control-group design.
    c. pretest-posttest control-group design.
    d. time-series design.

Answer: a

26. (obj. 8) Of the following procedures for testing statistical significance, the one most likely to be used in analyzing the data from a pretest-posttest control-group design is
    a. path analysis.
    b. analysis of covariance.
    c. two *t* tests, one comparing the pretest and posttest means of the experimental group and the other comparing the pretest and posttest means of the control group.
    d. a *t* test comparing the posttest means of the experimental and control groups.

Answer: b

27. (obj. 8) What is the preferred statistical technique for analyzing the data from an experiment that employs a posttest-only control-group design?
    a. a *t* test comparing the posttest means of the experimental and control groups.
    b. multiple regression.
    c. analysis of covariance.
    d. the correlation ratio.

Answer: a

OPEN-FORM ITEMS

1. (obj. 1) List and describe five types of extraneous variables that are threats to the internal validity of an experiment.

Answer (any 5 OK):

1. *History.* Treatments extending over a period of time allow variables other than the experimental treatment that happen to be occurring during that time period to affect the results.
2. *Maturation.* During the experimental treatment, changes occur that are due to natural developmental changes in the research participants rather than to the treatment.
3. *Testing.* Experience with a pretest can lead to better performance on the posttest.
4. *Instrumentation.* Faulty instruments can lead to apparent changes when no real change has occurred (such as using a posttest that is easier than the pretest).
5. *Differential selection.* The basis for selection of the treatment and control groups is different.
6. *Experimental mortality.* Differential loss of research participants occurs for reasons that have nothing to do with the experimental treatment.
7. *Statistical regression.* In any test-retest research design, regression toward the mean can occur for research participants whose scores are at the tails of the score distribution. This phenomenon suggests a change in the research participants when no real change has occurred. It is a serious problem in studies dealing with extreme groups, such as children with severe learning disabilities.
8. *Selection-maturation interaction.* Groups are selected (i.e., treatment vs. control) that differ in maturation level.
9. *Experimental treatment diffusion.* Members of the control group obtain access to the experimental treatment.
10. *Compensatory rivalry by the control group.* Control group participants perform beyond their usual level because they perceive that they are in competition with the experimental group.
11. *Compensatory equalization of treatments.* The control group receives goods and services similar to those that are part of the treatment received by the experimental group.
12. *Resentful demoralization of the control group.* Control group participants become discouraged because they perceive that the experimental group is receiving a desirable treatment that is being withheld from them.

2. (obj. 1) What does it mean to say that an experiment has good internal validity?

Answer:

It means that extraneous variables have been well controlled by the researcher, so that any observed effect on the dependent variable can be attributed solely to the treatment variable.

3. (obj. 2)
   a. Describe *pretest sensitization.*
   b. Is it a threat to the internal or external validity of an experiment?

Answer:

a. The pretest can sensitize research participants to the experimental treatment and bring about different results from what would have been obtained if no pretest had been given.
b. This is a threat to ecological validity, which is a form of external validity.

4. (obj. 3) Representative design is an attempt to make experimental conditions more representative of the natural environment. What are two recommended approaches for making educational research more representative?

Answer (any 2 OK):

1. When appropriate, conduct the research in the actual field setting to which you wish to generalize your findings.
2. Incorporate several environmental variations into the design of the experiment. For example, if the purpose is to evaluate a new instructional method, it is advisable to have not one teacher but rather a sample of teachers using it.
3. Observe what research participants are actually doing during the experiment. These observations may prove helpful to the researcher in interpreting the experimental results.
4. A related technique to *c* above is to observe the social context in which the experiment is being conducted. Certain events that occur in schools or in other educational settings may affect the experimental treatment. If these events are observed and recorded, the research findings should be more interpretable.
5. Prepare research participants for the experiment. The typical practice is for researchers to give simple instructions to the research participants and perhaps a few minutes of training prior to the start of an experiment. However, more extensive preparation may be necessary to ensure a smooth transition from participants' current mental set to the one required by the experimental task.
6. Incorporate a control treatment that allows research participants to use their customary approaches to learning.

5. (obj. 4) What are two techniques that a researcher can use to avoid experimenter bias?

Answer:

a. Train naive experimenters to work with the research participants.
b. Avoid suggesting to the experimenters that one experimental treatment is better than another.

6. (obj. 5) How can randomization be achieved if individuals within intact groups cannot be randomly assigned to the experimental and control groups?

Answer:

Select a sample of intact groups and randomly assign these groups to the experimental and control conditions.

7. (obj. 6)
   a. What is one advantage of the pretest-posttest control-group design over the posttest-only control-group design?
   b. What threat to external validity is present in the pretest-posttest control-group design?

Answer:

a. (any 1 OK):
   1. The former design gives the investigator assurance that the treatment groups are initially comparable.
   2. The former design permits adjusting for initial group differences.
b. Pretest sensitization is a threat to the external validity of this design.

8. (obj. 7)
   a. What is the most important limitation of the one-group pretest-posttest design?
   b. What kinds of variables can be studied by using this design?

Answer:

a. Because there is no control group, the investigator cannot estimate how much the pretest-posttest change is due to extraneous variables such as history or maturation and how much change is due to the treatment.
b. This design is useful in studying changes in very stable variables, e.g., those for which change is very unlikely in the absence of a specific treatment. Attitudes of adults, for example, have been found to be stable. This design also is appropriate in training studies in which there is almost no chance for research participants to learn the content unless they are trained.

9. (obj. 8) A researcher conducts an experiment that employs a pretest-posttest control-group design. The pretest and the posttest are similar tests of American history. Describe the statistical technique that should be used to analyze the pretest and posttest scores.

Answer:

Use analysis of covariance, assuming its assumptions are satisfied. The posttest mean of the experimental group is compared with the posttest mean of the control group, with the pretest scores as the covariate.

APPLICATION PROBLEMS

Problem 1

A researcher is planning to test the effectiveness of a new reading program. A sample of 40 teachers distributed evenly among five schools in one school district has volunteered to use the program for a semester. Using only this sample, the researcher wishes to form two equivalent groups, one of which will participate in the special program while the other receives the regular program. State methods for achieving equivalence between the groups through random assignment.

Sample Answer:

a. One method is to assign teachers randomly to the experimental and control treatments.
b. Another method is to assign students randomly in each classroom to the experimental and control groups.

Problem 2

A team of researchers want to test the effectiveness of providing high school students with a note-taking outline of each chapter that they are assigned to read in a history class. They have permission to conduct the experiment with two history classes, each containing 30 students. They randomly form two groups within each class: The experimental group receives a note-taking outline each time it is assigned a chapter, whereas the control group receives the same assignment but not a note-taking outline. On the basis of this information, what flaw have the researchers introduced into the experimental design?

Sample Answer:

This experimental design creates the threat of experimental treatment diffusion. It will be difficult to ensure that none of the students in the control group will try to obtain the note-taking outline (which is the experimental treatment) from a classmate who is in the experimental group. If some of the control-group students obtain the outline, the experiment is no longer a pure comparison between two types of experimental treatment.

Problem 3

A researcher is planning an experiment to test the effectiveness of the discussion method at the high school level. One teacher has agreed to use the discussion method in her class several times a week for a semester. Another teacher has agreed to teach the same content but without using the discussion method. The researcher will collect the following data: student scores on an achievement test and on a scale measuring attitudes toward the instruction. What recommendations can you offer to improve the representativeness of this experimental design?

Sample Answer:

a. Instead of one teacher each in the experimental and control treatments, recruit a sample of teachers to be in each treatment. The courses represented in each treatment (e.g., English or history) also might be varied.
b. Plan for observation of in-class activities during the experimental period. The observational data may help in the interpretation of the results.
c. Provide a reasonable amount of preparation for students who are to be in the treatment involving discussion. They may be unfamiliar with the discussion method, and thus they may react negatively to its introduction into the curriculum unless they are adequately prepared beforehand.

Problem 4

Study the following research plan and identify any variables and/or conditions that may pose a threat to the internal validity of the experiment. Name the most likely threats to internal validity, and explain each briefly in terms of the research plan.

Research plan: The researcher wants to determine the effect of a special reading program on the reading achievement of inner-city children. The study will be longitudinal, extending from the beginning of grade 2 to the end of grade 3. He identifies 50 children who are nonreaders at the end of grade 1; these children will receive the special program. He randomly selects 50 other children in the same school and grade level to serve as a control group. The researcher administers the same reading test to both groups at the start of grade 2 and at the end of grade 3. By the end of grade 3, there are 27 children who have remained in the special program and 36 children in the control group. The researcher compares the reading gains of the two groups and finds that each group has gained an average of 1.6 years in reading grade placement.

Sample Answer:

a. *History*. Over a two-year period, other events could have influenced the reading performance of the research participants. These events may not have been the same for the experimental and control groups, because the treatment cases were nonreaders while the controls were randomly selected.
b. *Statistical regression*. Because the treatment group was at the lowest level of reading achievement at the start of the experiment while the controls were randomly selected, the posttest scores of the treatment group probably would regress upward, while no similar regression would occur for the control group.
c. *Differential selection*. The bases for selecting the treatment and the control groups were different.
d. *Experimental mortality*. The greater loss of research participants from the treatment group is likely to compromise the equivalence of the treatment and control groups.
e. *Testing effect*. It is conceivable that a testing effect occurred, because both groups took a particular reading test twice. In other words, the children might have become test-wise. However, the fact that two years passed between the pretest and posttest makes it very unlikely that a testing effect occurred.

Problem 5

A researcher is planning to test the effectiveness of a new reading program. A sample of 40 teachers distributed evenly among five schools in one school district has volunteered to use the program for a semester. Using only this sample, the researcher wishes to use random assignment to form groups, one of which will participate in the special program while the other receives the regular program. State methods for achieving equivalence between the groups through random assignment.

Sample Answer:

a. One method is to assign teachers randomly to the experimental and control treatments.
b. Another method is to assign students randomly in each classroom to the experimental and control groups.

Problem 6

A researcher wants to determine whether students learn more when they take unannounced pop quizzes or regularly scheduled, announced quizzes. The measure of learning will be a 50-item achievement test on the content covered in a semester-long course. Describe the steps involved in designing and conducting an experiment based on this information.

Sample Answer:

a. Randomly assign some classes to the experimental treatment group (pop quizzes) and other classes to the alternate treatment group (announced quizzes).
b. Administer the achievement test as a pretest to both groups at the beginning of the semester.
c. Implement the two treatments: pop quizzes and announced quizzes. Check for treatment fidelity.
d. Administer the achievement test as a posttest to both groups at the end of the semester.
e. Use analysis of covariance to analyze the data. The posttest scores are the dependent variable and the pretest scores are the covariate.

TEACHING ACTIVITIES

Activity 1

Identify a research article that describes an experimental study that employed one of the designs covered in chapter 12 of the textbook. Have all students read the study as a homework assignment and then discuss in class the technical aspects of the study's research methodology and the study's strengths and weaknesses.

Activity 2

Have students choose a research question that they would like to explore through experimental research. Have them design an experiment using one of the more powerful designs covered in the chapter, namely, the pretest-posttest control-group design or the one-variable multiple-condition design. In class, take students through the following steps in creating the design:

a. Have the class reach consensus on an experimental treatment to be investigated.
b. Create an appropriate control-group condition.
c. Consider possible threats to the internal validity of the experiment and steps that can be taken to minimize or avoid the threats.
d. Consider how the experiment can be designed to enhance its external validity.
e. Consider features of representative design that can be incorporated into the experiment.
f. Specify one or more tests that can be administered to measure the dependent variable(s).
g. Design a technique for checking treatment fidelity.
h. Create hypothetical pretest and posttest means for the experimental and control groups, and select the most appropriate statistical technique(s) for analyzing the data.
i. If students have read about research designs in other chapters of the textbook, ask them whether it would be possible to investigate the effects of the experimental treatment using one of these other designs. If the answer is yes, ask students to compare the advantages and disadvantages of their experimental design with those of the other type of research design.

Activity 3

If you know a researcher who is doing or has done an experiment involving one of the designs covered in this chapter, invite this person to be a guest presenter. Ask the researcher to discuss why she chose to do an experiment, problems that arose in conducting it, how she handled these problems, what she learned by doing the experiment, and what direction future research on the phenomenon might take.

CHAPTER 13
EXPERIMENTAL RESEARCH: DESIGNS, PART 2

Note: The phrase in parentheses following the item number for both closed-form and open-form items, for example, "(obj. 3)", refers to the textbook chapter objective to which the item is keyed.

CLOSED-FORM ITEMS

1. (obj. 1) The statistical procedure that typically is used to analyze data from an experiment that employs a nonequivalent control-group design is
   a. analysis of variance.
   b. analysis of covariance.
   c. a *t* test for independent means.
   d. a *t* test for correlated means.

Answer: b

2. (obj. 2) 0 X 0
   0   0

The graph above describes the
   a. nonequivalent control-group design.
   b. time series design.
   c. counterbalanced design.
   d. static-group comparison design.

Answer: a

3. (obj. 2) A static-group comparison experiment
   a. involves only a single group of research participants, all of whom receive the same treatment.
   b. requires that the research participants remain in the same location during the entire experiment, so as to avoid threats to the experiment's internal validity.
   c. involves a treatment and control group, but only the treatment group is given the posttest.
   d. involves a treatment and control group, but of which are given a posttest, but no pretest.

Answer: d

4. (obj. 3) The main threat to the internal validity of a static-group comparison experiment is that
   a. research participants may be sensitized to the experimental treatment by the pretest.
   b. this design does not include a control group.
   c. posttest differences between groups may be due to preexisting group differences rather than to the experimental treatment.
   d. the experimental treatment may diffuse to the control group.

Answer: c

5. (obj. 3) The main threat to the internal validity of a nonequivalent control-group experiment is
   a. the control group will feel resentful, because control groups generally perform at a lower level on the pretest than do treatment groups.
   b. the possibility that observed differences between the experimental and control groups might reflect preexisting differences between the groups rather than treatment effects.
   c. differential attrition in the two groups across the duration of the experiment.
   d. all of the above.

Answer: b

6. (obj. 4) Match each example with the type of treatment variable it represents.
   __1. Traditional vs. innovative method of teaching reading
   __2. Male vs. female students
   __3. High vs. low scorers on an achievement test
   __4. High vs. low socioeconomic level of a school's student population
   __5. Vocational vs. academic curriculum
   a. Potentially manipulable aspects of the environment
   b. Relatively fixed aspects of the environment
   c. Manipulated variables
   d. Response characteristics of research participants
   e. Organismic characteristics of research participants

Answer: 1 = c   2 = e   3 = d   4 = b   5 = a

7. (obj. 4) Students' scores on a test are an example of
   a. a manipulated variable.
   b. an organismic characteristic of research participants.
   c. a response characteristic of research participants.
   d. a relatively fixed aspect of the environment.

Answer: c

8. (obj. 5) In a factorial experiment, the researcher
   a. analyzes the treatment variable into two or more factors.
   b. analyzes the dependent variable into two or more factors.
   c. determines the effect of one treatment variable on a dependent variable.
   d. determines the effect of two or more treatment variables on a dependent variable.

Answer: d

9. (obj. 5) Aptitude-treatment-interaction research is primarily concerned with
   a. the exploration of matches between learner characteristics and different instructional methods.
   b. the use of the experimental method to develop aptitude tests.
   c. the combined effects of response and organismic characteristics on research participants' performance.
   d. whether the intensity and duration of treatments can increase students' aptitude for mastering different academic subjects.

Answer: a

10. (obj. 5) A 3 X 2 factorial design means that there are
   a. six interaction effects.
   b. three levels of one factor and two levels of another factor.
   c. six factors.
   d. three factors, two of which are manipulated.

Answer: b

11. (obj. 5) The main purpose of the Solomon four-group design is to determine the presence of
   a. experimenter bias.
   b. an aptitude-treatment interaction.
   c. an attribute-treatment interaction.
   d. pretest sensitization.

Answer: d

12. (obj. 5) Experiments can vary in the
    a. number of independent variables.
    b. number of research participants in each treatment or control group.
    c. treatment and control conditions that each research participant is assigned.
    d. all of the above.

Answer: d

13. (obj. 6) The single-case experiment is particularly well suited to
    a. survey research methodology.
    b. research on behavior modification.
    c. use in cross-cultural studies.
    d. case studies.

Answer: b

14. (obj. 6) Careful training of observers, operational definition of behaviors, and control of observer bias are all used to ensure __________ in single-subject experiments.
    a. precise description of the experimental conditions
    b. baseline and treatment stability
    c. reliable observation
    d. all of the above

Answer: c

15. (obj. 6) Because of the need for repeated measurements in single-case designs, it is important to
    a. obtain measurements of behavioral products rather than behavior.
    b. standardize the measurement procedure.
    c. discontinue treatment as soon as improvement occurs.
    d. keep baseline observations to a ratio of 1 for every 5 intervention observations.

Answer: b

16. (obj. 7) The A-B-A-B design
    a. avoids the problem of ending an experiment with withdrawal or reversal of the treatment.
    b. eliminates the possibility that an observed treatment effect will be dependent on the particular baseline conditions included in the experiment.
    c. has lower internal validity than the A-B-A design.
    d. all of the above.

Answer: a

17. (obj. 7) Conditions other than the naturally occurring target behavior are used as controls in
    a. an A-B design.
    b. an A-B-A design.
    c. an A-B-A-B design.
    d. a multiple-baseline design.

Answer: d

18. (obj. 7) In the analysis of single-case data, it has been found that
    a. graphical data plots are best, because they cannot be used to distort treatment effects.
    b. the observations made at different intervals of the experiment are susceptible to serial dependency.
    c. the percentage of treatment data points that exceed the highest baseline data point yields highly misleading results.
    d. analysis of variance for repeated measures is superior to any other statistical technique.

Answer: b

19. (obj. 8) The A-B-A-B design
   a. is the best single-case design for studying multiple treatments.
   b. ends with treatment reversal.
   c. yields findings about treatment effects that are dependent on the particular baseline conditions included in the experiment.
   d. is low in internal validity.

Answer: c

20. (obj. 8) The major threat to the external validity of single-case experiments is
   a. the use of one or a few cases in most single-case experiments as a basis for generalizing to a population.
   b. the small number of observations during the course of a typical single-case experiment.
   c. the focus on observing behavior rather than the research participant's cognitions during the course of most single-case experiments.
   d. the use of a withdrawal procedure rather than a reversal procedure in the second baseline of most single-case experiments.

Answer: a

21. (obj. 9) If the range of difficulty of test items is limited, the test may be subject to
   a. statistical regression.
   b. instrumentation effects.
   c. a lack of replicability.
   d. a ceiling effect.

Answer: d

22. (obj. 9) An appropriate technique for determining the statistical significance of pretest-posttest change in experiments is
   a. analysis of variance for repeated measures.
   b. the t test for independent means.
   c. the t test for correlated means.
   d. a Mann-Whitney U test.

Answer: a

23. (obj. 9) The validity of gain scores based on repeated administration of the same test to research participants
   a. does not depend on whether the test has equal intervals across all of its measurement points.
   b. depends on whether the test has equal intervals across all of its measurement points.
   c. does not depend on whether a given score on a test measures more than one ability.
   d. depends on the number of factors manipulated in the experiment.

Answer: b

OPEN-FORM ITEMS

1. (obj. 1) Explain the key difference between an experiment and a quasi-experiment.

Answer:

An experiment involves random assignment of research participants to the experimental and control groups, whereas a quasi-experiment does not involve random assignment.

2. (obj. 1) In an experiment that includes a pretest and posttest, describe a statistical technique that can be used to reduce initial group differences resulting from nonrandom assignment of research participants to the experimental and control treatments. Indicate the function of the pretest and posttest in the statistical technique.

Answer:

Analysis of covariance can be used. The posttest scores are the dependent variable and the pretest scores are the covariate.

3. (obj. 2)
   a. What is the main difference between a static-group comparison design and a nonequivalent control-group design?
   b. Which design is stronger in internal validity, and why?

Answer:

   a. The nonequivalent control-group design includes both a pretest and a posttest for the experimental and control groups, but the static-group comparison design includes only a posttest.
   b. The nonequivalent control-group design is stronger in internal validity, because the availability of pretest scores makes it possible to assess whether pre-existing group differences can be ruled out as a cause of observed effects on the dependent variable.

4. (obj. 3)
   a. What threat to external validity is controlled by the Solomon four-group design?
   b. How is the threat to external validity controlled by this design?

Answer:

   a. Pretest sensitization
   b. This external validity threat is controlled by including one treatment group that is given a pretest and another treatment group that is not given a pretest. A comparison of these groups indicates whether the pretest had an effect on the dependent variable.

5. (obj. 4) Five types of independent variables can be employed in an experiment. Name and describe three of these types of independent variables.

Answer (any 3 OK):

   1. Manipulated variables, such as teaching method, assignable at will by the experimenter
   2. Potentially manipulable aspects, such as school subject studied, that the experimenter might assign in some varied way to the research participants but rarely does
   3. Relatively fixed aspects of the environment, such as community or school or socioeconomic level, not under the direct control of the experimenter but serving as explicit bases for stratification in the experiment
   4. Organismic characteristics of the research participants, such as age, height, weight, and gender
   5. Response characteristics of the research participants, such as their scores on various tests

6. (obj. 5)
   a. What is the purpose of aptitude-treatment interaction (ATI) research?
   b. What type of experimental design is employed in ATI research?

Answer:

   a. The purpose of ATI research is to determine whether the effects of different instructional methods are influenced by the cognitive or personality characteristics of the learners.
   b. ATI studies employ a factorial design because there are at least two independent variables, such as instructional method and learner characteristics.

7. (obj. 5) Using a factorial design, a researcher conducted an experiment to determine how prior vocabulary knowledge and a new reading program influence students' reading comprehension. The new reading program is the experimental treatment, and the existing reading program is the control treatment.
   a. Identify what would be a main effect in this experiment, and define what is meant by a main effect.
   b. Identify what would be an interaction effect in this experiment, and define what is meant by an interaction effect.

Answer:
   a. The type of reading program is a main effect, and vocabulary knowledge also is a main effect. A main effect is an observed direct effect of an independent variable on the dependent variable.
   b. An interaction effect would be the finding that the effect of the type of reading program on reading comprehension is influenced by students' prior vocabulary knowledge. An interaction effect occurs when the effect of one independent variable on the dependent variable is influenced by another independent variable.

8. (obj. 6) Why is the A-B-A-B design considered more acceptable from an ethical standpoint than the A-B-A design?

Answer:
These designs are used for the most part to reduce an undesirable behavior or increase a desirable behavior. In the A-B-A design the treatment that brings about favorable change is withdrawn, returning the research participant to the original condition. In the A-B-A-B design the treatment (B) is reintroduced, which leaves the research participant in the improved condition.

9. (obj. 7) What is the main difference between an A-B-A design and a multiple-baseline design in a single-case experiment?

Answer:
An A-B-A experiment uses the natural occurrence of the target behavior as a control condition for assessing treatment effects, whereas a multiple-baseline experiment uses other conditions (e.g., different cases or multiple target behaviors) as a control condition.

10. (obj. 8) Which of the two single-case designs, A-B or A-B-A, has superior internal validity? Why?

Answer:
The A-B-A design has superior internal validity, because if withdrawal of the treatment (i.e., the second A) results in return of the research participant's behavior to the original baseline (i.e., the first A) it provides strong evidence that the treatment actually caused the change in the dependent variable brought about in condition B. In the A-B design, the change in the dependent variable could have been brought about by extraneous variables such as history or maturation, and the effect of extraneous variables cannot be separated from treatment effects.

11. (obj. 9) Describe two potential problems that can occur when raw gain scores (posttest scores minus pretest scores) are used to measure the amount of learning that individuals achieve as the result of an experimental intervention.

Answer (any 2 OK):

1. The range of difficulty of the test items might be too limited for research participants to be able to display their actual learning gain.
2. Inndividuals who earn extremely high or low scores on one administration of a measure might demonstrate a learning gain because of statistical regression rather than because of actual learning.
3. Individuals might start with different pretest scores and gain the same number of points as measured by the posttest, but this gain will not mean the same thing for all individuals if the test does not have equal intervals across all points of the score distribution.
4. Two individuals might obtain the same score on a test, but this score can reflect a different pattern of abilities for each individual.
5. Gain scores can have low reliability if (1) the reliability of the pretest and posttest scores is low and (2) the correlation between the pretest and posttest scores is high.

12. (obj. 9) Describe two alternatives to the use of gain scores to analyze research data from a correlational or experimental study that included administration of a pretest and a posttest.

Answer (any 2 OK):

1. Part correlation, in which the gain scores are correlated with another variable after adjusting the gain scores so that the research participants' pretest scores are partialled out (i.e., held constant)
2. Multiple regression, in which the pretest scores are entered into the multiple regression equation first so that their effect on the posttest scores is partialled out
3. Analysis of covariance, in which the posttest means of an experimental group and a control group are compared, with the pretest scores serving as a covariate
4. Analysis of variance for repeated measures, in which a determination is made as to whether the pretest-posttest difference for the experimental group is reliably different from the pretest-posttest difference for the control group

APPLICATION PROBLEMS

Problem 1

A research team conducted an experiment in which they administered a mathematics test before and after students had participated in a new individualized curriculum. Parallel forms of the test were used as the pretest and posttest, and the range of possible scores was 0-100 on each. In analyzing data from the experiment, the researcher found that students in the lowest quartile on the pretest ($M = 15.5$) made a good gain (posttest $M = 37.6$), whereas students in the highest quartile on the pretest ($M = 83.7$) declined slightly (posttest $M = 80.1$). From these differences in gain scores, they concluded that the new curriculum is more effective for students of low ability than for students of high ability. What are two other interpretations that can be made of the differences in gain scores?

Sample Answer:

a. Regression toward the mean could have occurred.
b. Students in the highest quartile may have made a substantial gain but it was not reflected in the posttest due to a ceiling effect; that is, the posttest may not have measured the entire range of possible achievement for the particular variables of concern.

Problem 2

A research team wishes to determine which of two types of staff development is more effective. The administrators of a school district agree to the experiment, and all the teachers in two high schools agree to participate and to take the pretest and posttest. However, the administrators insist that the teachers cannot be randomly assigned to the staff development programs. All teachers in one high school must participate in program A, and all teachers in the other high school must participate in program B.

a. If the researchers agrees to this condition, what type of experimental design must she use and why?
b. What is the main threat to internal validity in this type of experimental design, and how can it be handled?

Sample Answer:

a. The researchers will need to conduct a quasi-experiment that employs a nonequivalent control-group design, because the assignment of teachers to the two treatments is nonrandom.
b. The main threat to the internal validity of this type of experiment is that the two groups of teachers might differ in one or more characteristics prior to the experiment. These characteristics rather than the treatment variable (i.e., type of staff development) may be responsible for any observed effect on the dependent variable. To control for initial group differences, the researchers can use analysis of covariance, which will statistically equate the two groups on the pretest administration of the dependent variable.

Problem 3

A researcher plans to test the effectiveness of self-paced instruction vs. conventional instruction for male and female students of varying levels of ability. There are a total of 150 students: 60 boys and 90 girls. Within each of these groups (boys and girls), there are an equal number of high-, middle-, and low-ability students. Make a chart that illustrates the experimental design for this research project, and show the number of students in each experimental group. Also, list each interaction effect that can be analyzed.

Sample Answer:

	Conventional Instruction		Traditional Instruction	
Ability	Boys	Girls	Boys	Girls
High	10	15	10	15
Middle	10	15	10	15
Low	10	15	10	15

Interaction effects:
A X B
A X C
B X C
A X B X C

Where:
A = treatment
B = gender of student
C = ability level of student

Problem 4
A new program has been developed to increase students' speed and accuracy in simple mathematical computations. You have been asked by the school district's curriculum specialist to evaluate its effectiveness. One of the first decisions you must make is whether to use a group or a single-case experimental design. What questions could you ask the curriculum specialist about the program and the purpose of the experiment to determine whether a group or single-case design is more appropriate, and what is the purpose of each question?
Sample Answer:

a. Is the curriculum specialist more interested in the learning of individual students or in the learning of students as a group? Single-case designs focus on the individual learner, whereas group designs focus on group trends.
b. Is it possible to give students many tests of the computational skills? Single-case designs require frequent measurement of the same variable.
c. Is it possible to meet the requirements of an A-B-A design or of a multiple-baseline design in the classes that will participate in the experiment? An A-B-A design (e.g., reinstating baseline conditions after withdrawal of treatment) or a multiple-baseline design (e.g., changing one computational skill at a time) each impose unique requirements on the participants in an experiment. The researcher needs to determine which research design is more acceptable to them.

TEACHING ACTIVITIES

Activity 1
Identify a research article that describes an experimental study that employed one of the designs covered in chapter 13 of the textbook. Have all students read the study as a homework assignment and then discuss in class the technical aspects of the study's research methodology and the study's strengths and weaknesses.

Activity 2
You can have students practice designing an experiment using one of the more powerful designs covered in the chapter, such as a nonequivalent control-group design, a factorial design, or an A-B-A design. You can give students a research problem for which one of these designs is appropriate, or you can have them generate both the problem and the design. You can have students follow each step for the design as specified in the textbook. Because there is no single correct procedure for each step, students can generate alternate procedures for each step and consider their strengths and weaknesses.

Activity 3
If you know a researcher who is doing or has done a study that involved one of the quasi-experimental designs covered in this chapter, invite this person to be a guest presenter. Ask the researcher to discuss why she chose to do the study, any problems that arose in conducting it, how she handled these problems, what she learned by doing the study, and what direction future research on the phenomenon might take.

CHAPTER 14
CASE STUDY RESEARCH

Note: The phrase in parentheses following the item number for both closed-form and open-form items, for example, "(obj. 3)", refers to the textbook chapter objective to which the item is keyed.

CLOSED-FORM ITEMS

1. (obj. 1) Which of the following is characteristic of qualitative case study research?
   a. the study of particular instances of a phenomenon
   b. the in-depth study of a phenomenon.
   c. the study of a phenomenon in its real-life context.
   d. all of the above.

Answer: d

2. (obj. 1) The key issue in selecting the case for a case study is to
   a. decide what phenomenon you want to be able to say something about at the end of the study.
   b. construct specifications for a case that would reflect the phenomenon to an extreme extent.
   c. find gatekeepers who have access to a range of instances of possible cases.
   d. identify a field setting in which the researcher already is a participant.

Answer: a

3. (obj. 1) Case selection typically involves all but which one of the following?
   a. Specifying the phenomenon of interest
   b. Defining a unit of analysis
   c. Deciding the focus on which data collection will concentrate
   d. Determining the population to which the results can be generalized

Answer: d

4. (obj. 2) In his case study the researcher sought to depict and conceptualize the phenomenon he studied. The primary purpose of this case study was
   a. evaluation.
   b. interpretation.
   c. explanation.
   d. description.

Answer: d

5. (obj. 2) A case study in which the researcher relates differences in how adults cope with reading comprehension problems to a theory of intellectual development most clearly illustrates the purpose of ___________ in case study research.
   a. description
   b. explanation
   c. confirmation
   d. evaluation

Answer: b

6. (obj. 3) The primary aim of thick description is to
   a. compile as many objective facts about a phenomenon as possible.
   b. illustrate communalities among a wide variety of phenomena.
   c. provide information to assess the worth of a phenomenon.
   d. depict a phenomenon and re-create the context within which it is situated.

Answer: d

7. (obj. 3) Rayna was late for school eight times in October, and gave the teacher varying explanations for the cause of her tardiness. A case study researcher is likely to describe this aspect of the case as a
   a. theme.
   b. construct.
   c. pattern.
   d. phenomenon.

Answer: a

8. (obj. 3) In case study research a *construct* refers to a(n)
   a. salient, characteristic feature of a case.
   b. concept inferred from observed phenomena and used to explain them.
   c. type of observed variation that is systematically related to another observed variation.
   d. variation in one phenomenon that is claimed to have a causal effect on another observed variation.

Answer: b

9. (obj. 4) The design of a case study is based primarily on
   a. a blueprint of methods and steps generated by prior case study researchers.
   b. the case study researcher's hypothesis about the phenomenon being investigated.
   c. the interpretive skills of the case study researcher.
   d. the acceptability of the design to the individuals being studied.

Answer: c

10. (obj. 4) In case study research the research design tends to
   a. be established prior to the start of data collection.
   b. be determined by the type of phenomenon the researcher chooses to study.
   c. involve the testing of existing theoretical models.
   d. emerge as data collection proceeds.

Answer: d

11. (obj. 5) Grasping the meaning of events, developing causal explanations, and conducting formative evaluations can all represent the _____________ of a qualitative research study.
   a. validity
   b. conceptual framework
   c. goals
   d. research questions

Answer: c

12. (obj. 6) The study of multiple cases rather than a single case invariably
   a. involves identification of more than one focus of investigation.
   b. provides a better learning opportunity for the beginning researcher.
   c. permits exploration of systematic relationships among aspects of the phenomenon.
   d. involves theoretical or literal replication.

Answer: c

13. (obj. 6) A researcher studies two cases and predicts the same results for each case. This is an example of
    a. literal replication.
    b. theoretical replication.
    c. purposeful sampling.
    d. thinking "finish-to-start."

Answer: a

14. (obj. 7) Case study researchers are more likely than traditional quantitative researchers to
    a. play a major role in the collection of research data.
    b. formulate their research problems in relation to prior theory.
    c. pay considerable attention to obtaining permissions from the research site.
    d. select a research problem of personal interest to them.

Answer: a

15. (obj. 7) Case study researchers who base their research on ecological ethics
    a. aim to produce the greatest good for the greatest number of people.
    b. judge the morality of their decisions by whether they reflect a caring attitude toward others.
    c. refer to absolute values in assessing whether they are behaving ethically.
    d. consider participants' culture the major determinant of the morality of the researchers' actions.

Answer: d

16. (obj. 7) In securing permission to collect data in a research site, the case study researcher should
    a. dress and speak more formally than usual.
    b. describe the code of ethics that the researcher espouses.
    c. contact people within the site whom the researcher knows personally.
    d. work with gatekeepers at the site.

Answer: d

17. (obj. 8) Thinking "finish-to-start" in doing a case study involves
    a. analyzing the data before ending data collection.
    b. predetermining the information to be sought from each contact or document.
    c. predetermining the relative emphasis to be given to description, analysis, and interpretation in the case study report.
    d. developing a timeline that is anchored by the date when data collection must end.

Answer: c

18. (obj. 8) The mixed-methods approach to research design
    a. is rarely used in case study research.
    b. involves the collection of both qualitative and quantitative data.
    c. makes quantitative research auxiliary to qualitative research.
    d. all of the above.

Answer: b

19. (obj. 9) Typically a researcher's disclosure of personal information about himself to case study participants
    a. is necessary for obtaining their cooperation.
    b. has minimal effect on the research findings.
    c. inhibits research participants' expression of their own experiences.
    d. is a violation of research ethics.

Answer: b

20. (obj. 9) A subjectivity audit is a process by which a case study researcher
    a. includes her intense personal feelings and experiences in the research report.
    b. notes research situations that arouse her strong feelings so as to determine how they shaped the research process and outcomes.
    c. explains her personal experience to research participants related to the phenomenon under study during data collection.
    d. judges her decisions and actions by referring to absolute values.

Answer: b

21. (obj. 10) Exhaustion of sources, saturation of categories, emergence of regularities, and overextension are all
    a. criteria for deciding when to end the data-collection stage of a case study.
    b. topics that should be explored in a subjectivity audit.
    c. examples of the types of themes that might characterize a case.
    d. criteria for judging the interpretive validity of a case study.

Answer: a

22. (obj. 10) A case study researcher probably should collect additional data rather than end data collection when
    a. new information far from the central core of viable coding categories is received.
    b. the data being collected reflect the emergence of regularities.
    c. key informants have provided minimal information.
    d. all of the above.

Answer: c

23. (obj. 11) In most case studies, researchers
    a. use only one method of data collection.
    b. begin data analysis before ending data collection.
    c. use contact summary sheets instead of taking field notes.
    d. do not decide the form for presenting the case study until all the data are analyzed.

Answer: b

24. (obj. 11) Structural analysis of qualitative data involves the researcher's
    a. inferences about the meaning of data segments.
    b. identification of patterns inherent in textual elements.
    c. use of intuition to portray the phenomena being studied.
    d. coding of the degree of occurrence of particular variables in each case.

Answer: b

25. (obj. 11) Text retrievers are used in case study research to
    a. identify all data fields that have been assigned to a given code.
    b. list the location and frequency of all the words in a document.
    c. determine whether specific coding categories overlap.
    d. segment the database prior to analysis.

Answer: b

26. (obj. 11) The qualitative research tradition of educational connoisseurship and criticism best illustrates the method of
    a. structural analysis.
    b. constant comparison.
    c. reflective analysis.
    d. interpretational analysis.

Answer: c

27. (obj. 12) Asking the individuals studied for more information to reconcile discrepancies in the case study report is an example of
    a. member checking.
    b. triangulation.
    c. pattern matching.
    d. representativeness checking.

Answer: a

28. (obj. 12) The extent to which a measure in a case study correctly operationalizes the concepts being studied is an indicator of the extent to which the study's design reflects
    a. construct validity.
    b. internal validity.
    c. external validity.
    d. reliability.

Answer: a

29. (obj. 12) Outlier analysis is used in case study research to determine
    a. the extent to which the emic and etic perspectives of the phenomenon being studied are congruent.
    b. why particular members of the sample disagree with the case study's conclusions.
    c. whether the findings for extreme cases are consistent with those for other cases.
    d. why some data for a case diverge from other data for the same case.

Answer: c

30. (obj. 13) Case study findings are likely to be applicable to other cases or settings in all but which one of the following situations?
    a. The researcher studied a typical case.
    b. The research was based on grounded theory.
    c. A random sample from the unit of analysis was studied.
    d. The report readers' field setting is similar to that described in the case study.

Answer: b

31. (obj. 13) Reflection on context and anticipation of action places primary responsibility on ________________ for determining the applicability of case study findings.
    a. theoreticians
    b. report readers
    c. researchers
    d. research participants

Answer: b

32. (obj. 14) Reflective reporting of a case study is most appropriate when the researcher
    a. made an interpretational analysis of the case study data.
    b. wants to maintain an objective stance.
    c. wants to have her voice strongly present in the report.
    d. wants to display how bits of information relate to each other.

Answer: c

33. (obj. 14) Researchers who report their case studies in the form of fiction, poetry, drama, satire, or other literary genres usually
   a. have a postmodern sensibility.
   b. are using an interpretational reporting style.
   c. have minimal concern for demonstrating the validity of their findings.
   d. have studied a single case.

Answer: a

34. (obj. 15) The thick description typical of case studies tends to
   a. bring a case to life better than the statistical methods of quantitative research.
   b. help report readers compare cases with their own situation.
   c. help reveal both researchers' etic perspective and participants' emic perspective.
   d. all of the above.

Answer: d

35. (obj. 15) A disadvantage of the case study method compared to traditional quantitative research designs is that
   a. it requires the use of a computer for coding the data.
   b. the case on which the study will focus can change late in the research process.
   c. it provides a less adequate basis for interpretation than a quantitative research report.
   d. it is difficult to generalize the findings to other situations.

Answer: d

OPEN-FORM ITEMS

1. (obj. 1) Describe the four defining characteristics of a case study.

Answer:
   1. It involves the study of a phenomenon by focusing on specific instances of the phenomenon, that is, cases.
   2. An in-depth study is made of each case.
   3. The phenomenon is studied as it occurs in its real-life context.
   4. Both the participants' (emic) perspective and the researchers' (etic) perspective of the phenomenon is sought.

2. (obj. 1) A researcher decides to study the educational philosophies of three teachers out of ten teachers in one school district whom a key informant identified as outstanding instructional leaders. In this case study, what are (a) the phenomenon of interest, (b) the focus, (c) the unit of analysis, and (d) the case or cases being studied?

Answer:
   a. The phenomenon of interest is instructional leadership.
   b. The focus is the educational philosophy of outstanding instructional leaders.
   c. The unit of analysis is the ten teachers identified as outstanding instructional leaders within the selected field setting.
   d. The case is the three teachers whom the researcher selects as his sample for the case study, and each of these three teachers also can be described as a separate case.

3. (obj. 2) Describe the three purposes for which case studies typically are carried out.

Answer:
   1. Description of a phenomenon in sufficient detail to re-create it and its context, along with the meanings and intentions inherent in the situation
   2. Explanation of a phenomenon, with a focus on the relationships observed among different aspects of the phenomenon and the causal patterns within those relationships
   3. Evaluation of specific instances of a phenomenon, in which the researcher uses case study findings to make judgments about their worth or value

4. (obj. 3) Explain what is meant by *thick description* in case study research.

Answer:

Thick description involves the researcher's depiction and conceptualization of a phenomenon in sufficient detail to recreate it in its real-life context and to convey the meanings and intentions inherent in that context.

5. (obj. 3) Explain (a) the meaning of a pattern in case study research and (b) the difference between a relational pattern and a causal pattern.

Answer:

a. A pattern refers to a systematic relationship between one type of observed variation and another type of variation in a case study.
b. A relational pattern involves a relationship in which no claim is made that one variation caused the other, while a causal pattern involves a relationship in which the researcher claims that one variation did cause the other.

6. (obj. 4) Give one reason why a researcher might collect both qualitative and quantitative data in a case study.

Answer (any 1 OK):

1. Using more than one method of data collection can enhance the validity of case study findings.
2. Quantitative data are particularly helpful for arriving at findings that can be generalized to other individuals or situations.
3. The two types of data put the phenomenon being investigated into a more complete context.

7. obj. 4) Describe two ways in which case study research may involve both quantitative and qualitative research methods.

Answer:

1. Although most case study research uses a qualitative epistemological orientation, researchers with a positivist epistemological orientation have contributed a great deal to the literature on case study design.

2. In mixed-methods research involving case study, both qualitative and quantitative data-collection methods are used to generate case study research findings.

8. (obj. 5) Describe two of the components of Joseph Maxwell's 5-component model of case study design, and give an example of a question that is relevant to each component described.

Answer (any 2 components, and any one question relevant to that component, are acceptable.):

1. Purposes. What are the ultimate goals of the study? What issues is the study intended to illuminate? What practices will the study influence? Why does the researcher wish to conduct the study? Why should others care about the results? Why is the study worth doing?
2. Conceptual context. What does the researcher think is going on with the things she plans to study? What theories, findings, and conceptual frameworks relating to these things will guide or inform the study? What literature, preliminary research, and personal experience will the researcher draw on? What theory about the setting or issues guides the study?
3. Research questions. What does the researcher want to understand by doing the study? What is not known about the things being studied that the researcher wants to learn? What questions will the research attempt to answer? How are the research questions related to one another?
4. Methods. What will the researcher actually do in conducting the study? What approaches and techniques will be used to collect the data? What approaches and techniques will be used to analyze the data? How do the methods of data collection and analysis constitute an integrated strategy?
5. Validity. How might the researcher be wrong in drawing conclusions and interpretations? What are the plausible alternative explanations and validity threats to the potential conclusions of the study? How will the researcher deal with the plausible alternative explanations and validity threats to the potential conclusions of the study? Why should others believe the results?

9. (obj. 5) Describe four of the eight goals described by Joseph Maxwell that qualitative research can help researchers achieve.

Answer

(Note: See Table 14.1 on page 456 of the textbook, which gives Maxwell's list of eight goals; any four of these goals are acceptable.)

10. (obj. 6) State one advantage and one disadvantage of studying multiple cases rather than a single case in a case study.

Answer:

An advantage of studying multiple cases is that the researcher can compare cases and discover systematic relationships among the phenomena that they involve. A disadvantage is that the study of multiple cases reduces the total attention that the researcher has available to give to a single case.

11. (obj. 7) Describe the role of the qualitative case study researcher in data collection and typical activities that this role involves.

Answer:

As the primary "measuring instrument," the researcher carries out data collection and becomes personally involved in the phenomenon being studied. Typical activities in this role are interacting closely with research participants, attending social events in the field setting, and using empathy and intuition to grasp the meaning of the phenomenon as experienced by those in the setting.

12. (obj. 7) Name and explain two of the ethical stances from which researchers can judge the morality of their decisions and actions in a case study.

Answer (any 2 OK):

1. Utilitarian ethics consider the consequences of the researcher's decisions and actions on all the people who are affected by them.
2. Deontological ethics consider absolute values such as honesty, justice, fairness, or respect for others.
3. Relational ethics consider whether the decisions and actions reflect a caring attitude toward others.
4. Ecological ethics consider the meaning of the decisions and actions as perceived in the context of the research participants' culture and the larger social systems of which they are a part.

13. (obj. 7) Name two skills a researcher needs in order to gain entry to a field setting and enlist the cooperation of case study participants.

Answer (any 2 OK):

1. The ability to identify an appropriate field site
2. The ability to work with gatekeepers at the site to obtain necessary permissions
3. A respectful and cordial manner of relating to prospective research participants
4. A personal appearance with which research participants feel comfortable

14. (obj. 8) Describe three types of researcher actions reflective of the common statement that the researcher is the primary "measuring instrument" in qualitative research.

Answer (any 3 OK):

1. Having personal involvement in data collection, e.g., by directly observing participants as they behave naturally in the field and holding informal conversations with them.
2. Disclosing their personal experiences, feelings, or beliefs to field participants during data collection.
3. Attend social events in the field setting.
4. Using empathy and other psychological processes to grasp the meaning of the phenomenon as it is experienced by participants in the study.
5. Using their unique interpretive skills to make conceptual and theoretical sense of the case.

6. Reporting the findings to reflect both the emic and etic perspectives and to make the findings' contribution to the research literature clear.

15. (obj. 8) Give two examples of the types of interpretive acts that are typical of a case study researcher.
Answer (any 2 OK):
1. Conceptualizing the study through questions, images, and ideas
2. Defining the phenomenon, case, unit of analysis, and focus of the case study
3. Deciding on approaches to data collection and the individuals, objects, or events on which data will be collected
4. Deciding how to analyze the data and carrying out the analysis
5. Deciding how to report the case study and generating the report or reports

16. (obj. 9) Describe (a) the purpose, and (b) the basic elements, of a subjectivity audit as described by Alan Peshkin.
Answer:
a. Peshkin urges researchers to seek out their subjectivity systematically while their research is in progress so that they can better determine how it might be shaping their inquiry and research outcomes.
b. A subjectivity audit involves taking notes about research situations that arouse the researcher's positive or negative feelings. Peshkin identified "discretely characterized I's" in one of his research studies, which reflected areas in which his own beliefs and backgound influence his perceptions and actions in the research setting, e.g., the *Ethnic Maintenance I* and the *Justice-Seeking I.*

17. (obj. 9) What does the chapter recommend with respect to researchers' personal involvement or disclosure in the research and research report?
Answer:
Avoid excessive self-disclosure, because case study participants might view it as a distraction or might question the researcher's qualifications and the trustworthiness of the study's findings. Include brief comments about the researcher's background and experience relevant to the case study to facilitate readers' understanding and trust of the findings and interpretations.

18. (obj. 10) Describe two theoretical criteria that a researcher should consider in deciding when it is appropriate to end data collection for a case study.
Answer (any 2 OK):
1. Exhaustion of sources, meaning that the researcher senses that little more relevant information can be gained from further contact with the data sources
2. Saturation of categories, meaning that the categories used to code the data appear to be definitively established and continuing data collection produces only tiny increments of new information relative to the effort expended
3. Emergence of regularities, meaning that sufficient consistency has been discovered in the data for the researcher to conclude that the constructs that have been generated to represent the phenomena are sufficient
4. Overextension, meaning that any new information coming in appears to be far removed from the central core of viable categories that have emerged and does not contribute significantly to the emergence of other viable categories

19. (obj. 11) Define and describe the steps in the approach to analyzing case study data known as interpretational analysis.

Answer:

In interpretational analysis, the researcher infers constructs, themes, and patterns from the case study data to describe and explain the phenomenon being studied. It involves the following steps:

1. Selecting or developing a category system that is appropriate for describing aspects of the phenomenon
2. Dividing the database into segments and coding each segment for the categories that fit it
3. Grouping all the segments pertaining to each category by the method of constant comparison and, if desired, determining the inter-rater reliability of the coding system
4. Drawing conclusions about the constructs, themes, and patterns that are salient, and about their generalizability across cases if a multiple-case design has been used

20. (obj. 11) Describe one difference between structural analysis and reflective analysis as approaches to analyzing case study data.

Answer (any 1 OK):

1. In structural analysis the researcher looks for patterns (e.g. the occurrence of specific textual elements) that are inherent in the data, while in reflective analysis the researcher uses subjective judgment to characterize the phenomenon.
2. Structural analysis often involves the generation of frequency counts of various data elements (e.g., individual words or phrases), while in reflective analysis it is not possible to specify standard procedures.
3. Software programs like text retrievers and text database managers are often used in structural analysis, while artistic portrayal and criticism are more typical of reflective analysis.

21. (obj. 12) Describe five of the strategies recommended for ensuring the quality and rigor of qualitative research.

Answer

(Note: See the section in Chapter 14 on pages 473-476, Ensuring the Quality and Rigor of Qualitative Research, which describes seventeen criteria; any five of these criteria is acceptable.)

22. (obj. 12) What is the meaning of triangulation or crystallization in case study research, and what is their relevance to judgments of the validity of research findings?

Answer:

Triangulation or crystallization involve using multiple data-collection methods, data sources, analysts, or theories in collecting, analyzing, and drawing conclusions from case study data. These processes increase the validity of case study findings by eliminating biases that might result from relying on only one data-collection method, source, analyst, or theory.

23. (obj. 12) Describe two types of documentation that might be included in an audit trail to demonstrate the validity of case study findings.

Answer (any 2 OK):

1. The source and method of recording the raw data
2. The data reduction and analysis products
3. The products of the data reconstruction and synthesis
4. Process notes
5. Materials relating to the researchers' intentions, decisions, and dispositions
6. Information about instrument development

24. (obj. 12) What is the main difference between positivist and interpretive approaches to determining the validity of case study findings?

Answer:

Case study researchers who are positivists claim that objective knowledge about the world is possible, and thus use an approach for determining the validity and reliability of research findings involving statistical inference about generalizability. Researchers who subscribe to the interpretive approach apply different criteria to determine the value and applicability of case study findings and use concepts such as plausibility, authenticity, credibility, and relevance to generate those criteria.

25. (obj. 12) Describe one of the criteria used by case study researchers who subscribe to a positivist philosophy of scientific inquiry to judge the quality of case study design.

Answer (any 1 OK):

1. Construct validity is the extent to which a measure used in a case study correctly operationalizes the concepts being studied.
2. Internal validity is the extent to which the researcher has demonstrated a causal relationship between *X* and *Y* by showing that other plausible factors could not have caused *Y*. (This criterion is not applicable to descriptive case study research, which does not seek to identify causal patterns in phenomena.)
3. External validity is the extent to which the findings of a case study can be generalized to other similar cases.
4. Reliability is the extent to which other researchers would arrive at similar results if they studied the same case, using the same procedures, as the first researcher.

26. (obj. 13) Describe one procedure that a researcher can use to increase the probability that case study findings can be applied to other cases.

Answer (any 1 OK):

1. Select a case that clearly is typical of the phenomenon in which one is interested.
2. If a unit of analysis has been defined, select a random sample of individuals within this unit of analysis for intensive data collection and analysis.
3. Place the responsibility for generalizing case study findings on the readers or users of those findings, and write the report in sufficient detail to help readers determine the applicability of the findings to their situation.

27. (obj. 13) Describe one strategy that a researcher can use to help the readers of a case study report determine the applicability of the findings to other situations.

Answer (any 1 OK):

1. Provide a thick description of the participants and contexts that make up the case.
2. Address the issue of how representative the selected case or cases are of the general phenomenon being investigated.
3. If a multiple-case design was used, conduct a cross-case analysis to provide information about whether the results for different cases constitute a literal replication or theoretical replication of the findings.

28. (obj. 14) Name one of the primary characteristics of reflective reporting as an approach to writing reports of case studies.

Answer (any 1 OK):

1. The author uses literary devices (e.g., direct quotes, story telling, or various literary genres like poetry or drama) to bring the case alive for the reader.
2. The researcher's personal voice has a strong presence in the report.

29. (obj. 14) Name one of the primary characteristics of analytic reporting as an approach to writing reports of case studies.

Answer (any 1 OK):
1. The author uses an objective writing style, that is, the researcher's voice is silent or subdued.
2. The report follows a conventional organization of topics to be covered, corresponding to a traditional quantitative research report.

30. (obj. 14) Name four literary genres for reflective reporting of a case study besides the extensive use of direct quotes.

Answer (any 4 OK):
1. Fiction
2. Poetry
3. Drama
4. Oral readings
5. Comedy
6. Satire
7. Visual presentations

31. (obj. 15) Describe one advantage and one disadvantage of qualitative case study research as compared to quantitative research methods.

Answer (any 1 from each set OK):

Advantages
1. Use of thick description brings the case to life in a way that is not possible with the statistical methods of quantitative research.
2. The detail in a case study gives readers a better basis for developing theories, designing educational interventions, or taking some other action than they would have from reading only quantitative research reports.
3. The detail in a case study helps readers compare the cases with their own situations.
4. The researcher typically reveals her personal perspective, so readers can compare their perspective to that of the researcher.
5. Case study research is well suited to the study of unusual or atypical phenomena.
6. Case study design is emergent and therefore flexible, so the researcher can more easily make changes while the research is in progress.

Disadvantages
1. Because case study research does not adhere to the sampling logic of quantitative research, it is more difficult to generalize the findings to other situations with assurance.
2. Ethical problems can arise if it proves difficult when reporting the case study to disguise the identity of the organization or individuals that were studied.
3. Case study research is highly labor intensive for the researcher.
4. The demands of case study research may exceed the verbal, analytic, or social skills of the researcher.

APPLICATION PROBLEMS

Problem 1

A researcher has obtained a grant to carry out a case study involving a multiple-case design to examine how policies about the education of migrant workers' children have changed over time. Describe the skills that the researcher will need to conduct this case study successfully.

Sample Answer:

a. The researcher should have sufficient expertise, and the ability to present a professional identity and\ appearance, to interact with gatekeepers within the school hierarchy (e.g., state education officers in charge of migrant or bilingual education and administrators of schools with a large migrant population).
b. The researcher should have sufficient familiarity with the needs and life patterns of migrant families to be comfortable and knowledgeable in collecting data from such families.
c. The researcher should have sufficient time available to collect qualitative data through whatever data collection methods are most appropriate, e.g., attending meetings and social events, analyzing historical documents that contain educational policy statements, and conducting interviews with school personnel and migrant children and adults.
d. The researcher needs to have the skills for managing the project so that each case receives sufficient attention as well as for analyzing the data so that important similarities and differences between the cases are revealed.
e. The researcher needs good verbal skills for interacting with participants in the field setting and for writing a case study report that brings this phenomenon alive for the readers.

Problem 2

The following narrative describes a graduate student's research proposal for a case study concerning classroom leadership among students from different ethnic groups. List criticisms that an experienced qualitative researcher might make of the proposal.

"This study is concerned with the social structure of a fifth-grade class made up of students representing the following ethnic groups: 12 whites, 8 African-Americans, 4 Hispanics, 2 Asian-Americans, and 1 Native-American (Ute Indian). The research hypothesis is that there is no relationship between ethnicity and leadership status in the classroom. A random sample of 10 students will be selected and observed in class for a one-week period. An observation form has been designed for use in checking the number of leadership remarks made by each student."

Sample Answer:

a. Case study researchers usually ground their theoretical interpretations in the data rather than stating a definite hypothesis before collecting data.
b. A random sample is not likely to include representatives from each ethnic group. It would be preferable to select a purposeful sample, or to observe all the students.
c. Instead of using a structured observation form, the researcher probably would learn more by continuous recording (ideally a video recording) of what went on in the classroom. Then the researcher would be able to develop coding categories, if desired, and code and recode each data segment until she was confident that she had captured all significant instances of students' leadership behavior (nonverbal as well as verbal) and understood their meaning from an emic perspective.
d. A one-week observation period probably is too short to collect sufficient qualitative data.

Problem 3

Evaluate the strengths and weaknesses of the following proposal for a case study with the questions for evaluating qualitative research reports in Appendix B of the textbook.

"The study will be carried out in an inner-city high school. It is aimed at studying teachers' interactions with each other and with students in as many school-related situations as possible, including faculty meetings, classes, and informal contacts in the cafeteria, teachers' lounge, on the playground, and in the halls. Two individuals who are employed half time as teachers in the school will serve as participant observers for one school year. Their role in the research will not be revealed until all data have been collected. Concurrent with the observations, two experienced researchers will conduct survey interviews with all teachers and a sample of students. Unstructured interviews will also be conducted at regular intervals with a group of key informants that includes teachers, students, and other school personnel."

Sample Answer:

a. As part-time teachers at the school, the participant observers should have a good opportunity to obtain data on most teachers and many of the students. Because they have teaching responsibilities as well, they need some convenient method of recording the data so that it is available for later analysis. As participants, it would not be appropriate for them to make audio or video recordings of teachers' interactions. They should agree on a note-taking method that provides detailed information and allows them to check inter-observer reliability.

b. Freedom of access should be good, in that the participant observers will have access to any meetings that they can legitimately attend in their role as teachers. Their access to other teachers' interactions with students, however (e.g., interactions during classes taught by other teachers), might be limited by the nature of the school organization

c. Because observations will be made for an entire school year, the participant observers should have a good opportunity to sample the varied types of interaction situations in which they are interested. Again, they need some method to ensure that they record all the situations of interest, so they probably need a preplanned schedule for how they will use their free time and where to locate themselves within the school during those times.

d. It should be possible to collect both qualitative and quantitative data. It might be appropriate to focus the participant observers' observations and the key informant interviews on qualitative data. The two researchers could also collect some quantitative data during the survey interviews (e.g., asking interviewees to rate the frequency of various types of interactions in which they engage).

e. Triangulation can be achieved in this study by gathering information on the same topics based on both the participant observers' field notes and the data from the interviews.

f. Participant observers will probably need to use concealment, if not outright deception, to keep others unaware of their research activities. Collecting data about other teachers and staff without their knowledge raises ethical issues, and could create problems once their role is revealed. It would probably be better to tell school personnel that these two teachers will be making observations as part of the research, but to keep their research role as unobtrusive as possible.

TEACHING ACTIVITIES

Activity 1

Have students describe some of the phenomena having to do with education (in its broadest sense) that they find interesting. Work through several examples as potential topics for a case study, having the class define a research problem involving the phenomenon, a manageable focus for studying the phenomenon, a unit of analysis if appropriate, and the case or cases to be selected or sampled within that unit of analysis.

Activity 2

Select a research article reporting a simple educational case study and assign it as homework reading. In class have students describe the phenomenon, focus, unit of analysis if any, and the case or cases that the study involves. Ask students to use the concepts presented in the chapter to summarize the researcher's role in data collection and describe the approach to data analysis and reporting used in the case study.

Activity 3

Ask students to collect some qualitative data from or about an individual whom they know and are in a good position to interview or observe unobtrusively. If desired, provide a handout listing guidelines for doing the assignment, e.g., how specifically they should state the research problem, how they should select their case, how long or short the interview or observation period should be, and whether they should prepare a written report of their findings. Using the section topics in the chapter as a guide, have students report on their research experiences in class.

Activity 4

Invite a colleague to describe a completed case study in which the colleague participated as a researcher. Ask the presenter to focus on the particular problems that the case study involved and how they were handled, how the decision was made.

CHAPTER 15
QUALITATIVE RESEARCH TRADITIONS

Note: The phrase in parentheses following the item number for both closed-form and open-form items, for example, "(obj. 3)", refers to the textbook chapter objective to which the item is keyed.

CLOSED-FORM ITEMS

1. (obj. 1) Most qualitative research traditions
   a. have been used extensively in educational research.
   b. derive from the same academic discipline.
   c. are guided by similar epistemological assumptions.
   d. tend to borrow from one another over time.

Answer: d

2. (obj. 1) The majority of qualitative research traditions
   a. involve the study of individuals' lived experience.
   b. are derived from specific philosophical and theoretical formulations.
   c. reflect postmodern conceptions of reality.
   d. all of the above.

Answer: b

3. (obj. 2) The tradition of cognitive psychology focuses on the study of
   a. lived experience from a positivist perspective.
   b. the world as it appears to individuals when engaged in unbiased reflection.
   c. the structures and processes involved in mental activity.
   d. cognitive phenomena that are common to all human beings.

Answer: c

4. (obj. 2) Most researchers in the cognitive psychology tradition of qualitative research believe that
   a. the activity of physical structures in the human brain lead to the development of specific cognitive structures and processes.
   b. principles of learning can be formulated without invoking mentalistic constructs such as memory and motivation.
   c. the biggest contribution of their tradition to education has been the development of tests of intelligence, aptitude, and other constructs.
   d. an individual's mental and intellectual capacities are more dependent on genetic factors than on learning and experience.

Answer: a

5. (obj. 2) A cognitive psychologist would tend to explain the observed differences between experts' and novices' performance of a mental task as primarily a function of the experts'
   a. use of different problem templates.
   b. use of protocol analysis.
   c. construction of a content-specific schema tailored to the task.
   d. greater level of knowledge about the domain that the task involves.

Answer: c

6. (obj. 3) A key criterion in selecting the participants for a phenomenological research study is that they
   a. want to expand their understanding of the nature and meaning of the phenomenon being studied.
   b. agree to carry out contrived tasks and share their thinking as they perform the tasks.
   c. share the researcher's conceptions and values concerning the phenomenon being studied.
   d. are willing to be observed for an extended time period as they carry on their daily life.

Answer: a

7. (obj. 3) In phenomenological research, a textural description is
   a. an account of an individual's intuitive, prereflective perceptions of a phenomenon from every angle.
   b. the researchers' process of analyzing commonalities among individuals' verbal accounts of their lived experience.
   c. a guide used by interviewers to ask each research participant about her perceptions of the phenomenon under study.
   d. a process for preparing oneself to experience a phenomenon with no preconceptions.

Answer: a

8. (obj. 4) Phenomenographic research most differs from phenomenology in the former's
   a. interest in how reality appears to individuals.
   b. analysis of how individuals' differ in their conceptions of a given aspect of reality.
   c. interest in the objective nature of reality.
   d. use of indepth interviews as a method of collecting data.

Answer: b

9. (obj. 5) Most life history researchers
   a. are interested in how individuals interpret their life experiences.
   b. rely mainly on interviews and observations to collect data about individuals.
   c. use theories of cognitive development to make sense of individuals' interpretations of their life experiences.
   d. choose to write about their own life experiences.

Answer: a

10. (obj. 5) If a researcher writes a life history about himself, the research report is most likely to be called a
   a. case study.
   b. biography.
   c. memoir.
   d. oral history.

Answer: c

11. (objs 1-5) The following research traditions involve the investigation of lived experience. Match each tradition with the type of phenomenon that it investigates.

   __ 1. Cognitive psychology
   __ 2. Life history
   __ 3. Phenomenographic research
   __ 4. Phenomenology

   a. Individuals' different conceptualizations of reality
   b. Individuals' life experiences from their perspective
   c. Mental structures and processes used by individuals in different situations
   d. Reality as it appears to individuals

Answer: 1 = c 2 = b 3 = a 4 = d

12. (obj. 6) The qualitative research traditions of symbolic interactionism and action research both involve
    a. the study of how the social transactions in which individuals engage contribute to their self-identity and the social structures within which they operate.
    b. the study of how individuals become affiliated with particular organizations.
    c. the investigation of society and culture.
    d. efforts to improve professional practice.

Answer: c

13. (obj. 6) The qualitative research tradition in which practitioners reflect on, and seek to improve the rationality and justice of, their work is called
    a. ethnography.
    b. action research.
    c. symbolic interactionism.
    d. cultural studies.

Answer: b

14. (obj. 6) The following qualitative research traditions examine societal and cultural phenomena. Match each tradition with the type of phenomenon that it studies.
    ___ 1. Symbolic interactionism
    ___ 2. Ethnomethodology
    ___ 3. Action research
    a. The rules that underlie everyday social interactions
    b. Self-relective investigation to improve the rationality and and justice of one's work
    c. How social transactions contribute to social structures and self-identity

Answer: 1 = c 2 = a 3 = b

15. (obj. 7) The research tradition that probably has most influenced the basic case study method as applied to educational research is
    a. cognitive psychology.
    b. life history.
    c. ethnography.
    d. symbolic interactionism.

Answer: c

16. (obj. 7) In qualitative research the assumed ability of individuals to shape the conditions of their lives is called
    a. cultural transmission.
    b. cultural acquisition.
    c. phenomenography.
    d. agency.

Answer: d

17. (obj. 8) A particularly desirable characteristic of ethnographic research is its
    a. emphasis on the researcher's etic perspective.
    b. use of a reporting style that gives voice to oppressed groups.
    c. adherence to the goal of the natural sciences to develop universal laws.
    d. in-depth study of phenomena in their real-life context.

Answer: d

18. (obj. 8) A particular strength of ethnography is the researcher's
    a. holistic orientation to studying a culture or aspect of a culture.
    b. focus on the idiosyncrasies of various members of the culture.
    c. concern for forming reciprocal relationships with those studied.
    d. preference for studying deviant or primitive cultures.

Answer: a

19. (obj. 9) An important difference between critical theory overall and the particular branch of critical theory called cultural studies is the former's concern for the
    a. investigation of the power relationships in a culture.
    b. emancipation of the members of cultural groups from systematized oppression.
    c. development of theories focused on large-scale social structure.
    d. understanding of the values and beliefs that underlie educational practice.

Answer: c

20. (obj. 9) The basic assumption of all critical theories is that
    a. all social inequalities need to be changed in order to make the world better place.
    b. no approach to seeking the truth is privileged over any other.
    c. cultural acquisition plays a minimal role in perpetuating forms of social and economic oppression.
    d. the members of oppressed groups are the best equipped to challenge the institutions that maintain their oppression.

Answer: a

21. (obj. 10) An approach that characterizes research and theory building in the cultural studies tradition is the
    a. analysis of the institutional system within which the researcher himself works.
    b. emphasis on long-term ethnographic investigation of subcultures within one's society.
    c. continual critique of the researcher's beliefs, the phenomena being studied and its methods of study.
    d. use of language that reflects the everyday vocabulary of oppressed groups.

Answer: c

22. (obj. 10) Instrumental rationality in educational research involves a(n)
    a. attempt to determine the purpose of controversial educational practices.
    b. analysis of the power relationships that are central to the operation of educational institutions.
    c. preoccupation with means or technology over ends or purposes.
    d. criterion for judging the validity of research.

Answer: c

23. (obj. 11) Ethnomethodology differs from phenomenology in the former's concern with
    a. the objective features of social reality.
    b. how groups develop intersubjective interpretations of reality.
    c. how social reality appears to individuals.
    d. the researcher's reflections on his own influence on the phenomena being studied.

Answer: b

24. (obj. 11) The type of data analysis used by ethnomethodologists is most similar to
    a. structural analysis.
    b. reflective analysis.
    c. interpretational analysis.
    d. emergent analysis.

Answer: b

25. (objs 6-11) The following research traditions involve the investigation of society and culture. Match each tradition with the type of phenomenon that it investigates.
    __ 1. Cultural studies
    __ 2. Action research
    __ 3. Ethnography
    __ 4. Ethnomethodology
    __ 5. Symbolic interactionism
    a. Characteristic features and patterns of a culture
    b. Contestation of oppressive power relationships in a culture
    c. Practitioners' self-reflective efforts to improve the rationality and justice of their work
    d. The influence of social interactions on social structures and individuals' self-identity.
    e. The rules that underlie everyday social interactions

Answers: 1 = b 2 = c 3 = a 4 = e 5 = d

26. (obj. 12) A researcher studies the terms used by students and teachers to describe cheating in class in order to determine how cheating behavior is conceptualized within the school system. This research is best considered an example of
    a. cognitive psychology.
    b. ethnographic content analysis.
    c. semiotics.
    d. cognitive ethnography.

Answer: d

27. (obj. 12) The study of the implicit rules governing the speech acts between two or more people is known as
    a. discourse analysis.
    b. conversation analysis.
    c. sociolinguistics.
    d. narratology.

Answer: b

28. (obj. 12) Sociolinguistics is the study of
    a. the interpretive processes that individuals use to produce accounts of reality.
    b. the effects of social characteristics such as age, socioeconomic status, and ethnicity on language use.
    c. the implicit rules governing the speech acts between two or more people.
    d. literary works that seek to represent and explain individuals' personal and social experience.

Answer: b

29. (obj. 13) The hermeneutic circle in hermeneutics refers to
    a. the process of alternating between interpreting each part of a text and interpreting the text as a whole.
    b. the flow of conversation between participants in a dialogue.
    c. the point at which participants' separate viewpoints recede into the background and consensus emerges.
    d. the fact that both the author and the reader of a text are engaged in interpretive acts.

Answer: a

30. (obj. 14) In semiotics the expression of an idea (e.g., H_2O) along with its meaning (e.g., water) constitute a
    a. referent.
    b. signifier.
    c. signified.
    d. sign.

Answer: d

31. (obj. 14) In order to examine people's conformity to and deviation from the intended meaning of signs, a semioticist would be most likely to
    a. analyze nonverbal sign systems rather than verbal sign systems
    b. combine fieldwork in a natural setting with a formal analysis of a sign system.
    c. focus her analysis on the denotative signs used by people.
    d. conduct a content analysis of the words used in people's dialogue.

Answer: b

32. (obj. 15) A principle that underlies structuralism as a research tradition is that
    a. the individual communicator defines social reality.
    b. historical analysis is central to understanding a communicative system as it exists at a given point in time.
    c. communicative systems have little continuity because of the constant action of forces toward change.
    d. communicative systems have self-regulating mechanisms that make them resistant to change.

Answer: d

33. (obj. 15) Poststructuralism is an approach to the study of systems based on the assumption that
    a. a communicative system is best understood by focusing on the individual elements within it.
    b. the researcher's task is to discover the most objective interpretation of a literary work or text.
    c. texts include within themselves everything that is necessary for their interpretation.
    d. it is not possible to find any inherent meaning or value in a given communicative system.

Answer: d

34. (objs 12-15) The following research traditions involve the investigation of language and communication. Match each tradition with the type of phenomenon that it investigates.
    __ 1. Ethnographic content analysis
    __ 2. Ethnography of communication
    __ 3. Hermeneutics
    __ 4. Narrative analysis
    __ 5. Semiotics
    __ 6. Structuralism
    a. Use of speech in the social life of members of a cultural group
    b. Organized representations and explanations of human experience
    c. Signs and the meanings they convey
    d. The content of documents in cultural perspective
    e. The process by which individuals arrive at the meaning of a text
    f. The systemic properties of language, text, and other communicative phenomena

Answers: 1 = d 2 = a 3 = e 4 = b 5 = c 6 = f

OPEN-FORM ITEMS

1. (obj. 1) Give two reasons why it is important for an educational researcher to become familiar with the major qualitative research traditions that have been used in educational research.

Answer (any 2 OK):

1. Researchers are likely to encounter these traditions in their reviews of the research literature.
2. Knowledge of the traditions will help a researcher formulate questions to guide a case study.
3. Knowledge of the traditions will help researchers develop methods for collecting and analyzing research data in case studies.
4. Knowledge of the traditions will suggest relevant theories to which researchers might connect their findings.
5. A case study will have added meaning and significance if it is grounded within an established research tradition.

2. (obj. 1) Define the term *research tradition.*

Answer:

A research tradition is a group of scholars who agree among themselves on the nature of the universe they are examining, on legitimate questions and problems to study, and on legitimate techniques for seeking solution. The term refers also to the work of such scholars.

3. (obj. 1) Describe four key characteristics of qualitative research traditions.

Answer:

1. Such traditions are derived from particular wide-scale philosophical formulations and theories and from the writings of individuals who have espoused them.
2. Traditions tend to blend with or borrow from each other, while others remain on the periphery or fade out of use.
3. A tradition usually includes both a focus on a particular type or class of phenomena and a selected research approach for studying the phenomena.
4. The forms of writing and representation used in the postmodern inquiries that predominate at this moment tend to be dynamic, problematic, open ended, and complex.

4. (obj. 1) Describe the three different types of phenomena on which different qualitative research traditions tend to focus.

Answer:

1. Lived experience
2. Society and culture
3. Language and communication

5. (obj. 2) Name one type of phenomenon that educational researchers working in the tradition of cognitive psychology have investigated extensively.

Answer (any 1 OK):

1. Teachers' thinking
2. Students' learning processes
3. Motivation to learn
4. Differences between the problem solving strategies of experts and novices.

6. (obj. 3) Describe four key procedures often used in planning and conducting a phenomenological investigation.

Answer:

1. Identify a topic of personal and social significance.
2. Select participants who have experienced the phenomenon being studied and who share the researchers' interest in understanding it.
3. Interview each participant to obtain a comprehensive description of their experience of the phenomenon being studied.
4. Analyze the interview data to identify meaning units and themes for each research participant (textural description) and regularities of thought across participants (structural description).

7. (obj. 3) What is the difference between a textural description and a structural description of a phenomenon that is studied through phenomenology?

Answer:

A textural description is an account of an individual's intuitive, prereflective perceptions of a phenomenon from every angle. A structural description is an account of the cross-case regularities of thought, judgment, imagination, and recollection that underlie and give meaning to different individuals' experiences of a phenomenon.

8. (obj. 3) Describe one advantage of phenomenology as a qualitative research tradition for use in education.

Answer (any 1 OK):

1. It can be used to study a wide range of educational phenomena.
2. The interview process used to collect phenomenological data is wide-ranging and therefore capable of detecting many aspects of experience that may prove to be important variables in subsequent quantitative studies.
3. The procedures of phenomenological inquiry are relatively straightforward, so less training might be required to do a phenomenological study compared to a study based on some of the other research traditions.

9. (obj. 4) How would a phenomenographic researcher's approach to studying teachers' views of the reasons for students' misbehavior in class differ from a phenomenologist's approach?

Answer:

A phenomenographic researcher would study a group of teachers to develop a classification of their different conceptions of the reasons for students' misbehavior. A phenomenologist would be concerned with each teacher's total experience of student misbehavior, including his feelings, reflections, and associations with other life experiences.

10. (obj. 5) List two of the reporting formats in which a life history might be presented.

Answer (any 2 OK):

1. Biography
2. Life story
3. Oral history
4. Case study
5. Testimonio
6. Portrait
7. Autobiography
8. Memoir

11. (obj. 6) What type of phenomena is the common focus of symbolic interactionism, ethnomethodology, and action research?

Answer:

These three research traditions focus on societal and cultural phenomena.

12. (obj. 6) State the goal of (a) symbolic interactionsm and (b) action research.

Answer:

a. Symbolic interactionism seeks to understand the influence of social interactions on social structures and individuals' self identity.
b. Action research seeks to engage practitioners in self-reflective efforts to improve the rationality and justice of their work.

13. (obj. 7) Describe one of the key characteristics of ethnography.

Answer (any 1 OK):

1. Its focus is on discovering cultural patterns in human behavior, that is, the communalities among individual human beings that are attributable to their culture.
2. It aims to convey the emic perspective of the members of the culture.
3. Its goal is to study the real-life settings in which culture is manifested and to study all key aspects of those settings.

14. (obj. 7) Describe one method that an ethnographer uses to achieve the goal of looking at a cultural phenomenon from the perspective of an outsider and then seeking to understand the phenomenon from the perspective of insiders.

Answer (any 1 OK):

1. The ethnographer can immerse herself in a culture that is far different from her own.
2. The ethnographer can study a subculture in her own community with which she is unfamiliar.
3. The ethnographer working in a familiar setting can take a different perspective from the one she normally uses, e.g., from a researcher perspective focused on theory rather than a teacher perspective focused on practice.

15. (obj. 8) Describe one of the key issues facing ethnography today.

Answer (any 1 OK):

1. Its increased focus on the emic perspective of unique cultures does not help promote understanding of cross-cultural commonalities.
2. An argument persists as to whether ethnographers should subscribe to the goal of the natural sciences to develop universal laws, subscribe to the goal of the humanities to understand the unique and particular case, or pursue both goals.
3. Critics argue that ethnographic reports impose a particular order on cultural phenomena that may not actually reflect the culture being described.

16. (obj. 8) Describe one strength and one weakness of ethnography.
Answer (any 1 from each set OK):

Strengths

1. It is particularly suited to investigating the complex phenomenon known as culture because of its holistic orientation.
2. It is able to identify the diverse elements of a culture and weave them into coherent patterns.
3. It enables the researcher to anticipate and interpret what goes on in a society or social group as well as in its individual members.

Weaknesses

1. Whether a given ethnography subscribes to the goal of the natural sciences to develop natural laws or to the goal of the humanities to understand the unique and particular case is often not clear.
2. Ethnographers impose their own order on cultural phenomena, which calls the validity of ethnographies into question.
3. Traditional ethnographies have not involved a reciprocal relationship with the members of the culture who were studied.

17. (obj. 9) What does cultural studies investigate, and what is its purpose?
Answer:

Cultural studies involves the investigation of power relationships in a culture, for the purpose of helping to emancipate members of the culture from the many forms of oppression that are perceived to operate within it.

18. (obj. 10) Explain the origin and meaning of the concept of *troubling* education and educational research.
Answer:

Troubling is a concept from anti-oppressive education, involving the questioning and exposure of assumptions that underlie accepted but oppressive cultural practices maintained by traditional educational operations.

19. (obj. 10) Explain three of the seven basic assumptions of the cultural studies tradition that were formulated by Joe Kincheloe and Peter McLaren.
Answer (any 3 OK):

1. Certain groups in any society are privileged over others.
2. Oppression has many faces.
3. Language is central to the formation of subjectivity (conscious and unconscious awareness).
4. The relationship between signifier and signified is never stable or fixed and is often mediated by the social relations of capitalist production and consumption.
5. All thought is fundamentally mediated by power relations that are socially and historically constituted.
6. Facts can never be isolated from the domain of values or removed from some form of ideological inscription.
7. Mainstream research practices are unwittingly implicated in the reproduction of systems of class, race, and gender oppression.

(Note: For judging the adequacy of students' explanations of these assumptions, see the text on pp. 509-512.)

20. (obj. 11) Describe one operating principle that guides ethnomethodological investigations of society and culture.
Answer (any 1 OK):

1. Ethnomethodologists reject the sociological view that human actors passively carry out prescribed actions on the basis of internalized social norms.
2. They seek to examine how various aspects of the life-world are produced, experienced, or accomplished interactionally and discursively.

3. They are concerned with how social reality appears to individuals, not with the objective features of social reality.
4. They are interested in how groups of individuals develop intersubjective interpretations of reality.

21. (obj. 12) Name and briefly describe one of the methods that can be used in narrative analysis.
Answer (any 1 OK):
1. Conversation analysis involves the study of the rules of speech acts between two or more people.
2. Sociolinguistics is the study of the effects of social characteristics such as age, socioeconomic status, and ethnicity on language use.
3. Narratology is the study of literary narratives.
4. Cognitive psychology is the study of the mental structures and processes used by individuals in different situations.
5. Ethnomethodology is the study of the rules that underlie everyday social interactions.
5. Event structure analysis is the study of the logical structures of social events.

22. (obj. 12) Explain the focus of ethnographic content analysis.
Answer:
This research tradition involves the examination of documents found in field settings as reflections of social interactions in the culture.

23. (obj. 13) Why has hermeneutics had so much influence on the general approach of qualitative researchers?
Answer:
Interpretation of meanings is at the heart of hermeneutics. Interpretation of meanings also is a major focus of investigation in qualitative research. Therefore, qualitative researchers have looked to hermeneutic philosophers and researchers for insights into the interpretive process.

24. (obj. 13) Explain the meaning of the hermeneutic circle in the qualitative research tradition known as hermeneutics.
Answer:
In hermeneutics the hermeneutic circle refers to a continuous process in which individuals alternate between interpretation of the meaning of each part of the text and interpretation of the text as a whole.

25. (obj. 14) Why would the qualitative research tradition of semiotics appear to have particular promise for educational researchers?
Answer:
Semiotics involves the study of sign systems, and many educational phenomena involve sign systems that are used to impart information and that thus affect what and how students learn.

26. (obj. 15) Explain the meaning of the structuralist principle, "the whole is greater than the sum of its parts" as it applies to the study of social groups.
Answer:
A social group is more than its individual members and how each interacts with the others. There is a sense of a group that exists independently of individual members and that influences the actions of each individual in the group.

27. (obj. 15) How does poststructuralism differ from structuralism in its assumptions about systems?
Answer:
Structuralism proposes to understand the inherent meaning of a system by the study of its elements, their relationships, and the overarching nature of the system itself. Poststructuralism, by contrast, argues that it is not

possible to find any inherent meaning in a system but that the only possibility is to examine the varied interpretations of a text, which are infinite.

APPLICATION PROBLEMS

Problem 1

Select a phenomenon of interest to you within the field of education, e.g., the effect of competitive athletics programs on students' experience of attending college. Describe one way in which you could study an aspect of that phenomenon through a tradition involving the investigation of (a) lived experience, (b) society and culture, and (c) language and communication.

Sample Answer:

The researcher could study students who are participants in an athletic program at a given university, e.g., the football team.

a. In an investigation of lived experience, the researcher could use the tradition of phenomenological research to have students reflect on how competitive athletics affects their experience of being students at the university.
b. In an investigation of society and culture, the researcher could use the tradition of cultural studies to examine how promising high school athletes with borderline achievement or from poor families are recruited with the promise of scholarships, tuition waivers, tutoring assistance, etc. to attend the university and participate in its athletic programs, and how athletic injuries alter students' present and future well being.
c. In an investigation of language and communication, the researcher could use the tradition of the ethnography of communication to study the language used by the coach and players during the half-time pep talk and how the language differs (e.g., in the use of metaphors involving battle and overcoming failure) depending on the score at half time.

Problem 2

Say that you are in the process of planning your master's or doctoral research study. You have decided first to select a research tradition that interests you and then to define a problem that can be studied by that tradition. Describe at least three of your personal characteristics (e.g., interests, abilities, and experience) that you might take into account in selecting the research tradition of greatest interest to you, and indicate some of the traditions that would appeal to you based on each of these characteristics.

Sample Answer:

1. You might take your own educational background into account. For example, a student who majored in sociology as an undergraduate might prefer to base her research on a tradition involving the investigation of society and culture, whereas a linguistics major might wish to use a tradition involving the investigation of language and communication.
2. You might consider whether you prefer a high level of structure when studying a problem or whether you prefer a low level of structure. If you like more structure, you might prefer ethnomethodology or structuralism, whereas if you prefer less structure you might want to base your study on symbolic interactionism or ethnography.
3. You might consider whether you have a critical view of educational systems in our society or a more positive view. If you have a critical view, cultural studies or critical race theory may be well suited to serve as a foundation for your research study.

Problem 3
A teacher decides to carry out an ethnography involving the study of the school in which he works. Describe (a) one way in which the teacher could define the research problem to make the study more manageable to carry out within a reasonable time frame and (b) one way in which he could "make the familiar strange" in order to balance the emic and etic perspectives of the phenomenon he investigates.
Sample Answer:

a. The teacher could make the study more manageable by limiting his focus to one aspect of the school phenomenon, e.g., the peer culture among students.
b. He could make the familiar strange by studying a subculture in the school with which he is unfamiliar, which again is exemplified by focusing on the peer culture among students. Another way to make the familiar strange would be to step back from his teacher role and emphasize his researcher role when he thinks about what he is learning from the data he has collected.

TEACHING ACTIVITIES

Activity 1
Assign an educational research article to students having to do with a qualitative research tradition with which you have some familiarity. Have students work in groups to identify the phenomenon that the research involved, the data-collection method or methods used to study it, the methods used to analyze the data, whether they agree with the researcher's interpretations of the findings, and what they consider to be the strong and weak points of the study.

Activity 2
Have students identify a research problem of personal interest. Ask them to select two different qualitative research traditions they think would be useful in studying this problem and make a tentative list of the steps in a research study on the problem that are based on each of these two traditions. Have them compare the two lists and identify possible advantages and disadvantages in using one tradition versus the other.

Activity 3
Have students do a literature search to identify a research report involving one of the traditions covered in this chapter, read the report, and make a presentation in class in which they summarize the problem, the methods of study, and the findings of the research.

CHAPTER 16
HISTORICAL RESEARCH

Note: The phrase in parentheses following the item number for both closed-form and open-form items, for example, "(obj. 3)", refers to the textbook chapter objective to which the item is keyed.

CLOSED-FORM ITEMS

1. (obj. 1) Unlike other types of social science researchers, historical researchers
   a. engage in causal inference.
   b. are concerned primarily with compiling facts.
   c. use subjective judgment to interpret events.
   d. discover rather than create data.

Answer: d

2. (obj. 1) An overarching goal of historical research is to
   a. test recent social science theories against historical data.
   b. interpret past events by using current concepts and perspectives.
   c. establish as many facts as possible about past events.
   d. gain an increased understanding of present-day phenomena by studying past events.

Answer: d

3. (obj. 1) Compared to historical research in the nineteenth century, contemporary historical research
   a. tends to be more factually complete.
   b. places more emphasis on the interpretation of historical events.
   c. places greater reliance on archival records.
   d. relies more on secondary sources.

Answer: b

4. (obj. 2) Match each example below with the use of historical research it best illustrates.
   __ 1. A historian in 2007 examines state department of education regulations passed between 1950 and 1990 for sexist content.
   __ 2. A historian analyzes the textbooks used to teach reading in a particular school district during the last 75 years.
   __ 3. A state education association newsletter presents a report card showing how various candidates seeking nomination to run for the U.S. presidency have voted on education-related bills.
   __ 4. A researcher studies reports of research on the relationship between intelligence and socioeconomic status since the first intelligence test was developed.
   a. Reviewing the literature in a specific area of interest
   b. Collecting information concerning past educational practices
   c. Sensitizing educators to past practices still in use that require reform
   d. Predicting future trends

Answer: 1 = c 2 = b 3 = d 4 = a

5. (obj. 3) Reading several historiographical works before undertaking a historical study particularly helps a historical researcher to
   a. identify the most appropriate historical sources to obtain.
   b. define the problem for the research study.
   c. specify the steps and procedures to be used in the research.
   d. avoid misinterpretations of historical data.

Answer: c

6. (obj. 4) Which of the following is *not* a typical topic for historical research?
   a. Histories of specific individuals
   b. Relating past ideas or events that were not previously viewed as related
   c. Comparing the objectives of a new curriculum program with those of an old curriculum program
   d. Revisionist reinterpretation of past events

Answer: c

7. (obj. 4) Revisionist history refers to the study of
   a. reform movements within various disciplines.
   b. the historical causes of current social problems.
   c. past events with the use of new interpretive frameworks.
   d. utopian conceptions of education and other social institutions.

Answer: c

8. (obj. 5) A useful classification of historical documents is
   a. primary vs. secondary.
   b. published vs. unpublished.
   c. intentional vs. unpremeditated.
   d. all of the above.

Answer: d

9. (obj. 5) The four main types of historical sources in educational research are documents, quantitative records, relics, and
   a. repositories.
   b. oral records.
   c. instructional devices.
   d. electronic databases.

Answer: b

10. (obj. 6) In historical research, secondary sources are defined as those documents in which the
   a. description is written from an objective viewpoint.
   b. individual describing the event was not present at its occurrence.
   c. individual describing the event was a direct witness.
   d. historian reports events using her own interpretive framework.

Answer: b

11. (obj. 6) A researcher doing a historical study in 2007 relies on sources published between 1910 and 1950 to investigate home schooling as practiced by pioneers who went West between 1800 and 1860. This study illustrates the error of
   a. excessive use of secondary sources.
   b. failure to reconcile discrepant accounts of past events.
   c. subjecting existing histories to radically new interpretive frameworks.
   d. attempting to work on a broad and poorly defined problem.

Answer: a

12. (obj. 7) Recording information from a historical source usually
    a. requires reproduction of the entire document.
    b. requires computer technology.
    c. must be done by an official archivist.
    d. is affected by the copyright status of the source.

Answer: d

13. (obj. 8) Internal criticism of a historical source involves consideration of all the following *except*
    a. the competence of the historical writer.
    b. whether the stated author actually wrote the document.
    c. possible indicators of the writer's bias, such as emotionally charged language.
    d. the accuracy of the facts presented in the document.

Answer: b

14. (obj. 8) Analysis of _____________ can be of assistance in external criticism of a historical source.
    a. the physical document, such as the paper used,
    b. the author's biases
    c. discrepant accounts of a historical event
    d. the individual's personal stake in the events being described

Answer: a

15. (obj. 9) Identifying forgeries, originals versus copies, and the date of origin of a historical document are all relevant to the ____________ of the document.
    a. internal criticism
    b. external criticism
    c. quantitative analysis
    d. historiographical analysis

Answer: b

16. (objs. 8-9) Match each of the following procedures of historical research with the most appropriate example of that procedure.
    __ 1. Internal criticism of a historical document
    __ 2. External criticism of a historical document
    __ 3. Making a synthesis of data
    __ 4. Revisionist reinterpretation of past events
    a. Collecting evidence to determine whether a historical source is a forgery
    b. Judging whether the writer was competent to report on the events described in the source
    c. Examining newly discovered historical documents to determine whether they reinforce existing interpretations of events
    d. Writing a history of World War II that makes no mention of the Holocaust

Answer: 1 = b 2 = a 3 = c 4 = d

17. (obj. 10) In historical research, an individual's public and private statements that give discrepant accounts of events are best viewed as
    a. two sources of data about the person making the statement.
    b. a sign of bias or prejudice.
    c. an example of antiquarianism.
    d. an indicator of the unreliability of observers' accounts.

Answer: a

18. (obj. 11) "History means interpretation" implies that
    a. there is no discernible objective reality in past events.
    b. all accounts and impressions of a past event are equally valid.
    c. historians make meaning of the past based on their own interests and experiences.
    d. current concepts rarely are useful for understanding earlier practices.

Answer: c

19. (obj. 12) The use of current concepts from other social science disciplines
    a. is a recent trend in historical research in education.
    b. rarely is useful for explaining past educational events.
    c. is an alternative to the traditional practice of external criticism in historical research in education.
    d. has helped check the movement toward revisionist history.

Answer: a

20. (obj. 12) Presentism is the practice of
    a. interpreting past events with the use of current concepts and perspectives.
    b. subordinating historical facts to the interpretive framework used to explain them.
    c. rejecting tradition in favor of change for its own sake.
    d. explaining current events in terms of the recent past rather than in terms of long-term historical trends.

Answer: a

21. (obj. 13) Historians generally believe that
    a. history repeats itself.
    b. ideology is the major causative agent in history.
    c. historical events are unique.
    d. determining the causes of past events is not an attainable objective.

Answer: c

22. (obj. 13) Finding consistency in the historical accounts of different reporters assures a historian that she
    a. has made the correct causal interpretation of a past event.
    b. has studied the entire range of perspectives on the phenomenon of concern.
    c. can generalize the findings from examination of a relatively small sample of the available primary sources.
    d. has obtained a representative sample of historical sources.

Answer: c

23. (obj. 13) The methods of quantitative history have proved to be particularly useful for
    a. causal interpretation of past events.
    b. making broad generalizations about the past.
    c. external criticism of historical sources.
    d. measuring individuals' attitudes toward past events.

Answer: b

24. (obj. 14) A historical research dissertation includes these chapter titles: "School Choice, 1920-1940"; "School Choice, 1941-1960"; "School Choice, 1961-1980." The historical facts in this dissertation appear to be organized
    a. similarly to dissertations involving other types of educational research.
    b. consistent with a revisionist historical perspective.
    c. in relation to topics or themes.
    d. in chronological order.

Answer: d

25. (obj. 14) If a student uses concepts and descriptions with strong affective or value connotations in a proposal for a dissertation involving historical research, the student should
   a. substantiate them by indicating the sources on which they are based.
   b. replace them with more moderate language in the final version of the dissertation.
   c. use direct quotes to convey each concept and description.
   d. summarize the student's personal experiences that underlie his choice of language.

Answer: a

OPEN-FORM ITEMS

1. (obj. 1) What is the main difference between contemporary and nineteenth-century historical research?

Answer:

Contemporary research emphasizes interpretation, whereas nineteenth-century research emphasized the compilation of as many objective facts as possible.

2. (obj. 2) State two purposes for studying the past.

Answer (any 2 OK):

1. For its own sake, because one is interested in a particular historical period or event
2. To help us understand the past, in particular, to learn from past mistakes
3. To gain knowledge and insights for building on past research and practice
4. To find evidence to support current proposals for social reform
5. To define and evaluate alternative future scenarios involving a particular educational phenomenon

3. (obj. 3) The initial step in doing historical research is to define the problem or question to be investigated. Briefly describe three subsequent steps that are typical of the historical research process.

Answer:

1. Search for sources of historical data.
2. Evaluate the historical sources.
3. Record information from the historical sources.
4. Interpret the historical data.
5. Report the historical research findings.

4. (obj. 4) Beach classified the problems and topics that can be addressed by historical research into five types, including current social issues such as home schooling and the growth of performance tests. Briefly describe and give an example of two other types of historical research problems.

Answer (any 2 OK):

1. Histories of specific individuals, institutions, or movements. Example: the educational experiences of members of a particular ethnic group
2. Exploration of relationships between ideas or events that previously appeared to be unrelated. Example: how the increased availability of personal computers has affected educators' conceptions of the teaching of writing
3. Efforts to synthesize old data collected by different historians or to merge old data with new historical facts. Example: using recent oral histories of teachers' lives to reexamine statements of educational policy earlier in this century
4. Reinterpretation of past events within new interpretive frameworks in order to sensitize educators to past practices that appear to have had unjust aims and effects but that have continued into the present and thus require reform. Example: how educational innovation in mid-nineteenth century New England schools served to thwart democratic aspirations

5. (obj. 5) List two of the main types of primary sources used in historical research, and give an example of each.

Answer (any 2 OK):

1. Written documents or records. Example: the diary of someone who was part of the Lewis and Clark expedition to Oregon
2. Quantitative records. Example: school records of student attendance, test scores, or program budgets
3. Oral records. Example: audio recordings of oral interviews with people who were students when the U.S. instituted busing as a strategy for integrating the public schools
4. Relics. Example: a collection of various types of computers used in the schools 10 to 20 years ago

6. (obj. 6) Describe the three main types of historical sources used by a historical researcher and the purpose of each.

Answer:

1. Preliminary sources are indexes that list secondary and primary sources relevant to historical research generally or to a particular historical period or topic. They are used to identify the appropriate secondary and primary sources to use in research on a specific historical problem.
2. Secondary sources are documents in which an individual who was not present at an event gives an account of the event. They are used to summarize information about a historical event that usually has been gained from numerous primary sources and perhaps from other secondary sources as well.
3. Primary sources are records (documents, quantitative records, oral records, or relics) that were generated by people who personally witnessed or participated in the historical events of interest. They are used to obtain and document the facts that historians present in historical research studies.

7. (obj. 7) A researcher has identified several primary sources that appear ideal for exploring her research topic. Describe two issues with which the researcher must deal before she is able to collect and record pertinent information from these sources.

Answer:

1. The researcher must determine whether the sources that she wishes to use will be made accessible to her, and under what conditions.
2. The researcher must find out whether information in the materials can be copied and reproduced in her research report.

8. (obj. 8) In examining a document, the historical researcher uses external criticism. (a) Explain what this involves, and (b) state one question that is likely to be asked in an external criticism of a document.

Answer:

a. External criticism deals with the evaluation of the authenticity of the source.

b. (any 1 OK):

1. Is it genuine?
2. Is it the original copy?
3. When was it written?
4. Where was it written?
5. By whom was it written?

9. (obj. 9) In examining a document, the historical researcher uses internal criticism. (a) Explain what this involves, and (b) state one question that is likely to be asked in an internal criticism of a document.

Answer

a. Internal criticism deals with the evaluation of the credibility of the information contained in the document.

b. (any 1 OK):

1. Is it probable that people would act in the way described by the writer?
2. Is it physically possible for the events to have occurred as described?
3. Do the quantitative data presented appear to be correct?
4. What is the writer's expertise, honesty, and role in the events, including possible conflicts of interest?

10. (obj. 10) Bias in a historical account involves the writer or informant having a strong set to perceive events in such a way that certain types of facts habitually are overlooked, distorted, or falsified. Briefly describe two common causes of such bias.

Answer (any 2 OK):

1. People often exaggerate their own roles in important events.
2. The truth is often elaborated upon or colored in order to make the account more interesting.
3. The person's position (e.g., a political or administrative role) may lead him to give socially acceptable rather than truthful information.
4. The individual's past experience with the phenomenon is such that he has reason to distrust the motives and actions of others.

11. (obj. 11) What is presentism, and how can it affect historical research?

Answer:

Presentism is the tendency of the historian to interpret past events using concepts and perspectives that originated after the events occurred. For example, terms such as *accountability* do not mean the same thing today as they did 30 years ago. The use of such a concept in interpreting past events can create misunderstanding of those events.

12. (obj. 12) Name one benefit and one possible drawback of a historical researcher's use of particular concepts to interpret historical data.

Answer (any 1 from each set OK):

Benefits

1. Concepts allow the researcher to show the relationship between many historical phenomena that otherwise might be seen as separate or insignificant.
2. Concepts allow the researcher to explore possible causal interpretations of historical events that have not previously been considered.

Drawbacks

1. The way in which a concept is defined places limits on what the historian chooses to explore.
2. If a concept meant something different at the time the historical event occurred than it does now, its use can create misunderstanding of the meaning of the event.

13. (obj. 13) Explain why it is difficult for historians to attribute a historical event to a single cause.

Answer:

A given event has many antecedents that could have influenced the event. Various plausible interpretations can be posed for any event, each of which explains some of the evidence, leaves other evidence unexplained, and suggests new questions to ask. Many of the possible causes may not even have been discovered. Thus it is difficult to justify attributing the event to a single cause.

14. (obj. 13) Briefly describe one problem faced by historians in generalizing from their findings.

Answer (any 1 OK):

1. Available sources almost always constitute a nonrepresentative sample of all the relevant records that once existed related to a given event.
2. In studying individuals a similar problem arises, in that the available records for one point in time may not accurately represent the individual's opinion or behavior at a different time.

15. (obj. 14) Describe three approaches to organizing the research findings in a historical research dissertation, and give an example of each.

Answer:

1. Present the historical facts in chronological order. Example: Each chapter in a dissertation about the educator Horace Mann covers a discrete period in his life: childhood, adolescence, young adulthood, and maturing years.
2. Present the historical facts according to topics or themes. Example: In a study of the growth of private schooling in the U.S., each chapter of the dissertation covers one of the major presumed causes for its growth: religious movements, reduced funding of public education, parental concerns about school violence, and trends in student achievement.
3. Combine the chronological and thematic approaches. Example: Each chapter in a study of the development of private tutoring services in the U.S. is thematic, covering a particular type of service (test preparation services, tutoring services focused on remediation, and tutoring services focused on fostering giftedness or creativity); and the internal organization of the chapter is chronological (pre-1950, 1950-1979, 1980-1989, and 1990 to the present).

APPLICATION PROBLEMS

Problem 1

A researcher is carrying out historical research about the impact of computers on instruction in the public schools between 1970 and 1990. While the study is primarily qualitative in design, suggest one type of quantitative information that the researcher might wish to report concerning this research problem.

Sample Answer:

The researcher might want to report the number and proportion of students of various types who received computer instruction or otherwise had access to computers, for example, by grade, gender, or ability level.

Problem 2

A historian plans a research study on how early twentieth-century school officials and psychologists influenced each other with respect to the advocacy of intelligence testing.

a. What concepts does the historian need to define in doing this research, and why?

b. List one factor that will affect the generalizability of the historian's findings.

Sample Answer:

a. *School official*, *psychologist*, *intelligence test*, and *early twentieth-century* need to be defined, because these concepts identify the range of phenomena to be included in the historical search.

b. Factors that will affect the generalizability of the findings (any 1 OK):

(1) The number of years in the early twentieth century for which historical sources will be obtained

(2) The range of psychologists and school officials whose views will be studied

(3) The geographical locales (e.g., the entire U.S., individual states, and/or European countries) for which historical sources will be sought

Problem 3
Suppose that you are doing a historical study on the teaching of pseudosciences in U.S. public schools during the period 1870-1899. You find the following article in the April 15, 1891, issue of the *Sonoma Farmer*, a rural weekly newspaper published in California:

Wonders of the Science of Phrenology

> Local citizens attending the County Fair this week are being amazed by Professor Horatio Horton, a leading practitioner of the science of Phrenology. Professor Horton can make infallible analyses of the character and personality of any man or woman by feeling the bumps on the individual's head. Most persons overheard by your reporter agreed that the Professor's analyses of people out of the audience were uncanny.
>
> Your reporter interviewed the Professor in his dressing room and learned that he is a leader in the movement to teach Phrenology in the public schools. The Professor himself has taught the science to thousands of students in colleges and high schools throughout most of the civilized nations of the world. Phrenology is now a required subject in the secondary schools of France, Italy and several other European countries. Students in these countries usually devote a year to the study of this valuable science.
>
> The Professor strongly recommends that local citizens apply pressure to county officials to bring about inclusion of Phrenology in the local curriculum. He is available to give teachers a short course in the science and has also written several books and pamphlets that would be useful to students. Your reporter feels that adequate training in Phrenology should be provided in our schools as soon as possible. After all, your children are entitled to a modern education.

Conduct an internal criticism of this source by listing several reasons why the accuracy of the information in the article can be questioned.
<u>Sample Answer</u>:

1. The reporter had not himself witnessed the teaching of phrenology referred to by the professor.
2. The reporter did not interview a purposeful sample of audience members but simply reported what he overheard.
3. The professor has a financial interest in making phrenology appear important.
4. The professor appears to have exaggerated his expertise to impress the reporter.

Problem 4
Suppose you are doing a study about policies for the allocation of funds to teacher salaries, books and other instructional materials, plant maintenance and operation, and administrative costs in three rural elementary schools during the period 1900 to 1930. One of your main sources for this study is the account books for each school, in which the principals listed by date each expenditure as it occurred and entered a brief description. In studying this source, how would you record the information needed for your data analysis?
<u>Sample Answer</u>:

A document summary form (see Chapter 14 of the textbook, p. 463)) can be prepared for recording the specific types of information needed for your research. You should note on each copy of the form the source of the information (e.g., Washington Elementary School account book, school year 1900-1901). For each entry you could list the date, the dollar amount, and the category that each entry reflects (teacher salary, textbooks, etc.). You could also record anything about the entry worthy of special note (e.g., payment of a teacher in goods rather than money). When you have prepared all the forms, you could sort them in different ways to answer specific questions, such as, How similar were the spending patterns of different principals? What trends occurred in expenditures for educational materials from 1900 to 1930?

TEACHING ACTIVITIES

Activity 1

Locate a published account of a historical event that is relevant to education and that generated considerable controversy (e.g., a newspaper story about the first African-American student's entry to the University of Alabama during the Alabama governorship of George Wallace). Have students determine whether the source is a primary or secondary source, and ask them to carry out an internal criticism of the source.

Activity 2

Identify a researcher in your area who has carried out a historical research study relevant to education, and invite this person to be a guest presenter. Ask the researcher to describe why he carried out the study, any problems that arose in collecting and analyzing the data, the findings, and what he sees as the value of the research for present-day understanding of educational issues.

Activity 3

Identify a research article that describes a historical study in education. Have the students read the study as a homework assignment and then discuss in class the study's strengths and weaknesses. You might want to indicate the particular aspects of the study to which they should pay attention, e.g., the statement of the research problem, the quality of the sources used, and the appropriateness of the researcher's interpretations.

CHAPTER 17
EVALUATION RESEARCH

Note: The phrase in parentheses following the item number for both closed-form and open-form items, for example, "(obj. 3)", refers to the textbook chapter objective to which the item is keyed.

CLOSED-FORM ITEMS

1. (obj. 1) Match each of the following examples of educational evaluation with the purpose for conducting an evaluation that it illustrates.
   __ 1. The developer of an innovative approach to teaching English to migrant children is asked for documentation of the success rates with this approach.
   __ 2. A high school principal asks an evaluator to collect data on the costs and benefits of the school's efforts to reduce student dropout.
   __ 3. Opponents of site-based management cite negative evaluations of this approach in a public hearing.
   __ 4. A researcher collects data to prepare a position paper on the costs, benefits, and problems of various means to promote adult literacy.
   a. A guide to policy decisions in education
   b. A basis for advocacy for political action
   c. A component of the management of educational programs
   d. Use of research to design new programs meeting specified criteria of effectiveness

Answer: 1 = d 2 = c 3 = b 4 = a

2. (obj. 1) The main reason that educational evaluation has attracted increased interest is
   a. the unique nature of the research designs used in evaluation research.
   b. the important role evaluation plays in policy analysis and program management.
   c. increased public demands for educational accountability.
   d. development of standards for program evaluation.

Answer: b

3. (obj. 2) Evaluation research differs most from other types of educational research in its emphasis on
   a. producing generalizable findings.
   b. demonstrating statistically significant differences or relationships between variables.
   c. yielding data that will facilitate decisions about an educational phenomenon.
   d. obtaining the opinions of individuals about educational phenomena.

Answer: c

4. (obj. 3) The most important factor in working with stakeholders when evaluating an educational program is to
   a. identify all groups and individuals with a potential interest in the program.
   b. develop a plan that allows all interested stakeholders to collaborate in the evaluation.
   c. determine and provide for different types of stakeholders the amount of involvement that they desire.
   d. assign different stakeholder groups to participate in evaluation of those program aspects with which they are most familiar.

Answer: c

5. (obj. 3) An outside evaluator is hired to evaluate a school program that has special funding. A teacher tells him that he actually was brought in to collect data to justify the principal's plan to reassign several staff members. The evaluator's most appropriate action in this situation is to
   a. interview a variety of key individuals in the field setting to explore further the basis for the evaluation request.
   b. ask the teacher to provide evidence to support her claim.
   c. terminate the evaluation effort in the interests of ethical principles.
   d. ask the principal to reconfirm the previously stated purpose of the evaluation.

Answer: a

6. (obj. 4) The outcome of program delineation is
   a. analysis of the program to determine the components for which evaluation data are available.
   b. the selection of the specific model of evaluation to be used to evaluate the program.
   c. the determination of the effectiveness of the program that is evaluated.
   d. an identification of the most important characteristics of the program that is to be evaluated.

Answer: d

7. (obj. 4) An example of a program resource is the
   a. set of criteria used to hire staff for the program.
   b. objectives that program staff are committed to achieve.
   c. observed benefits of the program.
   d. staff needed to implement the program.

Answer: d

8. (obj. 4) Match each question with the component of an educational program that needs to be evaluated to answer it.
   __ 1. How will students have changed following completion of the program?
   __ 2. What are the obvious and hidden costs of the program?
   __ 3. What school improvements are anticipated from implementation of this program?
   __ 4. To what extent did teachers actually use the techniques recommended in the program?
   __ 5. Did the principal's supervision of the teachers help them improve their use of program techniques?
   a. Program goals
   b. Program resources
   c. Program procedures
   d. Program management
   e. Program outcomes

Answer: 1 = e 2 = b 3 = a 4 = c 5 = d

9. (obj. 5) Gathering a comprehensive list of evaluation questions from stakeholders is the ___________ phase in selecting questions for an evaluation study.
   a. program delineation
   b. divergent
   c. goal definition
   d. convergent

Answer: b

10. (obj. 5) The convergent phase of an evaluation involves
   a. the evaluators' reduction of all possible evaluation questions being considered to a manageable number.
   b. stakeholders' determination of the final foci for the evaluation.
   c. stakeholder's identification of additional questions to be considered for evaluation.
   d. The evaluators' development of an evaluation time line.

Answer: a

11. (obj. 6) An important question to consider in creating a design for a program evaluation is,
    a. Which stakeholders should conduct the evaluation?
    b. How can the evaluation be conducted so as not to incur any extra costs?
    c. Can an outside evaluator be found who has a major stake in the program?
    d. How much internal and external validity can be built into the research design?

Answer: d

12. (obj. 6) Probably the most common type of quantitative research design used in evaluation studies is the _____________ research design.
    a. correlational
    b. single-case
    c. experimental
    d. causal-comparative

Answer: c

13. (obj. 6) The *Standards for Evaluations of Educational Programs, Projects, and Materials* were developed to
    a. disseminate information about the exemplary quality of the standards currently used in evaluation research.
    b. reflect the varied political orientations of individuals working in the field of evaluation.
    c. assemble into one source several sets of standards that various research and educational organizations had thoroughly tested in the field.
    d. improve the professionalism of educational evaluation.

Answer: d

14. (obj. 6) The main focus of the *Standards for Evaluations of Educational Programs, Projects, and Materials* is
    a. optimizing the instrumental use of evaluation research.
    b. selecting the best strategy for assessment of educational personnel.
    c. assessing the feasibility of including an evaluation component in a program design.
    d. comparing individuals' test performance with the appropriate norms.

Answer: a

15. (obj. 7) The data collection and analysis phases in an evaluation study
    a. are typically much more extensive than in other types of research.
    b. involve primarily quantitative measures of a program's outcome.
    c. are similar to that in other types of research.
    d. are usually carried out by an external evaluator.

Answer: c

16. (obj. 8) The report of an evaluation study typically differs from the report of a research study in that the former
    a. is simpler, because stakeholders only want the "bottom line."
    b. is often prepared in different forms for different stakeholder groups.
    c. contains a more extensive review of the literature.
    d. places more emphasis on the generalizability of the findings.

Answer: b

17. (obj. 8) A meta-evaluation is
    a. similar to a pilot test of a research study.
    b. a summary of any weaknesses in the research design or execution.
    c. a description of the extent to which the evaluation findings can be generalized.
    d. an assessment by stakeholders of how well the evaluation was carried out.

Answer: b

18. (obj. 9) Evaluation research as a special application of educational research can be traced back most clearly to
    a. the growing interest in qualitative research.
    b. research and development (R&D) in industry and medicine.
    c. the need for public funds to support compulsory education.
    d. the individual intelligence testing movement.

Answer: d

19. (obj. 9) Goal-free evaluation
    a. helps alert developers to adverse effects of the program.
    b. typically is carried out in the early stages of program development.
    c. involves collecting primarily data that are unrelated to the program's stated goals.
    d. is a collaborative effort between the evaluator and key stakeholders.

Answer: a

20. (obj. 9) Goal-free evaluation differs from other approaches to evaluation mainly in that it
    a. requires the evaluator to be uninformed of the intended goals of the program.
    b. requires unique statistical techniques.
    c. is used to evaluate programs in the formative stage.
    d. is concerned primarily with negative program effects.

Answer: a

21. (obj. 9) The main rationale for the development of objectives-based evaluation was that
    a. information about individual differences in student aptitude is needed for selection decisions.
    b. students might perform poorly in school not because of a lack of innate ability but because of weaknesses in the curriculum.
    c. the merit of an educational program must be assessed in relation to the values and beliefs of different stakeholders.
    d. it is difficult to specify the most desired instructional outcomes in behavioral terms.

Answer: b

22. (obj. 9) The goal of a college education for all citizens who desire one is an example of a need stated as
    a. an expectation.
    b. a norm.
    c. a minimum.
    d. an ideal.

Answer: d

23. (obj. 9) Match each example of the findings of evaluation research listed below with the type of evaluation in the CIPP model that it illustrates.

__ 1. Recruitment programs should be implemented for doctoral students who have the desired characteristics to become special education faculty members.

__ 2. The recruitment program has succeeded in attracting more Hispanic graduate students in special education, but the proportion of African-American students recruited has not changed.

__ 3. Not enough special education students are receiving doctorates to fill available faculty positions in special education.

__ 4. Attendance at recruitment program meetings designed to attract more minority students into special education revealed that a lower proportion of African-Americans and Hispanics attend the programs than their representation in the general graduate student body at this university.

a. Context evaluation
b. Input evaluation
c. Process evaluation
d. Product evaluation

Answer: 1 = b 2 = d 3 = a 4 = c

24. (obj. 9) Match each of the procedures below with the type of educational evaluation that uses this procedure.

__ 1. The degree of congruence between program standards and actual program performance is determined.

__ 2. The relationship between program benefits and the resources needed to achieve those benefits is calculated.

__ 3. Data are collected about present needs, required resources and strategies, program operation, and goal achievement.

__ 4. Evaluators conduct research to discover the actual effects of the program in operation.

a. Goal-free evaluation
b. Context-Input-Process-Product evaluation
c. Needs assessment
d. Cost analysis

Answer: 1 = c 2 = d 3 = b 4 = a

25. (obj. 10) Which of the following is a characteristic of responsive evaluation?

a. It makes extensive use of subjective inquiry.
b. It focuses on objective response patterns.
c. It refers to psychological theories of development.
d. A research design is first developed and the evaluation responds to the demands of that design.

Answer: a

26. (obj. 10) A desirable requirement for a graduate student wishing to use responsive evaluation as a model for an evaluation study for a dissertation is that the student should

a. be experienced in carrying out a variety of research designs.
b. work with an experienced team of evaluators on a joint project.
c. study a stratified sample of stakeholders.
d. be a stakeholder in the program to be evaluated.

Answer: b

27. (obj. 10) Which of these evaluation models involves independent development of pro and con arguments concerning program-related issues?
    a. The Context-Input-Process-Product model
    b. Discrepancy evaluation
    c. Adversary evaluation
    d. Goal-free evaluation

Answer: c

28. (obj. 10) An important difference between adversary evaluation and judicial evaluation is that the former
    a. involves a public hearing in which witnesses testify before a panel that makes recommendations..
    b. is based on the use of legal procedures to review program characteristics.
    c. involves a debate between two evaluation teams, with victory or persuasion as the desired outcome.
    d. has been widely used in educational research.

Answer: c

29. (obj. 10) Unlike other qualitative models of evaluation, educational connoisseurship and criticism is unique in that
    a. the questions that motivate the evaluation are set by the evaluator alone.
    b. it combines both qualitative and quantitative research methods.
    c. the evaluative orientation toward the phenomena being studied is based on critical theory.
    d. it is based largely on the research tradition of cognitive anthropology.

Answer: a

30. (obj. 10) Empowerment evaluation differs most from other qualitative models of evaluation primarily in
    a. the prominent role of stakeholders in the evaluation design.
    b. the use of the latest technological tools to facilitate data collection and analysis.
    c. its focus on establishing the mission or vision of the community as a basis for program improvement.
    d. all of the above.

Answer: d

31. (objs. 9-10) Responsive evaluation models and objectives-based evaluation models differ on several important characteristics. Place an *R* in front of the characteristics of responsive evaluation and an *0* in front of the characteristics of objectives-based evaluation in the following list.
    __ a. Uses a formal rather than an informal approach.
    __ b. Focuses on identifying concerns and issues.
    __ c. Is modeled after the procedures of experimental psychology.
    __ d. Employs careful preplanning of the evaluation design.
    __ **e. Involves purposeful sampling of stakeholders.**

Answer: a = O b = R c = O d = O e = R

32 (obj. 11) A decision by an educational research and development (R&D) specialist to abort further development of an educational program would most likely be made at the _______________ stage of the R&D cycle.
    a. instructional analysis
    b. formative evaluation
    c. instructional revision
    d. summative evaluation

Answer: b

33. (obj. 11) Formative evaluation
  a. involves collecting data about an educational program while it is still under development in order to improve it.
  b. enables the researcher to generalize the findings to other programs and samples.
  c. involves testing research hypotheses about a program prior to submitting it to summative evaluation.
  d. is conducted by using primarily quantitative research methods.

Answer: a

34. (obj. 11) The three-level process of formative evaluation described in the text
  a. corresponds closely to the evaluation procedures used by major textbook publishers.
  b. moves progressively from a focus on qualitative methods to a focus on quantitative methods of evaluation.
  c. moves progressively from a focus on quantitative methods to a focus on qualitative methods of evaluation.
  d. involves a review of the program by stakeholders at each stage.

Answer: b

35. (obj. 11) In contrast to formative evaluation, summative evaluation
  a. involves a critical review of each program component by key stakeholders.
  b. is carried out by an evaluator working alone.
  c. is considered an integral part of the instructional design process.
  d. is likely to involve quantitative research methods.

Answer: d

36. (obj. 11) An important purpose of summative evaluation is to
  a. help developers determine what the goals of a program should be.
  b. determine how successful the program is under normal operating conditions.
  c. discover the goals of a program by observing the program while it is being developed.
  d. identify unintended outcomes for which the program has application.

Answer: b

37. (obj. 12) A common criticism of behavioral objectives is that they tend to
  a. omit the situational context in which the behavior is to be performed.
  b. not give stakeholders an adequate sense of what those who succeed as a result of the program will be able to do.
  c. not provide much help in designing test items to evaluate program effectiveness.
  d. reduce education to a matter of teaching only that which is easily measured.

Answer: d

38. (obj. 12) Behavioral objectives are particularly helpful in
  a. determining the level of resources needed to develop an instructional program.
  b. determining the causes of students' failure to learn from an instructional program.
  c. designing test items to assess students' capabilities before and after experiencing an instructional program.
  d. one-on one testing of hypotheses derived from instructional design theory.

Answer: c

39. (obj. 13) Educational research and development holds great promise for improving education primarily because it
    a. requires collaboration between a variety of stakeholder groups in the evaluation.
    b. requires the use of behavioral objectives to evaluate student learning.
    c. provides a great deal of evaluation information for a relatively low cost.
    d. involves a close connection between systematic program evaluation and program development.

Answer: d

40. (obj. 13) A good way for a graduate student to design an educational research and development project to make it more manageable to conduct is to
    a. serve as both the developer and the evaluator for the project.
    b. compare the effectiveness of two alternate versions of the developed program.
    c. end the dissertation study after the preliminary field test stage.
    d. use only qualitative methods of evaluation.

Answer: c

OPEN-FORM ITEMS

1. (obj. 1) Describe two purposes for which educational evaluation studies are carried out.

Answer (any 2 OK):
1. To determine the worth or merit of particular educational methods, materials, programs, organizations, or individuals
2. To provide information needed to guide educational policy making
3. To provide a basis to support or oppose particular political decisions
4. To assist in the management of educational programs

2. (obj. 1) The chapter lists eight steps in program evaluation, beginning with clarifying the reasons for an evaluation. List three of the other steps of a program evaluation.

Answer (any 3 OK):
1. Selecting an evaluation model
2. Identifying stakeholders
3. Deciding what is to be evaluated
4. Identifying evaluation questions
5. Developing an evaluation design and time line
6. Collecting and analyzing evaluation data
7. Reporting evaluation results

3. (obj. 2) Briefly state one of the differences between educational evaluation and educational research.

Answer (any 1 OK):
1. Evaluation usually is designed to aid a local decision, whereas research is concerned with producing knowledge.
2. Evaluation usually is less generalizable, because it deals with a specific purpose or a limited question.
3. Evaluation produces judgments of value, whereas research produces descriptive or theoretical knowledge.

4. (obj. 3) If evaluators are asked to conduct an evaluation, what procedure should they use to clarify the reasons for doing the evaluation?

Answer:

The usual procedure is to interview a variety of key individuals involved in the program to be evaluated in order to obtain an overall picture of the reasons, including any covert or unethical reasons, that an evaluation is desired.

5. (obj. 3) (a) Define the term *stakeholder* as used in evaluation research, and (b) give two reasons why stakeholders need to be identified as part of an evaluation study.

Answer:

a. A stakeholder is anyone involved in the program being evaluated and/or anyone who may be affected by the results.

b. Reasons for identifying stakeholders

(1) Stakeholders can help the evaluator clarify the reasons for doing the evaluation; the questions that should guide the evaluation; and the best way to design the research, interpret the findings, and report the results.

(2) If some stakeholders are ignored, they can sabotage the evaluation or try to discredit the results.

6. (obj. 4) List two of the procedures that should be followed in determining which aspects of the overall program should be evaluated.

Answer (any 2 OK):

1. Program delineation, i.e., describing the most important characteristics or components of the program to be evaluated
2. Deciding which program components will be evaluated
3. Specifying the program goals
4. Identifying program resources
5. Identifying program procedures
6. Describing the program's management system
7. Identifying program outcomes

7. (obj. 4) (a) Identify the five key components of a program to be evaluated that the chapter describes, and (b) explain what one of them involves.

Answer:

a.

(1) Program goals
(2) Program resources
(3) Program procedures
(4) Program management
(5) Program outcomes

b. (any 1 OK):

(1) A program goal is the purpose, effect, or end point that the program developer is trying to achieve.

(2) Program resources are the personnel, equipment, space, and other cost items needed to implement the program.

(3) Program procedures are the techniques, strategies, and other processes used in conjunction with program resources to achieve program goals.

(4) Program management involves the system used to monitor the effectiveness of program resources and procedures in achieving program goals, and may include efforts by practitioners to monitor their own efforts.

(5) Program outcomes are the results that the program is intended to achieve, as well as unintended results of the program.

8. (obj. 5) What is the difference between the divergent phase and the convergent phase in selecting questions for an evaluation study?

Answer:

In the divergent phase, the evaluator gathers a comprehensive list of questions from all stakeholders and interested parties, whereas in the convergent phase the evaluator reduces the list to a manageable set of the most important questions.

9. (obj. 6) Briefly describe two of the questions that should be considered in developing an evaluation design.
Answer (any 2 OK):
1. Should the evaluation be qualitatively or quantitatively oriented?
2. Should an internal or external evaluator conduct the evaluation?
3. How much internal and external validity should be built into the design?
4. How can potentially negative effects of the evaluation be minimized?
5. Can the evaluation be completed in the time available?

10. (obj. 6) What is one negative effect that can occur from the evaluation of an educational program?
Answer (any 1 OK):
1. Personnel working in the program may resent the evaluator or feel threatened by the evaluation.
2. A good program can be destroyed by a poorly conducted, negative evaluation.
3. Evaluation activities use resources that thus are not directly available to enhance the program.

11. (obj. 6) *The Standards for Evaluations of Educational Programs, Projects, and Materials* developed four major criteria for good evaluation studies: utility, feasibility, propriety, and accuracy. Describe one specific standard for each of these broad criteria.
Answer:
See the list of Standards on pp. 570-571 of the chapter; any one item from each part of the list is acceptable.

12. (obj. 7) Describe one type of data-collection method that might be useful in the evaluation of an instructional program.
Answer (any 1 OK):
1. A questionnaire to assess various stakeholders' perceptions of the program
2. Obtaining student achievement test scores before and after they receive instruction based on the program
3. Interviews of teachers who have taught the instructional program
4. A questionnaire to assess students' likes and dislikes of the program

13. (obj. 8) Describe two desirable features of a dissertation involving educational evaluation.
Answer (any 2 OK):
1. **Several forms of the report may be prepared for different stakeholder groups.**
2. **The report includes a discussion of how all evaluation findings were used.**
3. **The larger significance of the study (e.g., its theoretical implications or replication of previous findings) is discussed.**
4. **The application of the particular model used in the evaluation is discussed.**
5. **A meta-evaluation of the evaluation is provided.**

14. (obj. 8) (a) Define meta-evaluation; (b) explain what a meta-evaluation typically includes; and (c) indicate whether meta-evaluation is necessary only in evaluation research, only in other types of educational research, or in both evaluation research and other types of research.
Answer:
a. A meta-evaluation is an evaluation of an evaluation study or a research study.
b. It typically includes a discussion of the limitations and weaknesses in the study that could affect the validity of the results.
c. Meta-evaluation is necessary in both evaluation research and other types of research.

15. (obj. 9) What is the main difference between the evaluation of individuals and objectives-based evaluation?
Answer:
The evaluation of individuals involves evaluating the individual against a standard and the study of individual differences, whereas objectives-based evaluation involves evaluating a program in terms of its success in promoting the achievement of desired program objectives by program users.

16. (obj. 9) Name the three components of a behavioral objective.

Answer:

1. A statement of the program objective as an observable, behavioral outcome
2. Criteria for judging successful performance of the behavior
3. The situational context (or "givens") within which the behavior is to be evaluated

17. (obj. 9) Name two possible problems associated with objectives-based evaluation.

Answer (any 2 OK):

1. Critics argue that it reduces education to a matter of teaching only that which can be stated and measured in the language of behavioral objectives.
2. Bias can be introduced in selecting the particular objectives to measure.
3. This approach does not offer much guidance if one wishes to understand why particular objectives are considered worthwhile or why certain stakeholders agree or disagree about the worth of certain objectives.
4. The politics of evaluation is not given much attention in this approach.
5. The evaluation process itself might hamper the very performance that is being assessed.

18. (obj. 9) What is meant by goal-free evaluation?

Answer:

Evaluation in which the evaluator does not know, or ignores, the goals of the program being evaluated. Thus, the evaluator is more likely to investigate both intended and unintended outcomes of the program.

19. (obj. 9) State one problem that can arise in doing a needs assessment.

Answer (any 1 OK):

1. Unless the concept of need is defined the same way by everyone involved in the needs assessment, confusion or disagreement may arise.
2. Many needs assessments do not make clear how urgent or optional are the desired states that are being determined.
3. The values that underlie various needs are often not clearly articulated.
4. Important individual differences in stated needs might be obscured by traditional methods of reporting group trends in a needs assessment.

20. (obj. 9) Briefly describe the four types of educational evaluation that are incorporated in the CIPP evaluation model.

Answer:

1. Context evaluation involves identification of the problems and needs in a specific educational setting and development of program objectives that will alleviate the needs.
2. Input evaluation involves identification of the resources and strategies needed to achieve the program objectives.
3. Process evaluation involves design of an evaluation system and collection of day-to-day evaluation data as the program is put into operation (similar to formative evaluation).
4. Product evaluation involves determination of the extent to which the program goals have been achieved (similar to summative evaluation).

21. (obj. 9) What is the main purpose of conducting a formative evaluation of an educational program?

Answer:

To obtain information that can be used to revise or modify the program to make it more effective, or to make a decision to abort further development

22. (obj. 10) What is the main way in which qualitative approaches to evaluation differ from quantitative approaches?

Answer:

Qualitative approaches to evaluation are not based on the assumption that objective criteria exist for judging the worth of an educational program. Instead they assume that worth depends on the values and perspectives of whoever does the judging.

23. (obj. 10) Describe the four stages of adversary evaluation.

Answer:

1. Generating a broad range of issues concerning the program by surveying various stakeholders
2. Reducing the issues to a manageable number
3. Forming two opposing evaluation teams, one of which prepares an argument in favor of the program on each issue and the other of which prepares an argument opposed to the program on each issue
4. Conducting prehearing sessions and a formal hearing in which the adversarial teams present their cases before individuals who must make a decision about the program

24. (obj. 10) Describe one shortcoming of adversary evaluation.

Answer (any 1 OK):

1. **The results can be biased if one of the evaluation teams is more skilled in argumentation than the other.**
2. By its nature, it promotes a combative, "innocent versus guilty" approach to program evaluation and thus may contribute to alienation among different types of stakeholders.
3. It requires a great deal of time and a large number of people, and thus is expensive.

25. (obj. 10) In the qualitative evaluation model known as educational connoisseurship and criticism, describe (a) what connoisseurship involves and (b) what criticism involves.

Answer:

a. Educational connoisseurship involves appreciating (in the sense of becoming aware of) the qualities of an educational program and their meaning.
b. Educational criticism involves describing and evaluating that which has been appreciated.

26. (obj. 11)

a. Describe the role that evaluation plays in educational research and development.
b. Describe the specific purpose of (1) formative evaluation and (2) summative evaluation in educational research and development.

Answer:

a. After a program has been developed, it undergoes a progressively more stringent series of field testing and revision cycles in which its effectiveness is evaluated in relation to whether learners exposed to the program can achieve its prespecified performance objectives.
b. (1) Formative evaluation is carried out by the program developers while the program is still under development in order to improve its effectiveness.
   (2) Summative evaluation is carried out by others after the program has completed development in order to determine how worthwhile the program is, especially in comparison with other alternatives.

27. (obj. 11) Explain one step of the educational research and development cycle that typically is performed before the step of writing performance objectives.

Answer (any 1 OK):

1. Identifying instructional goals for the R&D program or product to be developed, often including needs assessment
2. Conducting an instructional analysis to identify the specific skills, procedures, and learning tasks involved in reaching the goals of instruction
3. Analyzing learners' entry-level skills and attitudes, the characteristics of the instructional setting, and the characteristics of the settings in which the new knowledge and skills will be used

28. (obj. 11) Describe when (a) formative evaluation and (b) summative evaluation occurs in the educational research and development process.

Answer:

a. Program developers may conduct formative evaluation during any or all of the first seven steps of the 10-step R&D cycle as a basis for revision of the program or product, or to determine whether further development should be aborted.
b. After program development is complete, outside evaluators conduct summative evaluation to determine how worthwhile the final R&D program or product is, usually in comparision to other competing programs.

29. (obj. 11) Describe the three levels of formative evaluation that Dick, Carey, and Carey recommend.

Answer:

1. Prototype materials are tried out one-on-one by one evaluator working with one learner.
2. A small group of six to eight students tries out the materials.
3. A field trial is conducted with a whole class of learners.

30. (obj. 11) Give two reasons why an educational program needs to be tested in a field setting that is similar to the context in which it ultimately will be used before it is released for dissemination.

Answer:

1. The external validity of the research findings for the program will be higher in a field setting, that is, one can generalize the results more safely to other, similar settings.
2. Often problems will occur in the field that would not occur in more controlled research situations. Thus a test in the field is necessary to provide valid data about the program's effectiveness.

31. (obj. 12) State one benefit of specifying performance objectives in developing an educational program.

Answer (any 1 OK):

1. Performance objectives provide a way to communicate clearly to stakeholders the goals of the instructional program.
2. Performance objectives can be presented in complete detail or can be summarized in more general terms depending on the needs and interests of different types of stakeholders.
3. Performance objectives provide a solid basis for the precise planning of the test items, instructional materials, and instructional delivery system to be developed for the program.
4. Performance objectives can serve as the ultimate criterion for the effectiveness of the program, allowing evaluators to determine whether and how well the program works.

32. (obj. 13) Describe one advantage and one disadvantage of doing an educational research and development (R&D) project for a thesis or dissertation study.

Answer (any 1 from each set OK):

Advantages

1. A good educational R&D project not only contributes to educational research, but it also can lead directly to improvements in educational practice through the application of the program that was developed.
2. An educational R&D project gives the researcher the opportunity to learn more about development, as well as about research.
3. An educational R&D project provides an opportunity to compare the effectiveness of two or more alternative instructional programs in operation.

Disadvantages

1. Taking a program though all the stages of the R&D cycle can be very time-consuming.
2. Educational R&D projects usually require funds and staff beyond the capability of most graduate students.
3. To conduct a successful educational R&D project the researcher must have not only an adequate level of research skills, but also adequate development skills.

33. (obj. 13) Name one goal that would make it worthwhile for a student to spend the considerable time and effort required to carry out a complete R&D project for her thesis or dissertation study.

Answer (any 1 OK):

1. The student wants to make a contribution that will lead to an immediate tangible improvement in educational practice.
2. The student wants to identify and recommend other R&D efforts that might be pursued by others in the future to improve some aspect of practice.
3. The student wants to develop the full range of skills needed for becoming an educational R&D professional.

APPLICATION PROBLEMS

Problem 1

You have been asked by an elementary school principal to conduct an evaluation of the school's three-year-old study skills program. When you ask the principal what aspects of the program he wants to have evaluated, he replies, "I don't know. What do you usually evaluate?" How might you respond to his question?

Sample Answer:

You might point out that most school instructional programs have various components (e.g., for staff development, parent involvement, instructional materials, peer tutoring, and keeping records on student progress). Each component can be evaluated with respect to one or more aspects: its goals, resources, procedures, management, and outcomes. The principal needs to explain what the most important characteristics of the study skills program are and make a tentative decision about which components and aspects of the program need to be evaluated. With that information, you can plan the scope of the effort and you have a place to start. Without it, you may come up with a plan that will not satisfy the principal or other stakeholders.

Problem 2
A friend of yours, who is the director of a new program to aid migrant students and their families in the region, is preparing an annual budget. She asks you, as someone who has conducted educational evaluations, to help her decide how much of the program budget, if any, should be spent on program evaluation. She realizes that the less spent on evaluation, the more funds that will be available for direct program operations. What arguments could you present in favor of allocating at least 10 percent of the program budget for program evaluation?
Sample Answer:

1. As the director she will need to make decisions continuously about the program (e.g., whether to reallocate resources, change timelines, or redesign operating procedures). Evaluation can provide data that will improve these decisions.
2. The director is probably accountable to others (e.g., clients and an executive board) for program results. Evaluation can give the director more valid data about program results than she would have if she relied exclusively on her own or others' subjective impressions.
3. Having solid information about the program's effectiveness could be a big help in obtaining additional money for the program from funding sources, such as foundation or government grants.

Problem 3
A curriculum developer plans to conduct a preliminary field test of a set of self-instructional materials designed to improve the writing skills of college freshmen. List questions that the developer might want to have answered about the materials' effectiveness.
Sample Answer:

1. To what extent do the materials achieve specific performance objectives involving students' writing skills?
2. Are the materials easy for instructors and students to understand?
3. Do the materials require more classroom time than is likely to be available in a typical college writing course?
4. How do typical college instructors feel about the worth of the materials, and what recommendations do they have for improving them?
5. How do college students judge the worth of the materials, and what recommendations do they have for improving them?

Problem 4
An instructional program has one stated goal--to train high school students who are nonswimmers to swim freestyle two lengths of an Olympic-size pool in under four minutes. You have been asked to evaluate the program, and you believe a goal-free evaluation is the most appropriate evaluation model. How would you approach the task of evaluation?
Sample Answer:

You would not ask for any further details about the program's goal. You would disregard the goal in designing the evaluation and focus instead on the program's actual effects. These effects might include changes in the pool's regular schedule as a result of the new program; other students' expressions of acceptance, avoidance, or ridicule of the students in the program; the average distance that the students swim and their average swim time after the program is completed; and the students' reported fear of swimming, even though they might have achieved proficiency.

TEACHING ACTIVITIES

Activity 1

Assign a research article that reports the evaluation of an educational program. Ask students to write a brief assignment in which they summarize the researcher's decisions and actions in relation to each step in the evaluation process as described in the textbook.

Activity 2

Distribute the 30 standards from the *Standards for Evaluations of Educational Programs, Projects, and Materials* among your students. Ask students to report in class how well the article used for Activity 1 above met each of the standards, and what changes, if any, could have improved the evaluation study or its reporting.

Activity 3

Bring to class a description of a real or hypothetical educational program (e.g., a textbook, videotape, or computer game) that a development team wants to develop, and have students examine it. Have students use figure 17.2 on page 590 in the text (the 10-step R&D cycle) to plan the development of the program. If possible, have them carry out at least one specific activity (e.g., develop an actual instructional goal, identify one characteristic of the learners, write one performance objective, etc.) for each step.

CHAPTER 18
ACTION RESEARCH

Note: The phrase in parentheses following the item number for both closed-form and open-form items, for example, "(obj. 3)", refers to the textbook chapter objective to which the item is keyed.

CLOSED-FORM ITEMS

1. (obj. 1) A key aspect which differentiates action research from other forms of research in education is its focus on
   a. helping students achieve intended learning objectives.
   b. promoting collaboration among researchers.
   c. developing practitioner's research skills.
   d. collecting and analyzing local data to improve practice.

Answer: d

2. (obj. 1) Action research is most often reported
   a. through informal sharing with colleagues.
   b. in academic journals.
   c. on the websites of action research networks.
   d. in dissertations and theses.

Answer: a

3. (obj. 2) The development of networks of practitioners engaged in action research primarily serves the __________ purpose of action research.
   a. personal
   b. professional
   c. practical
   d. political

Answer: b

4. (obj. 2) Action research done for personal purposes is primarily intended to
   a. provide full participation for all individuals who are affected by the research.
   b. produce more variety in practitioner's work styles.
   c. promote practitioners' self-knowledge and fulfillment.
   d. promote increased collaboration among practitioners.

Answer: c

5. (obj. 3) Action research is cyclical primarily in the sense that in action research it is
   a. usually desirable to collect more data to determine the effects of one's actions.
   b. usually desirable to repeat certain research stages after others' review of one's research.
   c. common for the researcher to conclude the research by initiating a new action.
   d. common for the researcher to return to an earlier stage as the research progresses.

Answer: d

6. (obj. 3) The stage of action research that involves _____________ typically initiates a new cycle of action research.
   a. selecting a focus
   b. analyzing and interpreting data
   c. reflecting
   d. continuing or modifying one's actions

Answer: d

7. (obj. 4) Action research perhaps differs most from other forms of research in its emphasis on ____________ as an important part of the research cycle.
   a. data collection
   b. reflection
   c. collaboration
   d. improvement of practice.

Answer: b

8. (obj. 4) Action research contributes uniquely to professional practice in its use of ______________ as a basis for action.
   a. trial and error
   b. ideas from colleagues
   c. collection and analysis of data
   d. strategies from the research literature

Answer: c

9. (obj. 4) Action research, unlike typical professional practice, seeks to improve practice primarily by
   a. systematically collecting and analyzing data about practice.
   b. focusing on qualitative rather than quantitative indicators of best practice.
   c. embracing an overt agenda of social change.
   d. trying out strategies practitioners learn through professional development experiences.

Answer: a

10. (obj. 5) An action researcher's autobiographical narrative contributes primarily to the _____________ stage of the research.
   a. focus-selection
   b. data-collection
   c. action-taking
   d. reflection

Answer: d

11. (obj. 5) Reflection as a part of action research is best carried out
   a. after the action stage.
   b. before the action stage.
   c. during the action stage.
   d. all of the above.

Answer: a

12. (obj. 6) The emergent nature of action research is probably most prevalent during the ____________ stage of the research.
    a. selecting a focus
    b. taking action
    c. reflection
    d. continuing/modifying action

Answer: d

13. (obj. 6) Sonata-form case writing with sidenotes is designed to ____________________ in the reporting of action research.
    a. give practitioners a stronger voice
    b. give research collaborators a stronger voice
    c. give practitioners and research collaborators an equal yet distinct voice
    d. give clients a stronger voice

Answer: c

14. (obj. 6) Action research is most likely to have a definite beginning and end when it
    a. is carried out for a dissertation or course assignment.
    b. is conducted for practical purposes.
    c. involves collaboration with the research participants.
    d. is carried out by practitioners as a part of their everyday work.

Answer: a

15. (obj. 7) The concept of validity when applied to action research corresponds to the extent to which
    a. other practitioners adopt the actions that were tested through action research.
    b. one's research participants respond positively to the actions that were implemented.
    c. the research promotes more humane and just educational practice.
    d. the researcher provides evidence to demonstrate the credibility and trustworthiness of the study's findings.

Answer: d

16. (obj. 7) When the action researcher engages in reflective dialogue with other practitioner researchers in the formation and review of his research findings and interpretations, this provides evidence of an action research project's __________ validity.
    a. democratic
    b. catalytic
    c. dialogic
    d. process

Answer: c

17. (obj. 8) Probably the most accurate determination of what a practitioner actually does in practice is based on
    a. observations made by colleagues.
    b. the practitioner's own reflections.
    c. observations made by academic research experts.
    d. data collected from the practitioner's clients.

Answer: a

18. (obj. 8) In Argyris and Schön's theoretical framework, an individual's theory-in-action corresponds to
    a. his beliefs about how he deals with problems of practice.
    b. his actual behavior in practice.
    c. the impact of his reflections on his actions.
    d. the process by which he reduces discrepancies between his beliefs and his actions.

Answer: b

19. (obj. 9) Action researchers face ethical issues beyond those faced by other researchers primarily because
    a. action research is cyclical in nature.
    b. action researchers must reconcile their role of researcher with their traditional role of serving clients.
    c. action research has an explicitly personal purpose.
    d. action researchers engage in personal reflection.

Answer: b

20. (obj. 9) According to Zeni, the unique ethical issues in action research tend to involve
    a. the presentation or publication of the research findings.
    b. the relationships between practitioners and academics.
    c. the determination of the action researcher's espoused theory.
    d. efforts to establish the outcome validity of the research.

Answer: a

OPEN-FORM ITEMS

1. (obj. 1) Describe the main difference between the approach of action research and typical professional practice to improvement of practice.

Answer:

Action research includes a process of systematic data collection and analysis as a means to improve practice.

2. (obj. 1). The text lists 10 differences between formal research and action research. Describe three of these differences.

Answer (any 3 OK):

1. Extensive training is needed for formal research, whereas practitioners can carry out action research on their own or with some consultation.
2. The purpose of formal research is generalizable knowledge, whereas the goal of action research is knowledge that applies to the local situation.
3. The focus of formal research is identified through a review of previous research, whereas action research addresses current problems or goals of practice.
4. In formal research an extensive literature review based on primary sources is the basis for research, but in action research the literature review is more cursory and based on secondary sources.
5. Sampling in formal research is random or representative, whereas in action research the research sample is the practitioner's clients.
6. The research design in formal research involves rigorous control and a long time frame, whereas action research uses more casual procedures that may change during the study, and a short time frame.
7. Measurement procedures in formal research involve evaluated and pretested measures, whereas action research uses convenient measures or standardized tests.
8. Data analysis in formal research involves use of statistical tests or in-depth qualitative research analytic techniques, whereas action research focuses on practical significance and the presentation of raw data or graphs.
9. Formal research is typically reported in a published report, journal article, or professional conference, whereas action research usually involves informal sharing with colleagues, a brief report, presentations at local conferences, or publication through online networks.
10. Application of the results in the former places emphasis on theoretical implications and contributions to general knowledge about teaching and learning, whereas the latter emphasizes practical significance and improved practice in a specific learning situation.

3. (obj. 2) Describe briefly the central focus of action research with a primarily (a) personal purpose, (b) professional purpose, and (c) political purpose.

Answer:

a. Efforts to improve the researcher's own day-to-day work practice
b. Efforts to extend one's research beyond one's own practice in order to study and influence directly the social and institutional contexts in which one works
c. Efforts to bring about fundamental social change toward the goal of greater social justice for all

4. (obj. 2) Name the three main purposes for which action research is usually carried out, and give an example of a typical action that reflects each purpose.

1. Personal purposes, e.g., to develop a greater understanding of individual students' thoughts and actions; to develop a deeper understanding of teachers' experiences with particular educational innovations; to provide teachers an opportunity for personal examination and generation of theory; to produce heightened self awareness in practitioners; to examine the impact of the research process on practitioners; to conduct research as an individual learning process that values experiential knowledge
2. Professional purposes, e.g., to engage in action research as a form of staff development; to seek to legitimize practitioners' role as producers of knowledge and contributors to the professional knowledge base; or to develop networks of action research practitioners to promote their colleagueship and professionalism
3. Political purposes, e.g., to seek to make one's own teaching practices more humane and just; to provide full participation in the research process of all those who are affected by it; to embrace an overt agenda of social change toward economic and social justice

5. (obj. 3) Explain one reason that action research is often cyclical in nature.

Answer (any 1 OK):

1. Researchers may not always carry out the steps of action research in the same order and thus may still have work to do on certain steps before their research is complete.
2. Researchers may need to return to an earlier step for additional work as their research progresses.
3. Researchers may decide to continue going through some or all of the steps again rather than bringing the research to an end.

6. (obj. 4) Describe one strategy that an action researcher might use to increase the applicability of her action research findings to other educational settings, and how that strategy could help increase the applicability of the findings to other settings.

Answer (any 1 OK):

1. Study typical cases in her action research, so that they are similar to cases that would be found in other settings.
2. Select a random sample for her research study, so that her sample will be representative of the larger population of cases to be found in other settings.
3. Include descriptive quantitative statistics in the research findings, so that readers can compare the characteristics of their setting with those of the study.
4. Give a rich, thick description of her qualitative research findings, so that readers can more fully compare their setting with the setting of the action research study.

7. (obj. 4) Chapter 1 of the textbook describes four types of knowledge that research contributes to education: (1) description, (2) prediction, (3) improvement, and (4) explanation. Using the examples of action research in Chapter 18 or obtained from your own reading or experience, identify a claim that an action researcher made involving one of these types of knowledge based on having collected and analyzed data to support his findings that would otherwise have been difficult to make.

Answer (any 1 OK):

1. Description: In the action research conducted by Thomas Scott and Michael O'Sullivan (described in Chapter 18 on pp. 603-604) the authors describe questionnaire results on the percentage of students reporting use of the Internet, use of the Internet specifically as a research tool to collect information for assignments, and use of search engines and online databases. The authors also summarize qualitative data contrasting with the quantitative finding that most students evaluated their own Internet search skills as excellent or good.
2. Prediction: A teacher education student we know of conducted action research for her final masters paper involving efforts to predict which parents of students at her school could be counted on as volunteers in classrooms or for school activities. While parents' income, age, or number of children in school did not correlate with the number of hours the parent completed as a volunteer, three items on a checklist administered to parents at the start of the school year positively predicted parent volunteering: "I've always liked schools and being in school" "I think teachers are heroes and deserve all the help they can get from community members," and "I'm glad my child attends this school."
3. Improvement: In the action research study conducted by James Lytle, a new school superintendent (described in Chapter 18 on pp. 602-603), the author describes his efforts to involve the district's principals in shadowing students, collecting varied forms of data, and reporting and sharing their findings with other principals "as a way of deepening our shared understanding of why students behave and perform as they do." Lytle noted discernible improvements in student performance over the three-year period of his action research project, and also made it clear that his efforts to foster other administrator's participation in data collection involved actions to transform district leadership.
4. Explanation: In the action research study conducted by Ellen Agosta, Janet Graetz, and Margo Mastropieri (described in Chapter 18 on p. 610) the authors describe their study of teacher-researcher partnerships to improve the social behavior of a 6-year-old boy with autism. The intervention utilized was tested through single-case experimental research and was found to be successful in reducing instances of the child's screaming and increasing instances of his sitting quietly during group class activities.

8. (obj. 5) Summarize three suggestions for keeping an action research journal as a basis for reflection.
Answer:
(Note: See Table 18.2 on p. 605; any three of the 11 points in the table are an acceptable response.)

9. (obj. 5) Describe one key component of the action research cycle that is rarely emphasized in reports of formal research.
Answer:
Action research typically involves reflection, in which practitioners step back from practice to ponder and share ideas about the meaning, value, and impact of their practice.

10. (obj. 6) Describe the six steps of action research in Glanz's model.
Answer:
1. Select a focus.
2. Collect data.
3. Analyze and interpret the data.
4. Take action.
5. Reflect.
6. Continue or modify action.

11. (obj. 6) (a) Describe a final step of action research that is not included in Glanz's model but is of great importance to foster the impact and growth of action research.
Answer:
Reporting the action research is an important final step of action research.

12. (obj. 6) Describe one form in which action research might be reported.
Answer (any 1 OK:
1. Informal sharing with colleagues
2. A presentation to the local community or at professional meetings
3. Publication in an online action research journal
4. Publication as an article in a hard-copy refereed journal

13. (obj. 7) Match each of the following criteria for determining the validity of action research with the example of the evidence that best demonstrates that validity criterion.
__ 1. Catalytic validity
__ 2. Process validity
__ 3. Outcome validity
__ 4. Democratic validity
__ 5. Dialogic validity
a. Actions occur that lead to a resolution of the problem under study or to the completion of a research cycle that results in action.
b. The processes used in different phases of the research are adequate to confirm the findings.
c. All parties with a stake in the problem being investigated participate actively in the action research process.
d. Participants are energized and open to transforming their view of reality in relation to practice.
e. The action researcher shares her findings and interpretations with peers to consider alternative explanations.

Answer:
1 = d 2 = b 3 = a 4 = c 5 = e

14. (obj. 8) Explain the meaning of and give an example of (a) espoused theory and (b) theory-in-action; and (c) explain the relevance of these theories to practitioners' attempts to improve their practice.

Answer:

a. An individual's espoused theory involves her beliefs about how she typically deals with specific problems of practice, e.g., her stated philosophy of effective classroom management practice at the start of a school year.
b. An individual's theory-in-action involves what the individual actually does in practice, e.g., the rewards and reprimands she metes out to specific students in the first weeks of the school year.
c. Action research enables practitioners to pinpoint, and take steps to reduce, discrepancies between their espoused theories and their theories-in-action in relation to specific aspects of their practice, either by bringing their actions into better agreement with their espoused beliefs or by clarifying what they are truly committed to and then initiating actions more consistent with those commitments.

15. (obj. 8) Name one of the ways in which practitioners can use action research to reduce the discrepancy between their espoused theories and their theories-in-action.

Answer (any 1 OK):

1. Collect data to compare their own observations with those of outsiders.
2. Collect data to help them explore areas of discrepancy, for example by using an audio recorder to record their practice and then assessing the extent to which they carried out the actions they intended to carry out.
3. Reflect on the match between their espoused beliefs and their actions, and bring them into agreement either by changing their actions to match their beliefs or by redefining their espoused beliefs to correspond to their actual practice.

16. (obj. 9) Describe the approach that Zeni recommends for action researchers to build a "covenant of trust" to address the ethnical issues that may arise in such research.

Answer:

Zeni recommends dialogue with others about such ethical issues, including colleagues, research participants, and others who read or hear their research reports.

17. (obj. 9) Name the two aspects of action research that typically raise unique ethical issues, and give an example of a question that the researcher could ask about each aspect to address such issues.

Answer:

1. Participation and collaboration in the research. Possible questions: "Does your inquiry focus on people with less power than you?" "How does your project demonstrate mutual respect and justice?"
2. Presentation or publication of the research report. Possible questions: "What do your students know of your research?" "Who told them about the research?" "What are the risks to them or their families of their knowing, or not knowing, what data are collected and what is reported?"

APPLICATION PROBLEMS

Problem 1

Suppose that you are a school principal. You want to do an action research project to improve your effectiveness at getting teachers involved in defining benchmarks to help students meet state standards. Name three people in your institution who could help you in the design of your project, and one way each of them might be able to help.

Sample Answer:

1.. A district curriculum/research specialist could help you select data-collection methods appropriate for your research problem.
2. Another principal who has addressed this problem could help you anticipate possible pitfalls in dealing with it.
3. **A teacher in your school could help you think about the potential impact of your proposed actions on the teachers and students in your school.**

Problem 2

Suppose that you are a school teacher who wants to carry out an action research project in order to try out some new procedures for assigning and grading your students' homework. Briefly describe three ways in which you might have some of your students' parents participate in the action research, and a benefit of each.

Sample Answer:

1. You could involve some parents as classroom teaching assistants to help communicate the new homework procedures to students and to collect and grade homework assignments. A benefit is that having their help with your classroom responsibilities would free up more of your time to reflect on the design and results of your action research; another benefit is that you could compare your perspective with the parents' perspectives to evaluate the effectiveness of the procedures.
2. You could involve some parents as observers in collecting data about the students before and after you institute changes in your homework procedures. A benefit is that it would give you practical assistance in carrying out data collection and also in interpreting the data.
3. You could include a sample of your students' parents as research participants, for example, interviewing them about how they interact with their children concerning homework. A benefit is that you might discover strategies that you could recommend to other parents for supporting their children in completing homework.

Problem 3

Suppose that you have taught basic English classes at a community college for several years. The high proportion of students who drop out before the end of each term is, in your view, an important problem that you need to address. You have two weeks before your next class begins, and you can spend about one hour a day (for a total of ten hours) deciding on a strategy to reduce the dropout rate. You are considering two options for how to spend the bulk of your time: (1) carrying out a literature review to identify previous studies related to the problem, or (2) designing and initiating your own action research. Name three factors you would consider in deciding which option to choose.

Sample Answer:

1. How much time, difficulty, or cost is likely to be involved in developing and testing a strategy to reduce student dropout. If considerable time, difficulty, or cost is likely to be involved, a thorough literature review might be preferred, because it could help you to identify more quickly a promising strategy to implement.
2. How much you already know about the problem from your preservice and inservice education, your administrative experience, the reading you have done, and so forth. If you already have a good knowledge base in the problem area, a thorough literature review might not be necessary, so quickly beginning your action research project might be preferable.

3. The degree of controversy or range of differing philosophies or viewpoints concerning the appropriate solution to the problem. Some areas are marked by controversy, for example, whether to use a whole-language or phonics approach to teach reading to nonreaders. If you sense that identifying an effective strategy is likely to involve controversy (e.g., if the effect of such factors as your students' race, gender, and class on their math skills, motivation, and economic ability to attend community college should be considered), a thorough literature review might be preferable, because it will help you clarify your own position before selecting a strategy. However, if the problem does not appear controversial (e.g., if you suspect that modifying your testing procedures will for the most part solve the problem), you might prefer starting your action research project by focusing on designing your solution.

Problem 4
(This application problem builds upon Teaching Activity 2 for Chapter 18.) Identify an existing or anticipated problem in your education practice that would be worth addressing through action research. Briefly outline how you might carry out each stage of action research to address the problem.
Sample Answer:

1 Selecting a focus. I'm a high school language arts teacher, and I want to start a program of writing across the curriculum for ninth graders. A history teacher and a math teacher have agreed to join me in designing and offering the program.
2. Taking action. I'll ask the teachers to brainstorm ways to build brief but meaningful writing activities into our classroom teaching. Then each of us will assign writing to our students on a different day of the week (Tuesday, Wednesday, and Thursday), and on Friday we will meet to debrief and plan.
3 Collecting data. In a few weeks we can prepare a questionnaire to find out how the students feel about the writing program. We can also ask students to keep journals, and collect them occasionally. We can create a standard system that we'll each use to rate the quality of each student's writing in our classes.
4. Analyzing and interpreting the data. We can divide up the task of analyzing the data, looking at: (a) response to the program and their ideas for improving it, (b) whether we see a trend of overall writing quality in their assignments, and (c) a comparison of particular students' writing skills in each of the three subjects.
5. Reflection. Based on what we find in stage (4), each teacher can consider possible improvements in his or her classroom activities, or think about ways to incorporate some new activities.
6. Continuing or modifying action. We'll collect data to test the effectiveness of our improvements in our classroom activities and our new activities. Before the end of the term, we'll also make a report of our findings at a meeting of faculty, students, and interested parents. Based on the results, we'll propose a specific plan to continue what we are doing or try some new strategies, and we'll ask for comments and suggestions.

TEACHING ACTIVITIES

Activity 1

Describe in class an action research project in which you participated. Describe the types of colleagues, if any, with whom you carried out the project, and give examples to illustrate how you (a) selected a focus, (b) took action, (c) collected data, (d) analyzed and interpreted the data, (e) reflected on your research, and (f) continued or modified your action.

Activity 2

Ask each student to identify one problem in his or her education practice that would be worth addressing through action research. With the students working in small groups, have them select the problem of one of its members and briefly outline how the student might carry out each of the stages of action research summarized in the text, and the order in which they recommend the stages be carried out. Ask each group to report its plan to the class and explain why they ordered the stages as they did. Encourage class members to offer suggestions to improve each plan, and note examples of how collaborative effort serves to strengthen an action research project. You might also wish to remind students that action research is emergent, so any plan is likely to change as the research proceeds.

Activity 3

Have students find a written report of an action research project, read it, and report to their group whether the project had primarily a personal, professional, and/or a political purpose, and the evidence on which they based their determination of the project's purpose. Ask students to determine which purpose is most prevalent and which is least prevalent in all the action research studies that they have reviewed.